AUSTRIAN SUBJECTIVISM
AND THE EMERGENCE OF
ENTREPRENEURSHIP THEORY

THE COLLECTED WORKS OF ISRAEL M. KIRZNER

ISRAEL M. KIRZNER

Austrian Subjectivism and the Emergence of Entrepreneurship Theory

Edited and with an Introduction by

PETER J. BOETTKE and FRÉDÉRIC SAUTET

LIBERTY FUND Indianapolis

Introduction and index © 2015 by Liberty Fund, Inc.

19 18 17 16 15 C 5 4 3 2 1
19 18 17 16 15 P 5 4 3 2 1

Library of Congress Cataloging-in-Publication Data

Kirzner, Israel M.

   Austrian subjectivism and the emergence of entrepreneurship theory / Israel M. Kirzner; edited and with an introduction by Peter J. Boettke and Frédéric Sautet.

     pages   cm.—(The collected works of Israel M. Kirzner)

     Includes bibliographical references and index.

     ISBN 978-0-86597-858-4 (hardcover: alk. paper)—

     ISBN 978-0-86597-859-1 (pbk.: alk. paper)

     1. Austrian school of economics.   2. Economics.   3. Subjectivity.   4. Entrepreneurship.   I. Boettke, Peter J.   II. Sautet, Frédéric E.   III. Title.

     HB98 .K556 2015

     338′.0401—dc23   2015004683

LIBERTY FUND, INC.

8335 Allison Pointe Trail, Suite 300

Indianapolis, Indiana 46250-1684

B'EZRAS HASHEM

CONTENTS

INTRODUCTION TO
THE LIBERTY FUND EDITION

This volume gathers papers on two fundamental themes in Israel Kirzner's work: methodological subjectivism and entrepreneurship theory. We decided to put these subjects in the same volume because in Kirzner's work the latter cannot be understood well without knowing the former.

Throughout the nineteenth century, scientists labored to eliminate all forms of anthropomorphism and animalism from chemistry, physics, and biology. After Lionel Robbins's definition of economics in the 1930s and the rise of the mathematical method, on the basis of same methodology, economists developed an explanation of human action. Imitating the natural sciences, economists expunged from their science man with his purposes and plans. Such an exercise resulted in the mechanomorphism of modern economics, reducing thinking creatures to mechanical automatons and turning a social science into "social physics."

Ludwig von Mises, reacting to these developments and reflecting on the epistemology of economics and the view of man, reaffirmed the purposive nature of human action and the role this principle plays at the core of economics. Man's purpose, according to Mises, defines economics' subjective character. Kirzner followed in Mises's footsteps and stated in *The Economic Point of View* that "purpose is not something to be merely 'taken into account': it provides the sole foundation of the concept of human action."[1] According to Friedrich Hayek, Mises carried out the idea of subjectivism more consistently than any other economist. It is no exaggeration to add that Kirzner refined Mises's insights on subjectivism and entrepreneurship more consistently than any contemporary writer in the Austrian tradition.

The scientist who treats human beings as purposeless cannot ultimately understand economic phenomena and their causalities. He is in the same situation as a Martian without knowledge of how humans use buses to go to work who would just be observing bodies jumping into moving boxes every morning: it would be difficult to understand what is going on beyond bodies and boxes moving with certain

1. See *The Economic Point of View* (Indianapolis: Liberty Fund, 2009), 168.

regularity.[2] By ascribing purpose, the scientist applies subjectivism, that is, the idea that whatever means and ends an individual may select, he selects them because of the way he perceives and understands their relevance to his situation.

The disincarnated view of man has led economists to a focus on maximization within given constraints, which produced an incomplete, if not misleading, mechanistic view of the market. Kirzner has consistently fought against this approach, arguing that economists should concentrate their efforts upon explicating processes rather than end states. Indeed, to understand the capitalistic mode of production, the theorist must trace economic phenomena back to the initial purposes and plans of individuals.

Once purpose is understood to be at the foundation of the concept of human action, it becomes clear that methodological individualism and methodological subjectivism are two major planks of economics. The objects of human action as the external observer sees them do not matter to economics; only how the actors themselves perceive them does. To understand why people use buses every morning, one must take into account the knowledge and beliefs individuals hold about the usefulness of buses and how this knowledge and those beliefs shape their decisions. Economics makes the world intelligible in terms of human motives and purpose, not simply in quantitative terms.

Moreover if one assumes individuals as merely solving an optimization problem, it is impossible to understand how, over time, new information (from the point of view of the actors themselves) is generated in the economic system. In Kirzner's framework, entrepreneurial activity is fundamentally about the introduction of novel information. It follows that only a consistent pursuit of a subjectivist approach can account for the discovery and the emergence of new information, in the sense relevant to economic theory.

It is only through the consistent application of subjectivism that one can understand why the entrepreneurial function is an aspect of all action, and not just a special ability of the few. We are all entrepreneurs in our capacity as human actors. This is also why the entrepreneur in Kirzner is alert to profit opportunities, and not (primarily at least) a profit

2. Kirzner uses this example in his paper "On the Method of Austrian Economics," reprinted in this volume.

maximizer. Utility and production functions do not exist independently of valuing agents in their particular setting of time and place.

This subjectivist approach provides the foundations to explain the market process as the outcome of the purposeful actions of individuals. In pursuing their ends, individuals make use of the signals of the market, such as money prices and profits and losses, which serve as guideposts to decision-making helping transform subjective phenomena of the mind into objective signals.

These issues of epistemology and methodology possess profound implications for practical policy. As Kirzner states in the foreword to Ludwig von Mises's *The Ultimate Foundation of Economic Science,* at the core of those discussions rests the defense of a free society. It is only by bringing back into economics "those insights that positivist thought treats, in effect, as meaningless nonsense"[3] that one can fully realize the advantages of the unhampered market.

In addition to eight papers on methodological subjectivism,[4] this volume contains four articles by Kirzner on the history of entrepreneurship theory, including Kirzner's seminal paper on entrepreneurship, "Methodological Individualism, Market Equilibrium, and Market Process." It was in this paper presented at the Mont Pelerin Society meeting in Vichy, France, in 1967 that Kirzner conceptualized the role of the entrepreneurial function in the market process for the first time in his work. This paper opened the door to Kirzner's research on the market process, leading six years later to the publication of *Competition and Entrepreneurship.* In doing so, it paved the way to the modern Austrian theory of the market process.

ACKNOWLEDGMENTS

We would first like to thank wholeheartedly Israel Kirzner for his unparalleled contribution to economic science. Kirzner's research program has deeply enriched the discipline and has shed light on some of economics' most difficult puzzles. Economists owe him an immense intellectual debt.

3. See *The Ultimate Foundation of Economic Science* (Kansas City: Sheed Andrews and McMeel, 1978), vii.

4. Note that the editors have selected "Knowing About Knowledge: A Subjectivist View of the Role of Information," a paper on subjectivism and knowledge, for inclusion in *Competition, Economic Planning, and the Knowledge Problem* (Indianapolis: Liberty Fund, forthcoming), a volume in the present series.

The publication of the Collected Works of Israel M. Kirzner would not be a reality without the participation of Liberty Fund, Inc. We are extremely grateful to Liberty Fund, and especially Emilio Pacheco, for making this project possible. To republish Kirzner's unique oeuvre has been on our minds since our time spent at New York University in the 1990s—where one of us was a professor (Peter) and the other a post-doc student (Frédéric). We are thrilled at the idea that current and future generations of economists and other scholars will have easy access to Kirzner's works.

Finally, we wish to thank Emily Washington for her invaluable help in the publication of this volume, as well as Dr. Diana W. Thomas for providing her expertise in the translation of quotations from German to English.

Peter J. Boettke and Frédéric Sautet

AUSTRIAN SUBJECTIVISM

ON THE METHOD OF AUSTRIAN ECONOMICS

One of the areas in which disagreement among Austrian economists may seem to be nonexistent is that of methodology. Yet I shall attempt to point out that even with respect to method there are differences of opinion among individual thinkers. Some light may be cast on these differences by drawing attention to two distinct strands of thought that run through the writings of Austrian economists on the question of method. By separating these strands and then focusing on each in turn, we may discover and define different perspectives on economic method and perhaps more clearly understand how these different perspectives grow out of the unique view of method shared by all Austrian economists.

The general outline of the Austrian position on methodology is well known. Austrian economists are subjectivists; they emphasize the purposefulness of human action; they are unhappy with constructions that emphasize equilibrium to the exclusion of market processes; they are deeply suspicious of attempts to apply measurement procedures to economics; they are skeptical of empirical "proofs" of economic theorems and consequently have serious reservations about the validity and importance of a good deal of the empirical work being carried on in the economics profession today. These are the general features of the position that we know very well; yet within this general view we can distinguish two independent strands of argument. It is upon this debate that I should like to focus my attention in this paper.

TWO TASKS FOR ECONOMIC EXPLANATIONS

It will be helpful to cite two statements—by prominent Austrian economists—about what economics as a discipline is supposed to achieve. The first is by Friedrich A. Hayek, and the other is by Ludwig M. Lachmann. Hayek in his *Counter-Revolution of Science* contended that the function of social science, and by implication economics, is to explain how conscious, purposeful human action can generate unintended consequences through social interaction.[1] The emphasis here is on the

From *Foundations of Modern Austrian Economics,* ed. Edwin G. Dolan (Kansas City: Sheed and Ward, 1976), 40–51. Reprinted by permission of the Institute of Humane Studies.

unintended consequences of individual human decisions. To explain phenomena that are not the unintended consequences of human decision making is outside the scope of the social sciences in general and economics in particular. Hayek's position was cited by Alexander Gerschenkron in his contribution to the Akerman *Festschrift,* and I think Gerschenkron was perceptive in focusing on exactly what is, in Hayek's view, the fundamental task of economic explanation.[2]

Let us contrast the Hayek view with one expressed by Lachmann. Lachmann's position on the purpose of economic explanations is dealt with at length in his contribution to the Hayek *Festschrift, Roads to Freedom.*[3] Here, however, I shall quote from a more recent statement of his position that appeared in his review of John R. Hicks's *Capital and Time:*

> Economics has two tasks. The first is to make the world around us intelligible in terms of human action and the pursuit of plans. The second is to trace the unintended consequences of such action. Ricardian economics emphasized the second task, the "subjective revolution" of the 1870s stressed the urgency of the first, and the Austrian school has always cherished this tradition.[4]

Thus, we have here two tasks for economics. Besides the task that Hayek emphasized—the tracing out of the unintended consequences of action—we have the requirement that it make the world around us intelligible in terms of human action.

It is worth reminding ourselves that the two tasks Lachmann identified are to be found in Carl Menger's writings. In the third part of his 1884 book on methodology Menger pointed out that actions do have unintended consequences, and he made it very clear, as Hayek had done, that economics is the science that is able to explain how these unintended consequences emerge in the market place.[5] But Menger was also aware of the other task Lachmann emphasized. In a letter Menger wrote Léon Walras, cited by T. W. Hutchison in several of his writings,[6] Menger insisted that the economist is not merely after the relationships between quantities, but the *essence* of economic phenomena: "the essence of value, the essence of land rent, the essence of entrepreneurs' profits, the essence of the division of labor."[7] This view is what Kauder meant when he described Menger as holding that economics deals with social essences,[8] and what Hutchison called "methodological essentialism."[9]

TWO BASIC AUSTRIAN TENETS

I have asserted that two distinct strands of thought may be identified in the writings of Austrian economists with regard to the meaning and purpose of economic explanation. I would now like to distinguish two distinct insights about the economic world that receive varying emphasis and are not often adequately differentiated. First, there is the insight that *human action is purposeful,* and, second, there is the insight that *there is an indeterminacy and unpredictability inherent in human preferences, human expectations, and human knowledge.* Now these two insights are really quite distinct, because one does not encompass the other in any logical or epistemological sense. That human action is purposeful is an insight by itself, and that human knowledge and expectations are largely unpredictable is another. Nor is the truth of these two propositions equally obvious. The purposefulness of human action is something we arrive at by introspection. In this sense it is "obviously" true. On the other hand, the insight that men's preferences are inherently unpredictable—that we cannot discover consistent patterns in what men prefer and that we cannot postulate that there are consistent patterns in what men know and expect to happen—cannot be arrived at by introspection. The truth claimed for this last insight depends on our observations of our fellow men, that we do as a matter of fact find them to be unpredictable in their actions and expectations about future states of the world.

To me, the different emphasis Austrian economists attach to these basic insights is largely responsible for their different attitudes regarding the purpose of economic explanation. The recognition of purposefulness is, of course, fundamental to our definition of economics as the logic of choice. We are able to use our logic to simulate the actions of other human beings only because we share the logic that other men's purposes lead them to harness in their own interests. The recognition of purposefulness is essential to our positive conception of economics as the logic of choice and to our enterprise of studying the consequences of purposeful action. But if we consider those aspects of the Austrian approach that are used, not to derive economic laws, but to criticize other areas of contemporary economic thought, then the second of these basic tenets comes into prominence. Our dissatisfaction with empirical work and our suspicion of measurement rest on the conviction that empirical observations of past human choices will not yield any regularities or any consistent pattern that may be safely extrapolated beyond the existing data at hand to yield scientific theorems of universal applicability.

THE SIGNIFICANCE OF PURPOSEFULNESS

Let us try to understand the role these basic tenets of Austrian economics play in the Lachmann-Hayek discussions concerning what economic explanation is all about. In 1938 T. W. Hutchison published *The Significance and Basic Postulates of Economic Theory.*[10] The book received a blistering Austrian-like critique from the pen of Frank H. Knight, who was on most other issues, such as capital theory, not in sympathy with the Austrian school. In that article Knight conveyed some brilliant insights about the relationship of economics to the study of human action. Knight noted that "the whole subject of conduct— interests and motivation—constitutes a different realm of reality from the external world." In addition to the external world, with which the natural sciences are conversant, there is a different realm of reality, a realm no less real than the external world, but nevertheless different from it. This other realm is that of human conduct, which Knight identified as interests, motivation, and purpose.

> The first fact to be recorded is that this realm of reality exists or "is there." This fact cannot be proved or argued or "tested." If anyone denies that men have interests or that "we" have a considerable amount of valid knowledge about them, economics and all its works will simply be to such a person what the world of color is to the blind man. But there would still be one difference: a man who is physically, ocularly blind may still be rated of normal intelligence and in his right mind.[11]

Here, surely, we have the first of the basic tenets of Austrian theory, that there is a realm of reality constituted of human motives, interests, and purposes, and that, although purposes cannot be seen or touched, they are nonetheless "there."

When Lachmann called upon economists to make the world intelligible in terms of human decisions and purposes, I take it that he was telling us the following: *It is the task of science to describe and explain reality. If reality consists of more than the external world, then a science that is confined to the facts of the external world is simply incomplete. It does not account for everything that is there.* The Austrian approach insists that there is something besides the facts of the external world and the relationships that may be postulated between these bare facts. What is that something else? It is the realm of reality that Knight pointed to, the realm of purposes. And even if one were able to explain the facts of the external world in terms of similar facts, without regard to the human purposes underlying these facts, one would not have explained everything there is to be explained, not have set forth everything there is to set forth. One would have failed to make the world intelligible in terms of human action, that is, in terms of human purposes. Thus, even if the second Austrian tenet (that there are no constants in human behavior) were false, even if one were able to postulate consistent chains of cause and effect that depend only on externally observable phenomena, still one has failed to fulfill one's scientific obligation. There is a realm of reality called purposes. It is there, and if we fail to point it out, then we fail in the task of making the world intelligible in terms of human action.

Let us consider a simple example. Suppose a man from Mars is doing research for his doctorate and, after focusing his telescope on a particular location on Earth, discovers a certain regularity. Through his telescope he observes a set of boxes lined up in a row. He further discovers that a smaller box moves past these boxes every day at 7:30 A.M., comes to a stop at one of the boxes, and then, after a short stay, moves on. Moreover the investigator discovers something else; out of one of these boxes a body emerges every morning, and when the moving box makes its daily stop, the body is swallowed up by the moving box. Discovering this regularity, the researcher postulates a definite law, the law of moving boxes and bodies. As he goes on with the research, however, he discovers that sometimes the box moves away before the body has entered it, leaving the body behind altogether; while sometimes the body moves at an unusually rapid speed, arriving at the daily moving-box stop just in time to be swallowed up before the box moves on. Now this Martian researcher may be able to predict just when the person is going to miss the box and when he is going to catch it. He may even be able to explain the movements of the body and the box entirely without reference to the fact that someone is trying to catch the bus because he wants to get to work on time. But if he does so, he has not told us everything there is to be learned about this situation. A theory of moving bodies and boxes that does not draw attention to the dimension of purpose gives a truncated picture of the real world. *This* is what economics, in the Austrian view, is all about. Economics has to make the world intelligible in terms of human motives. It is more than simply moving boxes or changing economic quantities. This is the task to which Lachmann drew our attention when he insisted that we must make the world intelligible in terms of human purpose.

A memorable passage in Hayek's *Counter-Revolution* is the one in which he explained that objects useful to human beings are simply not objective facts.

> In fact most of the objects of social or human action are not "objective facts" in the special narrow sense in which this term is used by the [natural] Sciences . . . they cannot be defined in physical terms. . . . Take the concept of a "tool" or "instrument," or of any particular tool such as a hammer or a barometer. It is easily seen that these concepts cannot be interpreted to refer to "objective facts," i.e. to things irrespective of what people think about them.[12]

Pursuing this point Hayek asserted (in a footnote reference to the work of Ludwig von Mises) that every important advance in economic theory in the preceding century had been a result of the consistent application of subjectivism.[13] Lachmann's advice to economists paralleled Hayek's. According to Hayek, when we deal with artifacts—with tools and instruments or other products of human beings—we have not exhausted the description of what it is that we are describing if we stubbornly confine ourselves to their physical entities. We have not described a hammer until we have drawn attention to its purpose. Lachmann, similarly, instructed us that when we deal with broader questions, with institutions and regularities in economic affairs, we have not completed our task if we have not called attention to the purposes and motives and interests that underlie these phenomena. A hammer is more than a handle with a metal head; so is a price more than a number, milk consumption more than a number of gallons, and its relationship to price more than a simple functional relationship. A whole world of interests and motives is "there," is real, and it is surely our responsibility as scientists to make it clear.

Critics of Austrian methodology often argue that since praxeology deals with unobservables, it is inherently incapable of telling us anything scientific about observables. The latest (and perhaps the clearest and most sympathetic) statement of this argument was by James Buchanan, in his contribution to the Hayek *Festschrift*,[14] when he drew attention to the distinction between (1) the logic of choice (what he called the abstract science of economic behavior) and (2) the predictive science of human behavior. Buchanan argued that if we treat economics as the logic of choice, it cannot in principle lead to refutable hypotheses because no particular preference ordering has been specified, and to that extent it cannot tell us anything about the real world.

In answer to Buchanan, our discussion indicates that the truth is the other way around. We are not only able to say something about the real world; we are also able to say a great deal about a large and important area of human experience about which other disciplines are necessarily silent—the realm of purpose. This needs to be stated and restated, emphasized and reemphasized, again and again! The real world is more than the external world; the real world includes a whole range of matters beyond the scope of the measuring instruments of the econometrician. Economic science must be able to encompass this realm.

It is helpful in pursuing this strand of thought in Austrian methodology to constrast the Austrian use of purpose with the rationality hypothesis often employed by economists. For many non-Austrian economists this hypothesis is invoked with apologies and is considered something of a necessary evil. It is used to get theoretical results and is justified on the grounds that these results seem to fit the facts of the outside world although the hypothesis is philosophically suspect. Thus we find Gary Becker eager to demonstrate how certain fundamental theorems of economics do not require the rationality hypothesis—that rather embarrassing piece of excess baggage.[15] For Austrian economists, on the other hand, the notion of purposefulness is not merely a useful tool to obtain results but an essential element of economic reality that cannot be omitted. Making reference to human plans and motivations is an essential part of the economist's scientific task.

THE UNPREDICTABILITY OF KNOWLEDGE: A DILEMMA

Let us turn to the second basic tenet of Austrian methodology, the proposition that there is an inherent unpredictability and indeterminacy with regard to human preferences, expectations, and knowledge. I have already pointed out that this proposition does not have the same introspectively obvious ring of truth that the idea of human purposefulness does. Are we really so certain that human wants and human preference-orderings and the manner in which they undergo modification are inherently unpredictable? In fact, I wish to suggest that asserting this creates something of a dilemma for the Austrian economist.

There is a passage in an essay by Hayek that deals with this very question. In that essay Hayek discussed the concept of equilibrium and raised the problem of whether or not there is a tendency toward equilibrium in the economic world. Hayek remarked:

> It is clear that, if we want to make the assertion that, under certain conditions, people will approach that state, we must explain by what process they will acquire the necessary knowledge. Of course, any assumption about the actual acquisition of knowledge in the course of this process will also be of a hypothetical character. But this does not mean that all such assumptions are equally justified. We have to deal here with assumptions about causation, so that what we assume must not only be regarded as possible . . . but must also be regarded as likely to be true; and it must be possible, at least in principle, to demonstrate that it is true in particular cases. The significant point here is that it is these apparently subsidiary hypotheses or assumptions that people do learn from experience, and about how they acquire knowledge, which constitute the empirical content of our propositions about what happens in the real world.[16]

Hayek, then, asserted that when postulating a tendency toward equilibrium, we do have to resort to a particular empirical proposition. Moreover, the empirical proposition in question would seem to contradict the other idea that there are an inherent unpredictability and an indeterminacy about human preferences and human knowledge. If we are to be able to say anything about the process of equilibration, especially if we are to say something about the course by which human decisions lead to unintended consequences, we shall have to rely upon the particular empirical proposition that men learn from market experience in a systematic manner. This is inconsistent with the second tenet underlying Austrian economics that there is an inherent indeterminacy in the way by which human knowledge changes.

Hayek's argument is straightforward. In disequilibrium man's knowledge is imperfect, some people are making mistakes; equilibrium is the situation in which nobody is making mistakes. A movement from disequilibrium to equilibrium must therefore be one in which men gradually learn to avoid mistakes, so that their actions become more and more coordinated. Where do we derive our confidence that this type of learning in fact takes place? Hayek stated very clearly that this is an empirical hypothesis. If we reject this hypothesis, then we reject the basis for viewing the market process as an equilibrating mechanism—that is, reject the claim that economics can tell us anything definite about the unintended market consequences of human actions. We may still be able to make the world intelligible—that is, we may explain that what happens happens because human beings pursue their purposes. We can assert that their interacting decisions generate certain changes in knowledge, but we shall no longer be able to say in which particular directions knowledge changes, and we can no longer postulate a determinate process toward equilibrium. We shall, to put the matter succinctly, not be able to go beyond the first Lachmann task in order to pursue the program advanced by Hayek. If, however, we confine ourselves to the enormously important task of making the world intelligible in terms of human purposes, we need not accept Hayek's empirical proposition about the coordination of plans and the progressive elimination of mistakes. But if we are to explain the unintended consequences of human action, that is, if we are to assert that there is a tendency for entrepreneurial profits to be eliminated, or for prices to move in one direction rather than another, we must be able to say something about the manner in which human knowledge and human expectations undergo modification. If one accepts this particular empirical hypothesis, one has surely weakened, perhaps irreparably, the second basic tenet underlying Austrian methodology.

CONCLUSION

We have identified two requirements of economic explanations that Austrian economists consider important. We have also identified two basic tenets that seem fundamental to Austrian methodology. It turns out, however, that while one of these basic tenets, that of human purposefulness, is sufficient to sustain one of these two requirements (that of making the world intelligible in terms of human action), the second, which asserts the unpredictability of human knowledge, is inconsistent with the requirement that economic explanations trace the unintended consequences of human action. It seems therefore that the future progress of the Austrian school in applying its basic methodological tenets requires some decision about the extent to which the second tenet about the inconstancy of human purposes and knowledge can be upheld as a general proposition.

NOTES

1. Friedrich A. Hayek, *The Counter-Revolution of Science: Studies on the Abuse of Reason* (Glencoe, Ill.: Free Press, 1955), p. 39.

2. Alexander Gerschenkron, "Reflection on Ideology as a Methodological and Historical Problem," in *Money, Growth, and Methodology*, ed. Hugo Hegeland (Lund: C. W. K. Gleerup, 1961), p. 180.

3. Ludwig M. Lachmann, "Methodological Individualism and the Market Economy," in *Roads to Freedom: Essays in Honour of Friedrich A. von Hayek*, ed. Erich Streissler et al. (London: Routledge & Kegan Paul, 1969), pp. 93–104.

4. Ludwig M. Lachmann, "Sir John Hicks as a Neo-Austrian," *South African Journal of Economics* 41 (September 1973): 204.

5. Carl Menger, *Problems of Economics and Sociology*, trans. Francis J. Nock, ed. L. Schneider (Urbana: University of Illinois, 1963). The title of the 1884 German edition of the work is *Untersuchungen über die Methode der Socialwissenschaften und der Politischen Oekonomieinsbesondere*, and it is therefore sometimes referred to as *Investigations into Method*, which more correctly indicates the character of its contents.

6. T. W. Hutchison, *A Review of Economic Doctrines, 1870–1929* (Oxford: Clarendon Press, 1954), p. 148; idem, "Some Themes from *Investigations into Method*," in *Carl Menger and the Austrian School of Economics*, ed. J. R. Hicks and Wilhelm Weber (Oxford: Clarendon Press, 1974), p. 17 n.

7. This letter was composed in 1884; see the reference to it in W. Jaffé, "Unpublished Papers and Letters of Léon Walras," *Journal of Political Economy* 43 (April 1935): 187–207; also see Léon Walras, *Correspondence of Léon Walras and Related Papers*, ed. W. Jaffe, 2 vols. (Amsterdam: North-Holland Publishing Co., 1965), 2:3.

8. Emil Kauder, *A History of Marginal Utility Theory* (Princeton: Princeton University Press, 1965), p. 97.

9. Hutchison, "Some Themes," p. 18; Hutchison explained that the source of this term is in Karl Popper, *The Poverty of Historicism* (New York: Harper & Row, 1961), pp. 28–38.

10. T. W. Hutchison, *The Significance and Basic Postulates of Economic Theory* (London: Macmillan & Co., 1938).

11. Frank H. Knight, "'What is Truth' in Economics," in *On the History and Method of Economics*, ed. Frank H. Knight (Chicago: University of Chicago Press, 1956), p. 160.

12. Hayek, *The Counter-Revolution*, pp. 26–27.

13. Ibid., pp. 24, 31, 209–10.

14. James M. Buchanan, "Is Economics the Science of Choice?" in *Roads to Freedom: Essays in Honour of Friedrich A. von Hayek*, ed. Erich Streissler et al. (London: Routledge & Kegan Paul, 1969), pp. 47–65; see also James M. Buchanan, *Cost and Choice* (Chicago: Markham Publishing Co., 1970).

15. Gary S. Becker, "Irrational Behavior and Economic Theory," *Journal of Political Economy* 70 (February 1962): 1–13.

16. Friedrich A. Hayek, "Economics and Knowledge," in *Individualism and Economic Order* (London: Routledge & Kegan Paul, 1952), p. 46.

CARL MENGER AND THE SUBJECTIVIST
TRADITION IN ECONOMICS

The republication of the facsimile edition of Menger's classic treatise presents a fitting opportunity to re-examine the nature of Menger's revolutionary contribution to economic understanding, and to re-evaluate it critically in the light of the mature insights discovered in the course of a century-long development of the Austrian tradition which Menger initiated. In the present commentary we shall focus on Menger's central "vision," the new way in which he persuaded economists to "see" the economic system as a whole. Menger himself, in the preface to the *Grundsätze* (1981: 49), pointed to his having placed "all price phenomena (including interest, wages, ground rent, etc.) together under one unified point of view." We shall maintain that this "point of view" reflects Menger's subjectivist vision of the system as a whole, a vision that forms the very core of his contribution.

In a now classic passage Hayek, probably the most famous twentieth-century representative of the Austrian tradition initiated by Menger, has drawn attention to the role of subjectivism in the development of economic thought. Writing at mid-century Hayek (1955: 31) suggested "that every important advance in economic theory during the last hundred years was a further step in the consistent application of subjectivism." We shall argue in these pages that, measured against this criterion, Menger's vision represented a major step forward in the history of economics—but one which, we can now recognize with hindsight, fell short of exploiting its own full potential. The same preface in which Menger referred to his unified point of view—the point of view expressing, as we shall see, Menger's subjectivist understanding of market forces—reveals Menger's conviction that he had discovered "the conformity to definite laws of phenomena that condition the outcome of the economic activity of men and *are entirely*

From *The Meaning of Market Process: Essays in the Development of Modern Austrian Economics* (New York and London: Routledge, 1992), 70–85. First published in the German language as "Carl Menger und die subjektivistische Tradition in der Ökonomie," in *Carl Mengers wegweisendes Werk,* in Klassiker der Nationalökonomie, ed. Wolfram Engels, Herbert Hax, Friedrich von Hayek, and Horst Claus Recktenwald (Düsseldorf: Verlag Wirtschaft und Finanzen, 1990).

independent of the human will" (Menger 1981: 48, emphasis added). Our interpretation of this conviction of Menger will illustrate the sense in which his own understanding of the economic system failed to appreciate later steps taken in the development of subjectivist economics—a development which was unquestionably initiated entirely and solely by Menger himself. Let us first set out what we believe Menger's central vision to be.

THE MENGERIAN VISION

In his highly critical introduction to the 1950 English translation of the *Grundsätze,* Frank Knight focused attention on what he believed to be the "most serious defect in Menger's economic system" (Knight 1950: 25). This, Knight claimed, is Menger's "view of production as a process of converting goods of higher order into goods of lower order." Now, we do not at all agree that Knight has put his finger here on any defect in Menger; but we do believe that he has identified, in this view of production, the root insight that nourished Menger's understanding of the economic process.

For Menger the entire economic system is seen as a complex of activities directly or indirectly inspired by the goal of satisfying consumer needs. Every single item or service bought and sold in the market is valued only in so far as it can, in the purchaser's judgement, contribute valuably, directly or indirectly, towards the satisfaction of consumer needs. An act of production, in the Mengerian view, is an act which brings such valued items or services closer to the fulfilment of this ultimate goal of satisfying consumer needs—it is an act of "converting goods of higher order into goods of lower order." No act of production, by definition, can fail to result in goods of "lower order" than those utilized in that act of production.

With this teleological perspective Menger, in a revolutionary manner, was liberating economics from the strictly physical view of production which had dominated classical economics. In that view production could easily be discussed as if its output had its own economic significance, quite independently of its designed function in the ultimate promotion of consumer satisfaction. Knight objected to Menger's view of production that "in the technical production process, the typical relation is the use of both iron and coal to produce both iron and coal" (Knight 1950: 25). Exactly. For the non-Mengerian view the typical process of production does not, in any necessarily obvious way, reveal itself as bringing us nearer the satisfaction of ultimate consumer needs. Menger recognized that we must refine our vision of each act of production to see how it fits into an overall, unified process of deploying given nature-endowed resources, in a systematic fashion, towards the satisfaction of consumer needs. All the phenomena of the market, Menger saw, can be understood from this perspective. All "price phenomena (including interest, wages, ground rent . . .)" fall into place, from this perspective, as expressive of the acts of valuation generated by and concurrent with the opportunities for, and acts of, production. It is this one, unified point of view which illuminates all these phenomena, explaining them all as the systematic reflection, direct and indirect, of consumer needs, as they impinge on the given complex of society's resources.

For Menger, therefore, production is not simply a physical process in which the combining of inputs results in desired outputs; rather it is a process in which the importance of needed valuable prospective outputs—ultimate outputs needed for their own sakes—imposes itself upon, and enforces the appropriate deployment of, available given resources, no matter how remote these resources may be from the finally desired output. The web of market transactions is not so much one which, in Walrasian terms, permits a complex of interdependent intertwined acts of exchange and of production coherently to be consummated. Rather that web of transactions is seen as the network of forces through which the various relative strengths of different consumer needs exercise their power over the discovery and deployment of relevant goods of highest order and their systematic conversion in patterns leading ultimately to the provision of the goods of lowest order.

To be sure, we find iron and coal used in production processes yielding iron and coal. Menger would see nothing at all strange in this. But he would point out the superficiality of the view which fails to recognize the difference between the two sets of iron and coal—between means and ends (including intermediate ends!). At least part of the produced iron and coal must be designed for utilization in further steps of production (other than the generation of iron and coal). And as for that portion of produced iron and coal destined for use in yet further processes of iron and coal production, at least part of *its* iron and coal output must be designed to be used in further steps of production (other than the generation of iron and coal). What inspires the production of iron and coal cannot be *solely* the goal of commanding inputs for the production of additional iron and coal *ad infinitum*. What inspires the production of producing iron and coal, what confers economic significance—Mengerian economic *value*—upon any input unit of iron or coal, is the degree of importance associated with ultimate consumer needs directly or indirectly dependent upon that unit. For Menger an act of production cannot be understood except in teleological terms—as an act of deploying means towards ultimate, or at least intermediate ends.

THE SUBJECTIVISM OF MENGER'S VISION

There is no doubt that Menger's vision constituted one of those steps in the application of subjectivism of which Hayek wrote. Every textbook in the history of economic thought recognizes Menger as the founder of Austrian subjectivism. But we wish to draw attention to a subjectivist element in Menger's contribution which is not always appreciated.

Standard accounts of the early years of Austrian economics focus on the discovery of the principle of diminishing marginal utility and on the Austrian marginal utility theory of value.[1] Important though these aspects of Menger's work certainly were, however, it seems to us that they do not go to the heart of Menger's subjectivist perspective. For us, Menger's subjectivism reveals itself in his vision of the entire economic system—every single act of production and every transaction of exchange—as inspired by the deliberate attempts of economizing individuals to promote, in the light of their own knowledge and understanding, the satisfaction of ultimate consumer needs. This perspective transmutes all the phenomena of the economy from being simply physical transformations, relationships or ratios into direct or indirect expressions of human valuations, preferences, expectations, and dreams. This subjectivist perspective of Menger extends far beyond an understanding of diminishing marginal significance and its implications, and far beyond the narrow confines of the utility-based theory of value. This perspective suffuses the Austrian understanding of every single facet of the economy.

It is widely recognized that Menger's vision included—already in 1871—the ideas essential for a marginal productivity understanding of factor prices and of the theory of functional income distribution. Where the other pioneers of the marginal utility revolution confined their early insights to the theory of product price (with two decades to elapse before the extension to the theory of factor price), Menger presented his understanding of the principles of factor pricing in the same 1871 work in which he offered his theory of product price. For Menger the marginal productivity theory of factor value is not an *extension* of the marginal utility theory of product price, but part of the very same, seamless whole. The very same vision which saw product price as the expression of the marginal valuations of consumers saw factor prices as the indirect expression of those very same valuations. Although Knight at one point belittles Menger's theory of distribution ("We find in Menger barely the germ of a theory . . . of distribution . . ." [Knight 1950: 23]), he does recognize that "the 'marginal utility' doctrine, with its application to indirect and complementary goods, 'logically' covers all there is to say about distribution theory" (p. 15). The truth surely is that Menger's central insight is precisely this, that distribution theory is to be seen as simply an implication of the marginal utility theory of consumer goods prices. Marginal utility value theory is not the pinnacle of Menger's subjectivist achievement, but its foundation.

THE INCOMPLETENESS OF MENGER'S SUBJECTIVISM—
THE ADVANTAGE OF HINDSIGHT

Revolutionary though Menger's subjectivist vision of the economic system undoubtedly was, we can now see its limitations very clearly. The consistent development of Austrian economics since 1871 permits us to identify the key weaknesses in the *Grundsätze*. Somewhat paradoxically, these weaknesses turn out to be inadequacies in Menger's subjectivism. The subjectivist perspective which Menger's disciples learned from their master has enabled them to pursue a line of discussion and to grasp insights which eluded the master himself.

As was the case in our discussion of the positive features of the subjectivism of Menger's contribution, our assessment of the limitations of that subjectivism will differ from the conventional wisdom concerning Menger. The standard accounts of the development of subjectivist insights following Menger focus principally on the inadequacies of Menger's theory of needs. While not disagreeing on the unfortunate (and nonsubjectivist) character of Menger's theory of needs, we shall emphasize a different set of limitations surrounding the subjectivism of his vision.

As is well known, Menger's utility theory took as its point of departure the existence of a set of individual needs, for each consumer, which seem disturbingly objective and concrete. It is as if the physiological and psychological make-up of the individual generates definite requirements with definite degrees of urgency—quite apart from any choices made freely by that individual. What is emphasized in Menger is not freely exercised preferences, purposes spontaneously and independently pursued, but rather the inevitable adjustment of economic behaviour to meet the requirements imposed by these given sets of individual needs.[2] One begins to understand Menger's reference to "the conformity to definite laws of phenomena that . . . are entirely independent of the human will." It is as if these given sets of individual needs exercise their own force upon the system, constraining the allocation of resources and determining economic values, entirely without as it were the intermediation of the human will. Commentators have justifiably seen this view as somewhat primitive, at least as judged from the perspective of the more developed and sophisticated subjectivism of the later Austrians. We wish to draw attention to a different sense in which we must point out the inadequacy of Menger's subjectivism. It turns out that this inadequacy is to be found precisely in that overall vision of the economic system which we noted for the revolutionary subjectivist nature of its understanding of the system. It will be helpful for us to recall, by way of introduction, a fascinating little episode involving Hayek's sharp criticism of a position taken by Joseph Schumpeter.

At the end of his celebrated 1945 paper "The use of knowledge in society" Hayek referred to a passage, in *Capitalism, Socialism and Democracy* (1950), in which Schumpeter belittled the problem of economic calculation under a centrally planned system. Mises had argued that, in the absence of markets for factors of production, socialist planners would have no indexes of the relative social importance of the various resources and would hence be unable to plan rationally. Schumpeter maintained that economic rationality can nonetheless be attained in a planned society. For the theorist, Schumpeter argued, "this follows from the elementary proposition that consumers in evaluating ('demanding') consumers' goods *ipso facto* also evaluate the means of production which enter into the production of those goods" (Schumpeter 1950: 175). Hayek found this pronouncement "startling." Only for a single mind to which would be simultaneously known not only "the valuation of the consumers' goods but also . . . the conditions of supply of the various factors of production" (Hayek 1949b: 90) would it be valid to claim that consumers' valuations logically imply corresponding evaluations of the productive services. Schumpeter, Hayek charged, has fallen victim to an approach which "habitually disregards . . . the unavoidable imperfection of man's knowledge and the consequent need for a process by which knowledge is constantly communicated and acquired" (p. 91).

Clearly what Hayek found wanting in Schumpeter was an appreciation for the market process through which the scattered information, concerning resource availabilities and consumer valuations, is mobilized and brought to bear upon the decisions governing production and the allocation of resources. What needs to be introduced into Schumpeter's vision of the economic system is recognition of the role of entrepreneurial alertness and imagination, in inspiring and driving this market process of knowledge mobilization—in the face of the stark uncertainties of an unknown future. It was Schumpeter's failure—towering pioneer though he was in understanding the entrepreneurial role—to grasp the subjective dimension of this market process which led him to believe that consumers' valuations automatically translate into valuations of productive factors (Kirzner 1979a: Ch. 4, especially pp. 68f.).

This lapse in Schumpeter's subjectivism, we wish to submit, parallels precisely a corresponding lapse in Menger's subjectivism. The Schumpeterian vision of consumer valuations automatically generating valuations of productive factors is identical, we shall see, with Menger's vision in which consumers' needs generate results that are "entirely independent of the human will. . . ." Precisely that vision in which Menger saw how the economic system transmits consumer judgements of economic significance to the arrays of goods of higher order is, we wish to suggest from the perspective of modern subjectivism, flawed in failing to recognize the entrepreneurial steps—taken imaginatively, daringly and spontaneously, in the face of the impenetrable fog of the uncertain future—through which these judgements must necessarily be transmitted. These entrepreneurial steps represent the imagination and vision of the entrepreneurs peering into the unknown. Any claim to the effect that consumers' preferences dictate the allocation of resources can have validity only to the extent that these preferences are sensed and transmitted by market entrepreneurs. Menger's recognition of the way in which market phenomena reflect the active imprint of consumer valuations (rather than the passive constraints of the physical environment) was indeed a pioneering step in the development of subjectivist economics. This recognition would eventually point the way to an understanding that this imprint (in so far as it relates to the markets for higher order goods and the decisions through which they are allocated) is achieved through human actions expressing the alertness and the expectations of the entrepreneurs. But this complete subjectivist understanding, we argue, escaped Menger. For him, we submit, it was indeed as if the economic regularities that link consumer preferences to relevant shifts in the allocation of resources operate automatically and mechanically. In this fundamental respect Menger's subjectivism must, from the perspective afforded by a century's hindsight, be judged incomplete. Let us look more closely at Menger's overall vision.

MENGER AND THE ASSUMPTION OF PERFECT KNOWLEDGE

We have cited several times Menger's reference in his preface to economic laws as being independent of the human will. This theme is raised again by Menger in the body of his book, especially in the context of his theory of price. In explaining the formation of price in a monopolized market, for example, Menger concludes: "Summarizing what has been said in this section, we find that . . . the entire course of economic events is throughout not fortuitous but capable of being reduced to definite principles. . . . The phenomena of monopoly trade present us therefore with a picture of strict conformity, in every respect, to definite laws." He then adds the following intriguing afterthought: "error and imperfect knowledge may give rise to aberrations, but these are the pathological phenomena of social economy and prove as little against the laws of economics as do the symptoms of a sick body against the laws of physiology" (Menger 1981: 215–16). Clearly Menger confined the scope of economic law to the range of human activity unaffected by error and imperfect knowledge. A careful examination of his entire Chapter 5, on the theory of price, confirms that for Menger the inescapable laws which, given consumer valuations, determine prices are deduced strictly on the assumption that each economizing individual is in fact fully aware of the circumstances relevant to his decisions.

We have here then a clear statement of an important feature of Menger's economics. For Menger what economic theory explains is the determination of "economic prices," the prices that would emerge under conditions free of the "pathological" influence of error and imperfect knowledge. In his 1883 *Untersuchungen* Menger elaborated on this theme: "There is scarcely need to remark that . . . as a rule *real* prices deviate more or less from *economic* ones (those corresponding to the economic situation)" (Menger 1985: 71). Menger attributed this discrepancy to various considerations, especially to vagueness and error on the part of market participants concerning what they want and how to achieve their goals, and to incomplete knowledge concerning the economic situation.

It is clear, then, that the economic laws, operating independently of human will, which Menger saw as governing all market phenomena pertain, strictly speaking, only to a world of omniscient economizing individuals. The Mengerian vision which sees the values of the services of land, labour and capital as being but "a necessary consequence of their economic character" (Menger 1981: 173) proceeds by presuming that the economic system indeed permits actual prices to approximate the true economic prices. "The prices of these goods (the services of land and capital) are therefore the necessary products of the economic situation under which they arise, *and will be more certainly obtained the more developed the legal system of a people and the more upright its public morals*" (pp. 173–74, emphasis added).

What Menger clearly believes (although he does not appear to present an argument to support this belief, nor even to articulate it explicitly) is that the assumptions required for the emergence of economic prices are sufficiently reasonable to permit us to conclude that the understanding of the laws of economics provides an understanding of the real world. Although Menger, more perhaps than any other economist of his time, refers again and again to the effects of error and uncertainty, nonetheless he seems prepared to assume them away in arriving at his overall understanding of the economic system (Kirzner 1979a: Ch. 4).

All this is not a serious flaw, perhaps, in Menger's theory of prices, understood as an abstract system. While it certainly seems highly desirable to have an understanding of the dynamic market process through which prices emerge, there is certainly also scope for the (separate) theory of the factors governing the position towards which these prices may be gravitating. There is room for both a theory of the equilibrating process and the theory of equilibrium itself. There is a legitimate place for enquiry as to what would be implied by perfect knowledge.

But when the perfect knowledge assumption is transferred (as Menger's overall vision of the economic system apparently requires it to be transferred) to the proposition that consumer valuations are in fact substantially transmitted to the markets for the services of land, labour and capital, we have reason to be worried. For we now, over a century later, understand that if such transmittal indeed occurs, it can only be as the result of the competitive pressures exerted by alert entrepreneurs. Nowhere does Menger display awareness of the need to introduce the operation of these competitive-entrepreneurial pressures. Nowhere does he display appreciation for the circumstance that such pressures cannot be understood as mechanical or automatic, but must be understood as made up of the spontaneous discoveries of alert human beings. Nowhere, in brief, does Menger display a sensitivity to this dimension of the subjectivism upon which market forces in fact depend.

The situation is, in one sense, even worse than merely a lack of awareness by Menger of the scope for subjectivism in understanding the market process through which relative consumer preferences are transmitted throughout the system. When Menger refers to error and imperfect knowledge as "pathological" phenomena, he portrays a most unfortunate (if widely shared) understanding of the operation of markets. The truth, however, is surely that it is *only* through entrepreneurial incentives (for winning pure profit) *created by error* that we can hope to attain any approximation at all to that state of omniscience which Menger treats as normal for a healthy body economic. Appreciation for the possibility that subjectively based errors may drive a wedge between real prices and economic prices does not begin to equal a recognition that such subjectively based errors are in fact to be seen positively as *stepping stones* towards any real world relevance for these economic prices—and for the overall Mengerian vision which they make possible. Having recognized this incompleteness in Menger's subjectivism, let us now return to appreciate certain often overlooked features of those major steps towards subjectivism which Menger's vision so daringly represented.

A METHODOLOGICAL DIGRESSION—
THE ESSENTIALISM OF MENGER

Professor Hutchison has drawn attention to a much neglected methodological feature of Menger's contribution. Menger, he explains, "insisted that what the economist is after is not only relationships between quantities (*Grössenverhältnisse*) but the essence (*das Wesen*) of economic phenomena: 'How can we attain' he asks Walras [in an 1884] letter, 'to a knowledge of this essence, for example, the essence of value, the essence of land rent, the essence of bi-metallism &c by mathematics?'" (Hutchison 1953: 148).

Emil Kauder, too, appreciated Menger's methodological essentialism. "Menger claimed that the subjects of science are not the constructions of our mind but are rather the social essences. Essence means the reality underlying a phenomenon" (Kauder 1965: 97). Kauder took note of the Aristotelian character of Menger's approach: "Menger's theory deals with the Aristotelian essences, with exact types, and typical relations. . . . Like his Greek master, Menger searched for a reality hidden behind the observable surface of things. This X-ray technique of investigation is far removed from the way in which Walras, Jevons, and their followers worked" (pp. 97–8). Most recently Uskali Mäki has intensively explored the epistemological character of Menger's essentialism (see especially Mäki 1990). Our present purpose is the modest one of reminding ourselves of this feature of Menger's work, and of pointing out its relationship to the subjectivist tradition he pioneered in Austrian economics. Once again a critical comment by Frank Knight alerts us to what is going on.

Knight refers disparagingly to Menger's treatment both of demand theory and of cost and supply theory. In particular he deplores what he believes to be the neglect (by Menger especially, but to some extent also by the other leading economic theorists of his time) of the *interrelationships* between demand and supply. Knight describes some observations by Menger on the impact of marginal utility on production cost expenditure as lame, and "a far cry from recognition of the true relations of mutual determination between these variables" (Knight 1950: 23). For Knight the "comparative roles of (relative) utility and (relative) cost in determining price depend on the comparative elasticities of demand and supply" (fn.; see also Knight 1935). Menger presents no such a theory, and is therefore seen by Knight as having only a crude understanding of the theory of price determination. I think it is fair to say that this Knightian criticism expresses an unarticulated, perhaps unperceived— but nonetheless highly important—difference between Knight's own understanding of what a theory of price is supposed to explain and Menger's understanding of that same task. It will be helpful to refer to a somewhat similar disagreement between Böhm-Bawerk and Irving Fisher concerning the task of providing a theory of interest.

Irving Fisher cites Böhm-Bawerk as having postulated "*two* questions involved in the theory of the rate of interest, viz. (1) why any rate of interest exists and (2) how the rate of interest is determined" (Fisher 1930: 13f.; see also p. 474). Fisher argued that there is only one question "since to explain how the rate of interest is determined involves the question of whether the rate can or cannot be zero." Fisher sees no point in any separate explanation for the *existence* of the phenomenon of interest. Böhm-Bawerk, on the other hand, was most vigorous in maintaining the distinction which Fisher wished to deny. Böhm-Bawerk distinguished, specifically, between "originating forces" and "determining forces." An explanation for the origin of interest may be sought separately from an explanation for the interest *rate*. Böhm-Bawerk employed an illuminating analogy to drive his point home. "When we inquire into the causes of a flood we certainly cannot cite the dams and reservoirs built to prevent or at least mitigate inundations. But they are a determining factor for the actual water-mark of the flood" (Böhm-Bawerk 1959: vol. III, 192). In the same way, we are to understand, an enumeration of all the interest-rate-determining forces would be misleading as an explanation for the phenomenon of interest. It seems very clear that the difference between Fisher's understanding of the task of a theory of interest and that of Böhm-Bawerk parallels most faithfully the difference we are discussing between a Mengerian and a Knightian theory of price.

If we have identified all the factors which jointly determine the rate of interest, we have, for Fisher, provided a theory of interest. We know, in principle, what is responsible for the particular rates of interest we observe. No other task (such as explaining why the phenomenon of interest is to be found) calls for our attention (since our theory will have explained why the rate of interest is what it is).

Quite similarly for Knight what is being sought in the theory of price is a complete identification of those factors which in fact determine price. If we know the demand curve and the supply curve, we have identified the forces which, through the mutual determination of the relevant variables, establish the equilibrium price. And, unless we have completely identified these variables and the way in which they determine each other (for equilibrium to prevail), we have not fulfilled our responsibilities as price theorists. For Knight a theory of price is not a theory to account for the phenomenon of market value, but a theory to explain, in principle, why any particular price is what it is. Of course Knight's understanding of the task for price theory is very much the view which pervades neoclassical economics. Fisher's view on the task of a theory of interest was merely part of this general neoclassical outlook on the function of price theory. Yet, once we grasp Menger's essentialist perspective, it appears clear that Menger's view was quite different.

For Menger, it appears, the prime responsibility of a theorist explaining prices is not that of identifying the forces, and the relative strengths of these forces, which are jointly responsible for the level of prices. Rather the theorist, in his search for the essence of price, is looking for the root causes which are responsible for the phenomenon of price. Menger would presumably not deny the truth of Knight's often repeated contention (in criticism of the Austrian theory of value) that in the long run the relative prices of beaver and deer cannot (whatever their relative utilities) systematically differ from the ratio of physical inputs respectively needed to acquire them. But he would still have maintained that prices do not arise because of needed inputs, but because consumers' needs for these goods impel them to offer other goods in exchange. The number of pounds of deer flesh paid as the price of beaver does not *essentially* express the relative difficulty of their capture (even if this price cannot indefinitely diverge from that ratio). Rather, the essential reality underlying this price phenomenon is that it expresses the intensity of the need felt for beaver (relative to the intensity of the need felt for deer). The essence of a price is that it expresses the intensity of consumer needs. All kinds of circumstances, including especially the physical circumstances surrounding supply possibilities, will help determine the particular volume of goods which a consumer will feel constrained to offer as the price of the good he wishes to buy. But if the focus of our theoretical interest is (as the essentialist would maintain) to account for the phenomenon of price (rather than for its level) then once we have identified the root cause for this phenomenon (and explained how this root cause impinges on the environment in which production and exchange take place), we will have fulfilled our task.[3] From this perspective the explanations given in Menger's Chapter 5 on the theory of price, in which he explains the limits within which the actual level of prices is determined, must not be misunderstood. What Menger is showing in this chapter is not so much what determines the level of prices but how the level of prices expresses in fact the root cause (i.e. the intensity of consumer need) of prices. What from Knight's perspective must indeed have appeared as not much better than a valiant but crude pioneering effort towards a complete explanation for the determination of prices appears quite differently when seen from the perspective of the rather different essentialist agenda.

That Böhm-Bawerk, as we have seen, appears to have shared in Menger's understanding of the theorist's task is surely significant. A distinct, entirely valid, task of a theory of interest is to identify its essence, the underlying reality causing the phenomenon to come into existence. This task is to be distinguished from that of accounting for the height of interest rates. The root underlying cause for a flood is not to be looked for in the existence of dykes, important though dykes may certainly be in the determination of the water level. That Böhm-Bawerk (quite unself-consciously) shared Menger's perspective in this regard seems to suggest that this perspective has something to do with the subjectivist perspective which these founders of the Austrian tradition shared.

We have argued earlier in this comment that the key contribution of Menger, and the kernel of his subjectivism, lay not in his theory of marginal utility but in his revolutionary vision of the economy. In that vision Menger saw the entire system as a complex of activities directly or indirectly inspired by the goal of satisfying consumer needs. Of course this complex of activities occurs against the background of the relevant resource constraints and technological possibilities, but that background remains—background. To be sure the concrete activities will reflect the specific character of that background, but the essential nature of these activities remains that of serving consumer desires. In one physical environment consumer need for bread may generate a labour-intensive mode of agriculture; in another environment that same need may be responsible for a land-intensive mode of agriculture. For Menger the essence of both agricultural regimes is their being inspired by (and explained by) consumer needs for bread. The specific price of bread in any set of production constraints will certainly depend, in a functional sense, upon the specifics of those constraints. But the "underlying reality" accounting for the phenomenon of bread prices is, for the Mengerian view, to be seen in the consumer needs which they express.

That such an essentialist understanding of the task of economic theory is so strange to modern ears is a measure, surely, of the distance which modern economics has moved away from Menger's subjectivism. It was the subjectivism of Menger's vision of the economy which shaped his understanding of the goal of price theory. It was that subjectivism, surely, which shaped Böhm-Bawerk's understanding of the goal of a theory of interest. From this vantage point the contemporary rediscovery of Menger's essentialism seems to offer scope for renewed appreciation of the subjectivism of Menger's vision.

MENGER—THE SUBJECTIVIST PIONEER

We have seen (a) that Menger's core contribution was the subjectivism of his vision of the economy and (b) that this subjectivism is bound up with Menger's essentialist agenda for economic theory. We have also taken note of the incompleteness of Menger's subjectivism. We conclude by pointing out briefly how Menger's contribution was the pioneering step in an Austrian tradition which substantially completed the subjectivist perspective which Menger initiated.

Menger's *Grundsätze* served, of course, as the foundation for the Austrian School that is recognized in the history of economic thought. When Hayek wrote his 1934 introduction to Menger's *Collected Works,* he could say, after referring to Menger's "brilliant followers, Eugen von Böhm-Bawerk and Friedrich von Wieser," that "it is not unduly to detract from the merits of these writers to say that [the Austrian School's] fundamental ideas belong fully and wholly to Carl Menger" (Hayek 1981: 12). At the time that Hayek wrote these words the state of Austrian economics was somewhat stagnant and self-satisfied. Its principal protagonists believed (with much validity) that not very much beyond style of exposition separated the substance of Austrian economics from that of other schools of economic theory; that the insights of Austrian theory had been successfully absorbed into economics generally. Yet certain features of Menger's subjectivism, set forth in his *Grundsätze,* were pointing the Austrian tradition in a direction sharply diverging from mainstream neoclassicism.

It was undoubtedly Menger's teachings which inspired Ludwig von Mises and Friedrich Hayek in their long and arduous journey of articulating the Austrian vision systematically in non-equilibrium terms—in terms which emphasize the subjectivism of ignorance and discovery, of entrepreneurship and dynamic competition. This long journey began with Mises' 1920 critique of the possibilities for rational economic calculation in the centralized economy (Mises 1920). It proceeded via the brilliant papers of the 1930s and 1940s, published in the course of the ensuing debate, in which Hayek unravelled the subtle roles of dispersed knowledge and dynamic competition.[4] And that journey led to Mises' most complete formulation of the Austrian subjectivist view, in his 1949 *Human Action* (Mises 1966). By the end of this journey the Austrians had travelled far indeed from the contemporary mainstream. An appreciation for the profound vision which the Mises-Hayek formulations presented must surely proceed through appreciation for the subjectivism and the essentialism which shine through Carl Menger's *Grundsätze der Volkswirtschaftslehre.*

NOTES

1. A useful correction of the popular view treating Menger's contribution as simply parallel to that of Jevons and of Walras is Jaffé (1976).

2. For a critique of this aspect of Menger see Lachmann (1978).

3. To be sure, a critic might wonder why Menger could not, with equal validity, have seen the root cause for the phenomenon of price in the physical constraints surrounding production. If a pound of beaver cannot in fact be produced without forgoing the production of deer, or of other things, may it not be maintained that it is *this* underlying reality which accounts "essentially" for the phenomenon that beaver commands a price (in terms of other things paid for it)? After all, men will not hunt beaver unless a price is paid to make it worthwhile. Here, of course, Menger's subjectivist view of economic life is the dominant element—a philosophical, rather than an analytical, element. For Menger the real reason for the phenomenon of price lies in consumers' purposes in their pursuit of their goals, including both beaver and "other things." The relative difficulty of producing beaver and these other things merely marks out the channels along which consumer purposes are able to be pursued; it is seen as a background phenomenon, indeed critically important for the determination of the specific prices paid, but not itself ultimately responsible for the phenomenon of price.

4. These papers form the core of Hayek (1949a).

REFERENCES

Böhn-Bawerk, E. von (1959) *Capital and Interest,* South Holland, IL: Libertarian Press (originally published as *Geschichte und Kritik der Kapitalzins Theorien,* 1884).

Fisher, I. (1930) *The Theory of Interest,* New York: Macmillan.

Hayek, F. A. (1949a) *Individualism and Economic Order,* London: Routledge & Kegan Paul.

Hayek, F. A. (1949b) "The use of knowledge in society," in *Individualism and Economic Order,* London: Routledge & Kegan Paul (originally published in *American Economic Review* 35 (4) (1945): 519–30).

Hayek, F. A. (1955) *The Counter-Revolution of Science. Studies on the Abuse of Reason,* Glencoe, IL: Free Press.

Hayek, F. A. (1981) "Introduction," in C. Menger, *Principles of Economics,* New York and London: New York University Press (originally published as "Introduction," in *Collected Works of Carl Menger,* London: London School of Economics, 1934).

Hutchison, T. W. (1953) *A Review of Economic Doctrines, 1870–1929,* Oxford: Clarendon Press.

Jaffé, W. (1976) "Menger, Jevons, and Walras de-homogenized," *Economic Inquiry* 14 (4): 511–24.

Kauder, E. (1965) *A History of Marginal Utility Theory*, Princeton, NJ: Princeton University Press.

Kirzner, I. M. (1979a) *Perception, Opportunity and Profit*, Chicago, IL: University of Chicago Press.

Knight, F. H. (1935) "Marginal utility economics," in *The Ethics of Competition and Other Essays*, New York: Harper, Chapter v (originally published in *Encyclopedia of the Social Sciences*, 1931).

Knight, F. H. (1950) "Introduction," in C. Menger, *Principles of Economics*, Glencoe, IL: Free Press.

Lachmann, L. M. (1978) "Carl Menger and the incomplete revolution of subjectivism," *Atlantic Economic Journal* 6 (3), September: 57.

Mäki, U. (1990) "Mengerian economics in realist perspective," in B. Caldwell (ed.) *Carl Menger and his Legacy in Economics*, Durham, NC: Duke University Press.

Menger, C. (1981) *Principles of Economics*, New York: New York University Press (originally published as *Grundsätze der Volkswirtschaftslehre*, Wien: Wilhelm Braumüller, 1871: translated and edited by J. Dingwall and B. F. Hoselitz, Glencoe, IL: Free Press, 1950).

Menger, C. (1985) *Investigations into the Method of the Social Sciences with Special Reference to Economics*, transl. F. J. Nock, New York: New York University Press (originally published as *Untersuchungen über die Methode der Socialwissenschaften und der politischen Oekonomie insbesondere*, Leipzig: Duncker and Humblot, 1883; translation first published as *Problems of Economics and Sociology*, Urbana, IL: University of Illinois, 1963).

Mises, L. von (1920) "Economic calculation in the socialist commonwealth," translated in F. A. Hayek (ed.) (1935) *Collectivist Economic Planning*, London: Routledge & Kegan Paul.

Mises, L. von (1966) *Human Action, a Treatise on Economics*, 3rd edn, Chicago, IL: Henry Regnery (originally published as *Human Action*, New Haven, CT: Yale University Press, 1949).

Schumpeter, J. A. (1950) *Capitalism, Socialism and Democracy*, 3rd edn, New York: Harper & Row.

LUDWIG VON MISES AND FRIEDRICH VON HAYEK: THE MODERN EXTENSION OF AUSTRIAN SUBJECTIVISM

Much has been written about Ludwig von Mises.[1] And a great deal has been written about Friedrich von Hayek.[2] However, not much seems to have been written about Mises and Hayek as a linked pair in the development of modern economics. In particular their decisive role in the post–Second World War continuation of the Austrian tradition has not received its scholarly due. It is true that, in their accounts of the development of the Austrian School of economics, historians of economic thought have routinely cited Mises and Hayek as being modern representatives of the Austrian School. But such citations have generally tended to view them more as representing the last gasps of a dying tradition (or, indeed, the post-expiration twitches of one already dead) than as authentic contributors to a still-unfolding series of fresh intellectual developments. Furthermore these brief discussions have not explored the degree to which the work of Hayek indeed represents a continuation and extension of that of Mises, in the face of the important disagreements that separate the two. The purpose of the present chapter is to fill, to some degree, these gaps in the literature concerning the role of Mises and Hayek in the twentieth-century history of Austrian economics.

THE PARADOX OF MISES AND HAYEK

The truth is that something of a paradox surrounds the conventional pairing of these two economists. There can be no doubt that, on key elements in the Misesian system, Hayek is no Misesist at all. For Mises the possibility of economic understanding rests entirely on insights achieved *a priori;* his *praxeological* view of economic science expresses this apriorism in consistent and unqualified fashion. Yet at a relatively early and pivotal stage in his career as economist, Hayek made it clear

From *The Meaning of Market Process: Essays in the Development of Modern Austrian Economics* (New York and London: Routledge, 1992), 70–85. Reprinted by permission of Böhlau Verlag; the original source is *Die Wiener Schule der Nationalökonomie*, ed. Norbert Leser (Vienna: Böhlau Verlag, 1986). © 1986 by Hermann Böhlaus Nachf. Gesellschaft m.b.H., Graz-Wien.

that he was unable to follow his mentor in this regard.[3] For Hayek the possibility of economic regularities capable of being comprehended by science rests squarely on an empirical basis. Unaided human logic, for Hayek, is able to generate no systematic truths concerning economic processes. If historians of thought have paired Mises and Hayek in their accounts of twentieth-century economics, it almost seems as if this is based (beyond the purely personal and academic bonds linking the two from the inter-war Vienna milieu) entirely on certain key similarities in their views concerning some rather narrowly focused theoretical issues, specifically (a) the possibilities for economic calculation under central planning (see Hayek 1935, 1949a: Chs 7, 8, 9) and (b) the malinvestment theory of the business cycle (see for example Mises 1980: 357–66; Hayek 1931, 1933). Perhaps the important commonalities in the political/ideological implications seen as flowing from their shared views on these specific theoretical topics has been responsible for their names being linked in the literature. But for historians of the Austrian School of economics these common positions seem not sufficient to justify treating Hayek's economics as a seamless further development of Misesian economics. To justify such a treatment it would be necessary to go beyond agreement on a few specific issues and to demonstrate a uniquely shared overall understanding of the economic system. Can such a uniquely shared understanding be postulated for Mises and Hayek in the face of the fundamental methodological and epistemological differences that separate them?

It is our contention in this chapter that the correct answer to this question is in the affirmative. The apparent paradox of Mises and Hayek can, we maintain, be resolved in a manner that illuminates the contribution each has made to the advancement of the Austrian tradition in economics. Since elaboration of this assertion is to be the theme of this chapter, it will be understood that no attempt is made to survey the entirety of the enormously prolific scholarly output of these two eminent economists, during three-quarters of a century. Our concerns here are strictly limited to a discussion of (a) the important continuity that links the contributions of Mises and Hayek, as (b) this continuity has represented a consistent development of the Austrian School (and has, indeed, nourished a significant current revival of interest in the School). It may be helpful at this point to provide a concise preliminary overview of our proposed discussion.

MISES, HAYEK AND SUBJECTIVISM

We shall argue that the development of the Austrian tradition is to be assessed in terms of the *subjectivism* which has traditionally informed the Austrian approach to economic understanding. Subjectivism in economics did not, we submit, spring full blown into fully articulated existence with Menger's *Grundsätze*. What is common, we shall claim, to both Mises and Hayek is a readiness to extend subjectivist economics *beyond the relatively unsophisticated stage represented in the work of Austrians (and others) during the 1920s*. As we shall see, the advances for subjectivism contained in the work of Mises are rather different from those present in Hayek's contributions. Yet it is by drawing upon *both* of these complementary sets of contributions towards a more sophisticated subjectivism that the contemporary Austrian revival has been able to carry forward those continuing refinements in subjectivist economic understanding that have, arguably, constituted the history of Austrian economics since Carl Menger.

Our argument therefore (a) will have to establish the inadequacies in the subjectivism of the earlier writers, (b) will have to identify the separate advances in this regard contained in the work, respectively, of Mises and Hayek and (c) will have to show how these separate advances can be integrated in such a fashion as to permit us to talk sensibly about a joint Mises-Hayek contribution to the development of the subjectivist Austrian tradition in economics.

In an oft-quoted passage, Hayek many years ago underscored the significance which he attaches to the progressive deepening of subjectivist influence upon economic analysis. "It is probably no exaggeration to say," he wrote in 1952, "that every important advance in economic theory during the last hundred years was a further step in the consistent application of subjectivism" (1955: 31). And in a footnote he paid glowing tribute to Mises in this regard: "This is a development which has probably been carried out most consistently by L. v. Mises and I believe that most peculiarities of his views which at first strike many readers as strange and unacceptable are due to the fact that in the consistent development of the subjectivist approach he has for a long time moved ahead of his contemporaries" (p. 210, n. 24).

In this chapter we propose that it is indeed this shared dedication to subjectivism on the part of Mises and Hayek that represents the thread of continuity that links their work together. Moreover, as we shall see, the sum total of the insights which emerged as a result of this shared dedication to subjectivism have constituted a significant historical episode in the modern development of that intellectual tradition in economics for which subjectivism has always been the central idea—the Austrian School of economics.

SUBJECTIVISM AND SUBJECTIVISM

From its very beginning, of course, the Austrian School was identified as being "subjectivist." Whereas the classical theory of value had sought explanations in terms of the objective conditions surrounding physical production, the Austrians emphasized the market processes initiated by the actions of valuing, choosing, consumers. But explorations of subjectivism in recent years have drawn our attention to several quite different levels at which individual choice may be discussed. In particular *two* levels have been identified: one terminology identifies them as (a) "static subjectivism" and (b) "dynamic subjectivism" (Buchanan 1982; O'Driscoll and Rizzo 1985: Chs 2, 3; Ebeling unpublished). After the late Professor Machlup's delightful survey of the numerous different uses made in economic terminology of the static-dynamic distinction, it is of course wholly unnecessary to spell out which of these two levels is to be considered the more profound (Machlup 1963). There are some differences between different formulations of the distinction. But a useful criterion for such a classification is supplied by the well-known contributions of G. L. S. Shackle to the analysis of human decision making. In a stream of works over the course of some two decades,[4] Shackle has been concerned to emphasize the radical *creativity* and *indeterminacy* of the human decision. Each decision is a spontaneous new beginning, not at all the inexorable outcome of some previously given configuration of preferences and obstacles. Social history is a fabric woven out of the continual emergence of such mutually interacting new beginnings. These decisions are made in the face of the need to speculate on the course of future events, when the future is shrouded in ineradicable uncertainty. Moreover the essential unpredictability of the future is itself partly the consequence of our complete certainty that the future will be shaped, in large part, by intrinsically unpredictable future human decisions. From this Shacklean perspective, a "dynamically" subjectivist view of social history sees it as being governed by forces that must be traced back to choices being made, at each and every moment, by individual market participants *whose decisions can in no manner or form be treated as flowing inexorably out of the objective circumstances* prevailing at the instant prior to these respective decisions.

This view of the subjective character of human choice is contrasted sharply with that other ("static") level of subjectivist analysis in which the creativity and inherent indeterminacy of decision making is, at least tacitly, suppressed. The "statically subjectivist" view portrays the decision as indeed expressing the subjective preferences of the decision maker, but makes it appear as if these preferences are somehow separate from (and even, in some versions, chronologically prior to) the decision itself, and as if these preferences then "determine" the specific decision taken. The course of social history is then seen as the "inexorable" flow of events emerging from these interacting decisions (it being understood that such "inexorability" is strictly relative, of course, to the independent, "subjective" preferences of potential decision makers).

As Shackle and others have pointed out, the human decision envisaged in such a "statically" subjectivist view hardly constitutes a genuine *choice* at all (Shackle 1972: passim; Kirzner 1979a: Ch. 13). The very circumstance that the "chosen" course of action is seen as already inexorably implied in the given configuration of preferences and constraints, of ends and means, makes the choice "mechanical" or "automatic"—and thus not a true choice at all. True choice surely requires the realistic possibility of more than one alternative; but for the statically subjectivist view the rejected alternative is *already, before* (or at least apart from) the moment of decision, an option declared to be a suboptimal (and thus a quite unthinkable) alternative. The circumstance that, in this statically subjectivist view, the scales of individual preference, or the relevant indifferent maps, are declared to be the expression of independent subjective likes and dislikes does not suffice to invest this "mechanical" model of decision making with the characteristics of genuine choice. A machine can calculate a required optimal option; we would not wish to say that the machine can *choose*.

Now, a plausible view of doctrinal history might see the contemporary neoclassical mainstream as representing the legacy of "static subjectivism" stemming from the approaches of Jevons, Walras, and especially Pareto. (Pareto's notorious remark to the effect that the "individual can disappear, so long as he leaves us a photograph of his tastes"[5] concisely but accurately captures his extremely limited concern with the subjectivism of individual choice.) On the other hand, this view would suggest, the Austrian School from Menger to Mises has been much closer to "dynamic subjectivism." From Menger's emphasis on independent consumer *valuation* of the significance of commodities (and, indirectly, of factor services) to Mises' concern with purposeful human action in an open-ended, uncertain world, the Austrian tradition has refused, it would appear, to treat choice as if it were inexorably determined by "given" preferences. While not entirely wrong, this view of the Austrian School is, we shall see, rather seriously oversimplified. The truth is that, despite significant elements of "dynamic subjectivism" in Menger (and perhaps in several of his followers), the early post–First World War developments in Austrian economics were generally in the direction of being "static" rather than "dynamic" in their subjectivism. That this was the case can be perhaps most effectively conveyed by briefly considering the Austrian provenance of that extremely influential work, Lionel Robbins's 1932 *Essay on the Nature and Significance of Economic Science.*

LIONEL ROBBINS, THE AUSTRIANS, AND NEOCLASSICAL ECONOMICS

If modern neoclassical microeconomics sees itself as based upon the analysis of *choice,* this is in no small measure due to the influence of Robbins's book. When a modern textbook devotes an entire (admittedly brief) chapter to credit Robbins with the breakthrough leading up to the contemporary view that "the core of pure economic science is the general theory of choice" (Walsh 1970: 17), this is by no means an exaggeration. What is now a commonplace was, in 1932, something of a revolutionary idea; since then this idea has decisively governed the direction of mainstream economic thought. What is important for our purposes in this chapter is to recognize (a) the Austrian influence on Robbins in this regard and (b) the circumstance that this influence came to be transmitted to the neoclassical mainstream (via Robbins) in "statically," rather than "dynamically," subjectivist terms. The latter circumstance will suggest rather strongly that the Austrian literature that influenced Robbins so powerfully was itself perhaps closer to the Paretian, rather than the Mengerian, brand of subjectivism.

In a recent paper Mark Addleson (1984) has reminded us of the pervasive Austrian influence which Robbins's book reflects (and which was widely recognized at the time of its appearance). He cites R. W. Souter's scathing 1933 review of the book, in the course of which Souter described it as a "scholarly and succinct account of the main tenets of 'The Austrian School'" (Souter 1933, cited in Addleson 1984: 509). As Addleson points out the "*Essay* is steeped in the Austrian tradition. This is reflected in the author's acknowledgement of his 'especial indebtedness to the works of Professor Ludwig von Mises. . . .' The names of economists like Schönfeld, Hans Mayer, Strigl, Carl Menger, Fetter, Hayek, Böhm-Bawerk, Morgenstern and Machlup, are evoked time and time again. . . ."[6]

So that, if the "static subjectivism" that is so characteristic of modern neoclassical choice theory is significantly attributable to Robbinsian influence, we must not be surprised to discover evidence of such limited subjectivism not only in Robbins himself, but also in at least part of the Austrian literature that he cited.

For Robbins, of course, the role of choice was indeed central for the economic side of human life. "Economics is the science which studies human behavior as a relationship between ends and scarce means which have alternative uses" (Robbins 1935: 16). "When the time and the means for achieving ends are limited *and* capable of alternative application, *and* the ends are capable of being distinguished in order of importance, then behaviour necessarily takes the form of choice. . . . It has an economic aspect" (p. 14). But Robbinsian choice offers little scope for what we have called "dynamic" subjectivism.

The outcome of a Robbinsian act of choice, it appears, is inescapably implied in the given pattern of ends and of means the relationship between which is the prerequisite for Robbinsian choice. This outcome emerges, it seems to be asserted, in a manner almost beyond the control of the decision maker—it is instead "the resultant of conflicting psychological pulls acting within an environment of given material and technical possibilities" (Robbins 1935: 35). To be sure the ends themselves, while given, are not fixed for all time. Ends can and do change: "sybarites become ascetics" (p. 26). But the replacement of one set of given ends by a second set occurs *before* (or at least *outside*) Robbinsian choice itself. Whatever the process through which Robbinsian man comes to be endowed with the system of ends with respect to which he must allocate his finite array of given means, this process not only lies wholly outside the scope of economic science, it lies outside the realm of economic choice itself. Economic choice, for Robbins, is circumscribed entirely by the framework of given ends and given means that makes systematic allocative behaviour necessary. As Talcott Parsons pointed out at the time (1934: 512), this unfortunate mechanical picture of choice is a consequence of the way in which Robbins treats ends as given, suppressing the futurity of the very notion of a human purpose.

But a "dynamically" subjectivist viewpoint must surely recognize that in expressing his purposes man must choose between alternative imagined future scenarios. His imagination of these alternative futures is very much an intrinsic element of choice. At the moment of choice ends are not all "given"; they are nailed down only through the act of choice itself. Whatever it is that accounts for the particular ends that are thus chosen to be aimed at, it cannot be the solution of a problem in constrained maximization for which these ends themselves are data.[7] A fully subjectivist treatment of choice could not, as Robbins does, avoid discussion of these matters. A fully subjectivist treatment of choice must grapple with the way the decision maker, with all his spontaneous creativity in the face of a radically uncertain world, *chooses* which of the infinite possible pictures of the future he adopts as the basis for the alternative scenarios among which he undertakes the path he is to pursue. Despite all its virtues, all its Austrian credentials, Robbinsian choice is portrayed in abstraction from (if not in complete denial of) the insights of dynamic subjectivism.

But, as Richard Ebeling has recently shown in an unpublished paper, the writings of leading Austrian economists during the 1920s, including especially Hans Mayer, Richard Strigl (whom Robbins had cited prominently) as well as Rosenstein-Rodan, expressed a conception of choice *which is precisely as limited in its subjectivism (as "static") as that of* Robbins. If it is reasonable to judge the work of Robbins as pointing towards a synthesis of the various post-1870 marginalist schools of economic thought, then it must be stated that the subjectivism which Robbins brought to the synthesis from Vienna was severely limited to the "static" aspects of subjectivism.

Here, then, we find the basis for our earlier claim that by the early 1930s the development of the Austrian tradition had produced a seriously limited variety of subjectivism. We shall now argue that the work of both Mises and Hayek can be illuminatingly viewed as introducing (separate) elements of dynamic subjectivism. It will prove useful for this purpose, however, first to re-examine the theoretical model of a market economy populated entirely by "economizing men."

We shall find it convenient to identify *two* distinct aspects of this world that must appear very troublesome for any realistic attempt to understand markets. It will turn out, not at all accidentally, that the Misesian "dynamically subjectivist" contribution entails an alteration of this world in so far as concerns one of these two offending aspects; the Hayekian subjectivist contribution would transform this world in the second of these two aspects. Taken together, we shall see, the two contributions successfully replace a statically subjectivist view of the market with a dynamically subjectivist view. It is this circumstance, it is our thesis in this chapter, which (a) justifies the traditional pairing of Mises and Hayek and (b) recognizes their important joint contribution in extending the vision of the Austrian School of economics.

The world populated entirely by Robbinsian economizers is in fact the world of contemporary neoclassical microeconomics. Thus the demonstration of how the Mises-Hayek subjectivist contributions together drastically transform that world offers at the same time a glimpse of how the contemporary Austrian theoretical vision, informed by those contributions, differs sharply from the dominant neoclassical view.

Economizing man, we have seen, "chooses" within a framework rigidly circumscribed by the pattern of ranked ends and available means assumed to be perceived as given (for the moment of economizing choice). His strictly allocative choice does not encompass the perception or identification of the elements making up this rigid framework. Now, in the market economy, neither the ranking of ends nor the availability of means can be considered as given to any agent apart from the decisions of other (similarly "economizing") individuals. No producer, for example, can treat output of his product as equivalent to the achievement of ends of given importance without specific expectations concerning the market prices to be offered for that output, and so on. No producer can treat inputs as available means without specific expectations concerning the market prices to be asked by the sellers of those inputs. But surely recognition of this circumstance, that a world of economizing individuals presupposes definite anticipations concerning the choices which the other (similarly economizing) individuals are in fact now in the process of making, presents us with a very serious dilemma.

Either the economizing choices actually being made are "correct," in the sense that they sustain the anticipated frameworks of ranked ends and available means identified respectively by market participants; or these choices fail to confirm these anticipated ends-means frameworks. On the first of these two alternatives all the allocative decisions being made can in fact be successfully, and without generating regret, carried out as planned—since the selected courses of action deemed optimal indeed turn out to be both feasible and most preferred. The feasibility and optimality of any chosen course of allocative action has not been frustrated by failure of any of the anticipated choices of others to occur as expected. On the second of these alternatives, on the other hand, things are quite different. On the second alternative decision makers find themselves unable to complete their chosen courses of action (because those courses of action presupposed decisions of others that turn out not to have been made); or else they discover that their chosen courses of action turn out—for symmetrical reasons—to have been by no means the truly optimal allocative programmes in the light of the actual hierarchy of ranked ends and available means which the pattern of market decisions in fact generates. Each of these alternative possibilities appears to raise serious difficulties.

If we are to assume that all the economizing decisions are indeed "correct," we have necessarily confined ourselves to the fully co-ordinated, equilibrium world—something imaginable only on the basis of universal mutual omniscience concerning what market participants can and will choose to do. To *confine* ourselves and our economic analysis to the context of full mutual omniscience is not merely to accept a wildly unrealistic assumption; it is to confess that our model of the economizing world *is unable to throw light upon any process of adjustment through which, perhaps, an approach towards the fully co-ordinated state of affairs (or, indeed, of any specific state of affairs) might occur* in the real world of imperfect knowledge. But the second alternative is no less troublesome in this regard.

We may indeed easily imagine a world in which a large proportion of attempted economizing decisions turn out to be disappointed in execution (because the necessary anticipated decisions on the part of others have not in fact been made) or turn out to be regretted (because hindsight reveals that the true relevant patterns of ends and means would have suggested even more desirable courses of allocative action). *But it is not at all clear how, in a world of exclusive economizers,* such disappointments *can be held to generate systematic modifications* in the allocative decisions to be made by market participants in subsequent time periods. We must remember that our economizers are not endowed with any propensities that might systematically modify expectations concerning the decisions being made by others. Economizers are, so to speak, *endowed* with given ends-means frameworks. There is *nothing* within the scope of the analysis of economizing activity that permits us to postulate a systematic series of modifications in the ends-means frameworks held to be relevant by market participants. Unless we transcend the assumption of purely Robbinsian economizers, our second alternative indeed results in frustrated economizing attempts—but such disequilibrium chaos cannot be held to result in *any* systematic modifications of choices, let alone any *equilibrating* sequences of such modifications (see Kirzner 1973: 36).

To use a model made up of economizing individuals in order to arrive at an explanation for systematic market adjustments (that might be generated by initial disequilibrium) it is clearly necessary to assume that market participants do indeed come to know where market events have shown their previously assumed frameworks of ends and means to require revision. But to do this is to jeopardize the integrity of the model by importing into it a totally arbitrary modifying feature, i.e. endowing the population of economizers with the propensity to replace discredited assumed ends-means frameworks by new frameworks revealed to be relevant by market experience. To postulate such an endowment is not only sharply to modify the scenario of pure economizers (who were, after all, supposed to have *given* endowments of ends-means frameworks). It is to leave unexplained how market experience communicates to these economizing individuals sudden awareness of exploitable opportunities *which already existed but which were previously overlooked by the same economizing individuals.*

Here, then, we have before us the two separate aspects of this purely economizing world that must surely engender grave misgivings. First, the model of such a world is clearly seriously deficient in its failure to pay attention to the role played by *knowledge* and *learning* in the initial endowment of assumed ends-means frameworks, and in subsequent modification of these endowments as a result of market experience. Second, the make-up of the model, in terms of a population consisting solely of pure economizers, is in fact inconsistent with the kinds of learning sequences which one would have to postulate in order to account for systematic market processes. We shall see that while the "dynamic" subjectivism expressed in Mises' writings opened up the possibility of dealing with the second of these difficulties, it was not until Hayek's contributions to the deepening of subjectivism that the first of these two inadequacies was eliminated. Misesian subjectivism replaced the mechanical, allocative activity of the rather wooden economizer by the dynamics of human action. Hayek's work compelled the economics profession to address explicitly the role of knowledge and learning in economic process. Together, the Mises-Hayek contributions offer a truly "dynamically" subjectivist understanding of market processes.

LUDWIG VON MISES AND THE SCIENCE OF HUMAN ACTION

For Mises economics is a *science of human action*. Every conclusion of economic theory is, for Mises, the outcome of the circumstance that economic life consists of interacting human *agents*. It is human action that is the basic unit of analysis. Although Mises never did, to this writer's knowledge, spell out the distinction between his own notion of *human action* and the Robbinsian concept of "economizing," there can be no doubt that the difference is a fundamental one. Human action is a far broader concept than that of economizing; while the allocation of scarce means among multiple competing ends may be an *example* of human action, human action need not be allocative at all. "Human action is purposeful behavior" (Mises 1966: 11). What acting man seeks to do is "to substitute a more satisfactory state of affairs for a less satisfactory" (p. 13). Nothing in these formulations confines them to the calculative allocation of scarce means with respect to competing goals.

We may distinguish two subjectivist elements contained in the Misesian concept that are absent from the narrower notion of Robbinsian economizing choice. First, human action is essentially *purposive;* its objective is not *maximization* (of, say, utility or profit) subject to side constraints, but the removal of felt uneasiness, the attainment of a better future state of affairs. No one could accuse Mises (as some had accused Robbins) of suppressing the sense of purposefulness that suffuses human activity; no one could accuse him of suppressing that subjectively felt sense of *futurity* that human beings attach to the goals they seek to achieve through their actions. Not only does the concept of human action emphasize its purposefulness; the notion of purposefulness really does exhaust its essence. For Mises human action may consist of deliberately remaining completely idle (Mises 1966); *in*action may be an example of action. The *essential* element in action is goal pursuit, not maximization, not allocative efficiency, or anything else. There is no possibility of abstracting from the subjective element in human action without completely eroding the very concept.[8] Second, the concept of human action (unlike that of Robbinsian economizing) contains within it an essential *entrepreneurial* element. "In any real and living economy every actor is always an entrepreneur" (Mises 1966: 252). The human agent "is endowed not only with the propensity to pursue goals efficiently, once ends and means are clearly identified, *but also with the drive and alertness to identify which ends to strive for and which means are available*" (Kirzner 1973: 34, emphasis added). Thus subjectivism in the analysis of decision making means more than merely the recognition that the ends-means framework relevant to a particular decision maker is that with which he has been peculiarly endowed. It means more, even, than the recognition that the decision maker is consciously pursuing his purposes, that his activity is suffused with the sense of driving to attain his objectives. Subjectivism in the analysis of Misesian human action includes the insight that any ends-means framework relevant to a human action has *itself been actively chosen* in the course of that very action—and that that choice expresses and reflects that agent's dreams, aspirations and imagination, his expectations and his knowledge, his hunches and his biases.

Once our picture of the economic agent has, following Mises, been broadened from that of a constrained maximizer (in the context of an endowed ends-means framework) to that of the human being actively following his own hunches, his own vision (as to what is worthwhile pursuing and as to what is the best available relevant course of pursuing action), the way is open for incorporating *learning by discovery* into our understanding of market processes. We are now no longer bound to a mode of theorizing in which the unit of analysis precludes us from serendipitous changes in relevant knowledge. We are no longer confined to a world in which everything deemed worthwhile knowing is either *already* known to agents or is now confidently planned to be learned, sooner or later, in the course of already-fully-envisaged systematic search procedures. We can now find scope, within the market process, for the *spontaneous discovery* of hitherto unnoticed opportunities, or for the realization that earlier anticipations have proved to have been over-optimistic. We can now look for a possibly systematically unfolding series of such discoveries, made possible by the changing arrays of opportunities which these sequences of discoveries themselves generate.

To put this somewhat differently, we can now, possibly, explain a changing pattern of decisions over time as the systematic outcome of changing patterns of knowledge, with the latter changes themselves being the result of discoveries stimulated, in turn, by the steadily shifting sets of interpersonal opportunities created through time by these very sets of changing decisions. In other words this implication of the Misesian contribution contrasts sharply with one of the two disquieting features of the Robbinsian world noted in the preceding section of this paper, namely that a world of economizers is inconsistent with the kinds of learning sequences needed to account for systematic market processes.

To state these systematic implications of the Misesian subjectivist contribution is not, however, to claim that Mises himself explicitly enunciated the character of market processes in these terms. In fact Mises himself did not emphasize the role of changing arrays of knowledge as constituting the unfolding market process. It was Hayek's contribution to a deepened subjectivism that brought this role into unmistakably clear focus. To that contribution we now turn.

FRIEDRICH VON HAYEK AND THE ROLE OF KNOWLEDGE

Hayek's contributions to modern economics (quite apart from his prolific work in other disciplines) extend across a formidable range of areas within the subject. His bibliography in economics alone includes now classic works in monetary theory, business cycle theory, capital theory, doctrinal history, the theory of socialist planning, economic methodology, and other important areas. Yet it seems correct to state that the portion of Hayek's work most frequently cited (if not always adequately understood) in contemporary economic discussion is that which concerns *the role of knowledge*. In this section we briefly refer to this celebrated Hayekian contribution and cite it as constituting, in our view, a decisive, explicit extension of subjectivism in modern economics.

Hayek's definitive introduction of knowledge into economics involved two separate (but certainly related) series of insights. The first (represented most clearly by his famous 1937 paper "Economics and knowledge"[9]) demonstrated (a) the nature of market equilibrium constructs as the working out of the implications of complete mutual knowledge on the part of market participants and (b) the nature of hypothesized equilibrating market processes as consisting of specific patterns of mutual *learning*. The second set of insights concerning knowledge (introduced already in the 1937 paper, and spelled out definitively in Hayek's equally famous 1945 paper, "The use of knowledge in society" (Hayek 1949b)) drew attention to the positive and normative implications of the circumstance that the sum total of knowledge available in an economy "never exists in concentrated or integrated form but solely as the dispersed bits of incomplete and frequently contradictory knowledge which all the separate individuals possess" (p. 77).

To recognize market processes as consisting of systematically changing patterns of individual knowledge about one another, to recognize the normative significance of social institutions that make possible the fullest utilization by members of society of "knowledge which is not given to anyone in its totality" (Hayek 1949b: 78), is to threaten revolution in both microeconomic theory and the theory of welfare economics. Modern neoclassical theories of microeconomics and welfare economics, as suggested earlier, have remained at the lower (or "static") level of subjectivism. Hayek's insights concerning knowledge pointed to a comprehensive fully (or "dynamically") subjectivist revolution of understanding in these areas. That these threatened revolutions somehow never succeeded in dislodging the neoclassical dominance is mute evidence of the very limited extent to which the modern profession has been hospitable to extensions of subjectivism.

Hayek himself drew explicit attention to the subjectivist character of his work on the role of knowledge. In his most detailed discussion of the importance of subjectivism for the social sciences, Hayek wrote of "the more complex phenomena with which economic theory is concerned and where in recent years progress has been particularly closely connected with the advance of subjectivism." He cited in particular "the new problems which these developments make appear more and more central, such as the problem of the compatibility of intentions and expectations of different people, of the division of knowledge between them, and the process by which the relevant knowledge is acquired and expectations formed" (1955: 33). For the purposes of this paper it is important to notice that these subjectivist contributions of Hayek contrast sharply with that other disquieting feature of the model of the Robbinsian world noted earlier in this chapter, namely its failure to focus on the role of knowledge and learning (both in the initial specification of the model and in the manner in which the model can be put through its paces in accounting for market processes).

MISES, HAYEK AND SUBJECTIVIST ECONOMIC UNDERSTANDING

We have taken note of the separate contributions to the extension of subjectivism made by Mises and Hayek. For Mises economics came to be transformed into a science of (radically subjectivist) human action; Hayek outlined the translation of economic theorems into new forms of understanding concerning human knowledge. We wish to argue here that these separate contributions together not only make up a decisive step from static to dynamic subjectivism but also, at the same time, help articulate a subjectivist understanding of market processes that constitutes an authentic extension of the work of economists of the Austrian School, in a tradition going back to Menger. If our argument in this regard is accepted, it will have vindicated the references in the literature to a strong linkage between Mises and Hayek, in the face of the very important differences that separate them. It will moreover add significance to the references in the literature to this pair of economists as being latter-day representatives of the classic Austrian School.

Carl Menger decisively changed the orientation of economic understanding. His subjectivist insight demonstrated how economic phenomena can be most successfully perceived as the reflection and expression of valuing and economizing individuals. Menger's own subjectivism appears, on a number of accounts, to have been refreshingly "dynamic." Menger's successors carried many of these insights and brought them into contact with the work of marginalist economists from other schools. But in the very course of refining Austrian marginal analysis, a certain "static" quality seems to have crept into the subjectivism which that work expressed in the immediate post–First World War period. (To state this is not to criticize the writers involved. There are unquestionably certain aspects of Austrian economics for which articulation of dynamically subjectivistic insights is simply not necessary.) As a consequence it became possible for a brilliant synthesist such as Robbins to inject key Austrian insights into mainstream neoclassical economic theory (to which "dynamic" subjectivism was virtually a complete stranger) without transcending the level of static subjectivism at all. Thus the subsequent advances in neoclassical microeconomics, enriched by Robbinsian-Austrian injections, continued along a line which is, in fact, starkly *incompatible* with a dynamically subjectivist perspective. It is no surprise, therefore, to find some modern exponents of dynamic subjectivism, such as Professors Shackle and Lachmann, compelled to reject the neoclassical paradigm virtually in its entirety. Mises and Hayek took a different path.

The importance of the contribution of Mises and Hayek consists, in fact, not merely in their drawing attention to subjectivist elements absent from the earlier Robbins-Austrian formulations. Their introduction of these new elements enabled the traditional Austrian approach to be extended by suggesting a deepened understanding of market process. While indeed sharply differing from the neoclassical mainstream on many crucial substantive and methodological points, this deepened understanding yet preserved those important areas of overlap which from Menger's time onwards, were shared in common by the Austrians and the other marginalist schools. What Mises and Hayek preserved was a vision of the market which firmly recognizes its *systematic* (rather than chaotic or haphazard) character while never losing sight of the "open-endedness" of the decision making environment—an open-endedness generated by the imminent passage of time, by the imperfect knowability of the future and by the consequent omnipresence of radical uncertainty. This feat they accomplished by pointing the way to an understanding of market processes as systematic "discovery procedures"[10]—i.e. spontaneous mutual learning procedures—continually being set in motion by entrepreneurial human agents. The drive, the alertness and the incentives which spur human action tend to guide these unmodellable entrepreneurial discoveries in the direction of enhanced mutual knowledge, of enhanced interpersonal co-ordination. Despite continual buffeting by unpredictable exogenous changes in the basic data, it is still possible, on this modern Austrian view, to perceive the powerful co-ordinative forces of entrepreneurial alertness, as they manifest themselves in the ceaseless agitation of the market. To be sure, the disruptive effect of those continual buffetings manifests itself more seriously in some markets than in others. Thus while this deepened modern Austrian understanding provides insights relevant to *all* markets, their deployment to arrive at concrete forecasts or judgements in *particular* markets calls for close attention to the relevant empirical and institutional detail.

All this surely does vindicate the widespread linkage associated with the names of Mises and Hayek. There is every ground for believing that their vision of the market is indeed basically a single one, and that the subtlety and power of this vision derives from the sophisticated character of their contributions to subjectivism. From this perspective the shared critique of the possibility of centralized economic calculation (enunciated by both Mises and Hayek during the inter-war years) is no accident at all. That shared critique derived, we can now clearly perceive, from that shared understanding of market processes as processes of spontaneous entrepreneurial discovery (see Lavoie 1985a). For this shared understanding, we have argued in this chapter, their separate contributions to a deepened subjectivism can be seen as providing crucially important ingredients. For all these reasons, therefore, the linked contributions of Mises and Hayek may be seen, in the broad sweep of twentieth-century economic-intellectual history, as representing a vigorous spurt of new progress in a still-very-much-alive tradition of Austrian subjectivism.

NOTES

1. Although a full-length analysis of the economics of Ludwig von Mises has yet to appear in print, the following works are relevant: Moss (1976), Sennholz (1978), Greaves (1978), Rothbard (1973), Andrews (1981), Ebeling (unpublished). For a comprehensive bibliography of Mises' writings see Bien (1969).

2. A number of recent works discuss the broader impact of Hayek's work in social and political science and philosophy. For detailed surveys of Hayek's economic writings see Machlup (1976) and O'Driscoll (1977).

3. See Hayek (1949c). See also Hayek (1979: 205, n.51) for a reference to a basic philosophical disagreement that Hayek perceives to separate the two.

4. Among the most important of these are Shackle (1970, 1972).

5. See Pareto (1927: 170). (I am indebted to Professor L. M. Lachmann for this reference.)

6. See Addleson (1984: 509). (The writer gratefully acknowledges his indebtedness to Mr. Addleson's paper—despite the significant differences that separate it from this writer's views on several rather important points.)

7. On the relationship between Robbinsian choice and the maximization of utility, see Robbins (1935: 15n).

8. On this aspect of Misesian human action, and its advance over the economizing notion, see Kirzner (1960: 161f.).

9. See note 3.

10. The phrase is, of course, Hayek's. See Hayek (1978b).

REFERENCES

Addleson, M. (1984) "Robbins's essay in retrospect: on subjectivism and an 'economics of choice,'" *Rivista Internazionale Di Scienze Economiche e Commerciali* 31 (6).

Andrews, J. K. (ed.) (1981) *Homage to Mises, the First Hundred Years*, Hillsdale, MI: Hillsdale College Press.

Bien (Greaves), B. (1969) *The Works of Ludwig von Mises*, Irvington-on-Hudson, NY: Foundation for Economic Education.

Buchanan, J. A. (1982) "Order defined in the process of its emergence," *Literature of Liberty* 5 (4): 5.

Ebeling, R. M. "Action analysis and economic science, the economic contributions of Ludwig von Mises," unpublished doctoral dissertation, University College, Cork.

Greaves, P. L. Jr. (1978) "Introduction," in *Ludwig von Mises, On The Manipulation of Money and Credit*, Dobbs Ferry, NY: Free Market Books.

Hayek, F. A. (1931) *Prices and Production*, London: Routledge.

Hayek, F. A. (1933) *Monetary Theory and the Trade Cycle*, London: Jonathan Cape.

Hayek, F. A. (1935) *Collectivist Economic Planning*, London: Routledge & Kegan Paul.

Hayek, F. A. (1949b) "The use of knowledge in society," in *Individualism and Economic Order*, London: Routledge & Kegan Paul (originally published in *American Economic Review* 35 (4) (1945): 519–30).

Hayek, F. A. (1949c) "Economics and knowledge," in *Individualism and Economic Order*, London: Routledge & Kegan Paul (originally published in *Economica* 4, February 1937).

Hayek, F. A. (1955) *The Counter-Revolution of Science. Studies on the Abuse of Reason*, Glencoe, IL: Free Press.

Hayek, F. A. (1978b) "Competition as a discovery procedure," in *New Studies in Philosophy, Politics, Economics and the History of Ideas*, Chicago, IL: University of Chicago Press (first presented as a lecture, 1968).

Hayek, F. A. (1979) *Law, Legislation and Liberty*, Vol. 3, *The Political Order of a Free People*, Chicago, IL: University of Chicago Press.

Kirzner, I. M. (1960) *The Economic Point of View*, Princeton, NJ: Van Nostrand.

Kirzner, I. M. (1973) *Competition and Entrepreneurship*, Chicago, IL: University of Chicago Press.

Kirzner, I. M. (1979a) *Perception, Opportunity and Profit*, Chicago, IL: University of Chicago Press.

Lavoie, D. (1985a) *Rivalry and Central Planning: The Socialist Calculation Debate Reconsidered*, Cambridge: Cambridge University Press.

Machlup, F. (1963) "Statics and dynamics: kaleidoscopic words," in *Essays in Economic Semantics*, Englewood Cliffs, NJ: Prentice-Hall (originally published in *Southern Economic Journal*, October 1959).

Machlup, F. (1976) "Hayek's contribution to economics," in *Essays on Hayek*, New York: New York University Press (originally published in *Swedish Journal of Economics* 76, December 1974).

Mises, L. von (1966) *Human Action, a Treatise on Economics,* 3rd edn, Chicago, IL: Henry Regnery (originally published as *Human Action,* New Haven, CT: Yale University Press, 1949).

Mises, L. von (1980) *Theory of Money and Credit,* Indianapolis, IN: Liberty Fund (originally published as *Theorie des Geldes und der Umlaufsmittel,* 1912: translated as *Theory of Money and Credit,* 1934; also New Haven, CT: Yale University Press, 1953).

Moss, L. (ed.) (1976) *The Economics of Ludwig von Mises, Toward a Critical Reappraisal,* Kansas City, KS: Sheed and Ward.

O'Driscoll, G. P. Jr. (1977) *Economics as a Coordination Problem, The Contributions of Friedrich A. Hayek,* Kansas City, KS: Sheed, Andrews & McMeel.

O'Driscoll, G. P. Jr., and Rizzo, M. J. (1985) *The Economics of Time and Ignorance,* Oxford: Basil Blackwell.

Pareto, V. (1927) *Manual d'économie politique,* 2nd edn, Paris.

Parsons, T. (1934) "The nature and significance of economics," *Quarterly Journal of Economics* May: 512.

Robbins, L. (1935) *An Essay on the Nature and Significance of Economic Science,* 2nd edn, London: Macmillan (1st edn 1932).

Rothbard, M. N. (1973) *The Essential von Mises,* Bramble Minibooks.

Sennholz, H. F. (1978) "Postscript," in *Ludwig von Mises, Notes and Recollections,* South Holland, IL: Libertarian Press.

Shackle, G. L. S. (1970) *Decision, Order and Time in Human Affairs,* 2nd edn, Cambridge: Cambridge University Press (originally published 1969).

Shackle, G. L. S. (1972) *Epistemics and Economics: A Critique of Economic Doctrines,* Cambridge: Cambridge University Press.

Souter, R. W. (1933) "The nature and significance of economic science in recent discussion," *Quarterly Journal of Economics* 47: 377.

Walsh, V. C. (1970) *Introduction to Contemporary Microeconomics,* New York: McGraw-Hill.

THE SUBJECTIVISM OF AUSTRIAN ECONOMICS

I have chosen subjectivism as my topic for this chapter and surely few will question the appropriateness and importance of this topic. Austrian economics has recently lost one of its great modern masters, Friedrich A. Hayek. It is therefore perhaps particularly fitting to open this chapter with Hayek's often quoted tribute to the role of subjectivism in the growth of economic understanding. It is, he wrote, "probably no exaggeration to say that every important advance in economic theory during the last hundred years was a further step in the constant application of subjectivism" (Hayek, 1955, p. 31). Our thesis will be that the subjectivism that developed out of those pioneering insights of Carl Menger who founded the Austrian School, has come to mean entirely different things to different doctrinal traditions within modern economics—each of which derives substantially or wholly from the Mengerian tradition. In calling for the endorsement of that one variety of subjectivism which informs modern Austrian economics, we shall argue that it is this variety that most faithfully preserves and deepens Menger's own fundamental insights.

THE SUBJECTIVISM OF THE AUSTRIAN SCHOOL

Subjectivism has never, of course, meant any challenge to the possibility of "objective truth" in economics. It has never claimed that "everything is merely a matter of subjective interpretation" by the would-be economist. What the subjectivism of the 1870s challenged was the basic—if unstated—classical tenet that ultimately the only determinant of social-economic phenomena is the objective physical environment. All economic science has endeavored to account for real-world phenomena. The classical economist believed that these phenomena are to be seen as having been inexorably determined by the underlying physical realities. The availability of scarce natural resources, in conjunction with population and its demographics, basically determine the course of human history. What emerges over history is inescapable; it cannot be substantially

From *The Driving Force of the Market: Essays in Austrian Economics* (New York and London: Routledge, 2000), 41–53. Reprinted by permission of Taylor & Francis Books UK; original source is *New Perspectives on Austrian Economics*, ed. Gerrit Meijer (New York and London: Routledge, 1995), 11–23. © 1995 by Taylor & Francis Books UK.

altered by human will. Economic history emerges as automatically determined by the objective conditions governing and surrounding production. It was against this premise that Menger did revolutionary battle in
his 1871 *Grundsätze*—written, we are told, in what he himself described as
"a state of morbid excitement" (Hayek, 1981, p. 16).

The central thrust of Menger's book, we argue, was not so much his
articulation of a subjective (marginal utility) theory of value, as his vision of the entire economic process of production as expressing the imprint, upon external reality, of the human factor. It was this vision that
led him to formulate his theory of goods of various "orders," in which it
is the preference of the final consumers that determines the place of each
potential resource in the structure of production, and that ultimately assigns market values to all of them. It was this vision that led him (some
twenty years earlier than his fellow pioneers in the marginalist revolution, in other schools) to glimpse, at least, the outlines of the theory of
marginal productivity within the very formulation of the marginal utility theory of value. What ultimately determines the economic phenomena that we observe in the real world is, in this Mengerian vision, not
the physical conditions governing production, but the needs of human
beings. It is the latter that determine production methods, and the assignment of market values to goods, and incomes to owners of agents of
production. Menger's vision is thus subjective in the fundamental sense
that what emerges in real-world economies is the expression of human
preferences as exercised against a background of given, passive resource
constraints and endowments.

This subjectivist view of Menger differs not only, as already seen,
from the classical view. It also differs, at least philosophically, from the
Marshallian version of the neoclassical view. In this latter view (which
has, largely due to the influence of Knight and his disciples, become
the contemporary mainstream view in the United States) economic
phenomena are seen as emerging from the interplay of the subjective
and objective elements of supply (expressing objective cost conditions)
and demand (reflecting consumer preferences). For Menger, as we have
seen, the relevant insight is that—while, to be sure, the objective situation has much to do with the specific market outcomes that emerge in
the course of the economic process—it is solely the actions of choosing consumers that in fact initiate and drive the process through which
these outcomes emerge.

THE INCOMPLETENESS OF MENGER'S SUBJECTIVISM

As we shall see, and as is well known, Menger's subjectivism was incomplete in several respects. But we shall claim that the above kernel of Menger's subjectivist insight remains valid and central for economic understanding. It is this kernel that, during the long and checkered history of twentieth-century (and especially Austrian) economics, sometimes came to be obscured (especially in the early decade of the century). It is the revival of this kernel of subjectivism in the mid- and late twentieth century work of Mises, Hayek and their followers, that constitutes, in this economist's view, the most exciting feature of the resurgence of Austrian economics. And it is, paradoxically, this kernel that has unfortunately become threatened by certain recent developments within Austrian economics itself.

With the benefit of hindsight it is in fact possible to discern within Menger's work precisely those elements in his economic vision that we now see to have been, subjectivistically speaking, profoundly flawed, and relate them to those valid, enduring aspects of his subjectivism that have been, as it were, rediscovered and reaffirmed in modern Austrian economics. And, if we describe these latter, valid elements in Menger's subjectivism as being threatened, paradoxically, by certain developments within Austrian economics itself, the solution to the paradox is perhaps not far to seek. It has been an overenthusiastic tendency on the part of certain Austrian economists in recent years, to escape the legacy of incompleteness in Menger's subjectivism, that seems to have inadvertently led them almost to reject those paramount, valid expressions of Menger's subjectivist vision.

We have seen this vision to consist in the insight that the essential causal determinant shaping economic phenomena is not the physical environment within which economic activity proceeds, but the preference structure of the consumers whose needs inspire that activity. The prime flaw in Menger's vision—as seen from the subjectivist perspective—is his odd belief that this shaping influence exercised by human wants occurs inexorably and automatically, as it were without the intermediation of the human will (Menger, 1981, p. IX). It seems plausible to link this unfortunate view to Menger's apparent (and equally unfortunate) assumption, in his price theory, that values (which he showed to be determined by marginal utilities) occur in the context of complete knowledge. Ignorance, Menger argued, is to be seen as a pathology which should not obscure the underlying economic laws relating to healthy, normal (i.e., omnisciently informed) economic activity (Menger, 1981, p. 200; 1985, p. 56; Kirzner, 1979, ch. 4; 1992, ch. 4).

An example of the baneful influence of Menger's view of the "automatic" translation of consumer needs into the appropriate market values and patterns of resource allocation occurs in a passage in Schumpeter in which he criticized the Misesian thesis concerning the possibility of rational economic calculation under socialism. And the extent to which post-Mengerian Austrian subjectivism was able to escape these unfortunate influences is expressed in Hayek's sharp reaction to Schumpeter.

Mises has shown how, in the absence of markets for productive resources, socialist planners would simply be unable to plan rationally, because they lack indexes of the relative social importance of the relevant resources. Schumpeter rejected this on what we can see to have been solid Mengerian grounds. The appropriate pattern of resource allocation is implied, for any form of economic society, in the pattern of consumer desires. This follows, for the theorist, Schumpeter (1950, p. 175) argued, "from the elementary proposition that consumers in evaluating ('demanding') consumer goods *ipso facto* also evaluate the means of production which enter into the production of those goods." Clearly Schumpeter (correctly) understood Mengerian theory as implying an automatic, *logical* relationship linking consumer preferences to the correct valuation of productive resources.

And it was this that provoked Hayek to refer to this view of Schumpeter's as "startling." Only for a single mind to which not only the valuation of consumer goods are known but also the conditions governing the supply of the various factors of production, would it be valid to claim such a logical relationship. Schumpeter has simply slid into the (Mengerian) error of disregarding "the unavoidable imperfection of man's knowledge and the consequent need for a process by which knowledge is constantly communicated and acquired" (Hayek, 1949, p. 91).

MENGER'S SUBJECTIVIST HERITAGE: THE DIVERGENT PATHS

We have seen the central subjectivist thrust of Menger's vision. And we have seen the incompleteness of that vision (in its assumption of the normalcy of perfect knowledge). It appears plausible to see this dominant, but flawed, subjectivism of Menger, as the reason for the divergent paths followed by subsequent generations of economists touched by Menger's influence. We may distinguish three such paths.

(a) *Mainstream economics.* Menger's influence has left a powerful imprint upon twentieth-century mainstream macroeconomics. This influence was introduced, it can be shown, primarily through Lord Robbins' important 1932 book, *The Nature and Significance of Economic Science.* Robbins' work reflected (as made clear in his Preface to the book) the character of Austrian economics to which he had been exposed during the later 1920s. This economics expressed Menger's subjectivism—with all its incompleteness. Austrian economics in the 1920s paid virtually no attention to the problems of ignorance and uncertainty. While Robbins succeeded in shaping modern microeconomics in a subjectivist direction, by making the economizing decision the decisively important analytical unit, he did so while in effect retaining the Mengerian assumption of complete relevant information. In the Robbinsian approach adopted by mainstream microeconomics, as absorbed into the Walrasian context, each market participant is assumed to confront a given and fully known ends-means framework (created symmetrically by the decisions being simultaneously made by the remaining, similarly situated, market participants). Clearly, what we identified as the disturbing flaw in Menger's subjectivism has, in this modern mainstream version of it, become its most central identifying feature.

As an almost natural result of this central feature (the assumption of perfect knowledge), mainstream microeconomics proceeded to extend the Robbinsian framework (in which the individual decision-maker is seen as facing a given, known ends-means complex) to the economy as a whole. The entire economy was seen as somehow facing an economizing problem, as if it was required to allocate given social resources in a pattern calculated to achieve maximum satisfaction of ranked social objectives. Although Robbins himself had assumed perfect relevant knowledge strictly at the level of each individual, the extension of his framework to encompass societal economizing decisions, in effect assumed the possibility of complete, centralized information concerning the entire economy and all its available options, desires and possibilities. With this extension the mainstream view had expanded the flaw in Menger's system to the point where the subjectivist element in Menger's heritage was virtually smothered. It was Hayek's 1945 paper, "The Use of Knowledge in Society," that decisively rejected this assumption, for any realistic understanding of the operation of the market system.

(b) *Radical subjectivism.* The second path taken by post-Mengerian subjectivists is that which, in the second half of the twentieth century, has
been represented most prominently by the work of Shackle and of Lachmann. Although Shackle was a student of Hayek in the 1930s, there is little to suggest that his subjectivism owes much to Menger's specific influence. Lachmann, on the other hand, explicitly drew his subjectivism from
Austrian (and especially Mengerian) economics. The Shackle-Lachmann
subjectivist path represents the outright rejection of those elements in
the mainstream view that we have identified with the flaws in Menger's
own subjectivism. But they go much further. Not only do Shackle and
Lachmann reject the assumption of perfect knowledge, they tend to emphasize the virtual *impossibility* of relevant accurate knowledge. Decisions
refer to courses of action that will have consequences in the future, the
future is unknowable; hence even *individual* decisions (let alone imaginary societal decisions) must never be seen by economists as being made
in the allocative mode central to mainstream microeconomics. The uncertainty of the future must confound and frustrate the (admitted) urge
to rationality which humans display. No longer can we see decisions as
dictated, in effect, by the given arrays of ends and means relevant to the
respective decisions. Decisions are, in this view, made in a manner expressive of the decision-maker's own assessments of what the options
are (and what consequences they are expected to generate). These assessments reflect the expectations held at the moment of the decision; they
are held, in this view, to be *undetermined* by objective phenomena. This
"subjectivism of expectations," to use Lachmann's phrase, undermines
traditional microeconomics because it injects an unprecedented degree
of subjectivist-generated indeterminacy into the economic picture. One
can no longer rely, as traditional microeconomics relied, upon equilibrating market forces (driven by rationally maximizing individual decisions)
to generate systematic market outcomes. Market outcomes express the
decisions made; the decisions made express the expectations that happen
to be held at the moment of decision; that is all. This radical subjectivism
has thus not only cast away the assumption of perfect knowledge which
Menger's incomplete subjectivism had no qualms in making. It has at
the same time entirely abandoned those central conclusions of Menger's
economics in which, we argued, his subjectivism found expression. In
the radical view we can no longer recognize any systematic processes
in which consumer preferences come to leave any powerful imprint upon

the production decisions governing the uses to which higher-order goods are to be allocated.

The preceding, mainstream "path" had led to the smothering of Mengerian subjectivism as a result of the drastic deepening of the "perfect knowledge" assumption. The radical path has, we have now seen, led to the denial of those central results of economic analysis in which Menger's own subjectivist view of the economic process was reflected. It is against this background that we turn to note the third path taken by economists touched by Menger's subjectivist influence.

(c) *The modern Austrian revival.* This path is that created by the work of Mises and of Hayek. It has brought about, during the past quarter of a century, a significant revival of interest in Austrian, and especially Mengerian, economics. We shall argue that this path preserves what is sound and valid in Menger's subjectivism, steering clear of both the incompleteness in Menger's view (which led to the death of subjectivism in mainstream microeconomics) and the nihilism of the radical subjectivists (which has led to the abandonment of the central subjectivist conclusions of Mengerian economics).

The key elements in this modern extension of Mengerian subjectivism (on this see further Kirzner, 1992, ch. 7) are the role of entrepreneurship in market processes, and the gradual expansion of knowledge generated in the course of the competitive market process. The first of these two key elements we owe to Mises; the second has formed the kernel of Hayekian economics since 1945. Briefly put, the Mises-Hayek theory of the market process sees it as a systematic process of knowledge expansion, the equilibrating character of which is the expression of entrepreneurial discovery. This vision of the market process not only preserves the key element of subjectivism in Menger's theory (i.e. recognition of the primary and dominant role exercised by consumer preferences). It does so without accepting the troubling Mengerian assumption of perfect knowledge. In fact, as we shall see, this modern Austrian view is able to reach Menger's central subjectivist conclusion *only* by introducing the new element of subjectivism needed in order to provide scope for entrepreneurial discovery. Not only are the flaws in Menger's subjectivism no longer necessary for his subjectivist conclusions, it turns out in fact that a new dimension for subjectivism is the necessary link in establishing anew the old Mengerian conclusions. All this deserves more careful attention.

THE MODERN AUSTRIAN SUBJECTIVISM

In this modern Austrian view subjectivist insights reveal two cardinally significant features of economic life. It is these features that make possible the claim (in Mengerian fashion) that markets do systematically tend to express the preferences of consumers. The first of these two features is in fact the direct denial of that feature in Menger earlier described as a flaw in his subjectivism. Whereas Menger's theory of price depended on the assumption of perfect knowledge, the Mises-Hayek understanding of markets emphasizes that, at any moment, markets are pervaded by widespread mutual ignorance on the part of market participants. Markets do *not* at each instant accurately reflect the patterns of consumer preferences of that moment. This recognition of ignorance is the foundation of all subsequent wisdom in regard to the systematic quality of market processes. And it is here that the second of the above two features in the modern Austrian subjectivist view enters our theoretical picture.

This second subjectivist feature recognizes that mutual error on the part of market participants creates opportunities for pure entrepreneurial profits. The emergence of these opportunities offers attractive incentives for entrepreneurial discovery. Subjectivism enters here by way of our appreciation for the way in which such entrepreneurial discoveries are made. The modern Austrian approach emphasizes that it is not sufficient, in order for these opportunities to be grasped (and thus eliminated), that they exist. Unnoticed opportunities are in fact the key feature of the economic world which is entailed by our understanding of market ignorance. For hitherto unnoticed opportunities to be noticed and grasped, they must be discovered; and such discovery requires a special characteristic on the part of potential discoverers, viz. the propensity to be alert. Entrepreneurial alertness is the new subjectivist element implicit, at least, in the work of Mises and Hayek, which is now seen to drive the Mengerian market process through which consumer preferences come to dictate productive decisions. This idea of entrepreneurial alertness was expanded in Kirzner (1973, 1979, 1985, 1989).

So long as unexploited opportunities for pure profit still remain, economic analysis demonstrates that consumer preferences have, in some sense, been defied. A pure profit opportunity expresses the situation where a unit of resource service is currently being assigned to a lower value use than is in fact available elsewhere in the market. This latter unfulfilled value is one through which "more urgent" consumer desires (as measured by money offered) are failing to be served as a result of the current allocation of resources services. The incentive for discovery provided by the available profit opportunity is the element that excites entrepreneurial alertness and thus drives the tendency towards a resource allocation pattern which, in the context of available resources, conforms to consumer preferences (as expressed by their money-backed demand). Modern Austrian subjectivist insights have served to illuminate the validity of Menger's vision of consumer sovereignty in the formulation of allocative decisions.

SCYLLA AND CHARYBDIS AVOIDED

It is instructive to notice how this modern Austrian version of subjectivism avoids the pitfalls inherent in each of the other two varieties of subjectivism we have seen to have derived from the Mengerian heritage. The Robbinsian subjectivism emphasized the allocative choice of market participants. But it did so, it seemed, by tacitly assuming (as in Walrasian theory) that all such allocative choices somehow correctly anticipated one another. There was nothing in the Robbinsian framework that could explain how any pattern of choices that failed so correctly to anticipate each other could systematically generate a more "correct" array of decisions. In other words, the perfect knowledge implicit in the Robbinsian framework (and thus in modern microeconomics) requires us to imagine that market outcomes are automatically dictated (to be sure, via the network of mutually compatible maximizing decisions) by the underlying data (i.e. production possibilities and consumer utility functions) without any human intervention that might be conceived of as arranging that appropriate choices in fact be made. It was this aspect of the Robbinsian system, we saw, that seemed to convert the flaw in Menger's subjectivism into one of its own central features. The modern Austrian subjectivism has avoided this trap both by explicitly rejecting the assumption of perfect knowledge and by introducing a new (subjectivism-friendly) analytical scheme for understanding the equilibrating propensity which markets display.

The Shackle-Lachmann more radical variety of subjectivism, we saw, pointed to the complete denial of systematically equilibrating market tendencies. Whereas Menger's subjectivism was, in Lachmann's terminology, the "expression of human 'disposition,'" modern radical subjectivism argues for subjectivism as "a manifestation of spontaneous action"

(Lachmann, 1986, p. 55). In the earlier view choice is the "*result* of the impact of constraints on human dispositions. In the new view choice is not a result of anything, but a *creative act*" (Lachmann, 1986, p. 55). The markets are not to be seen as the systematic result of any set of objective circumstances whatever. Each decision is, in Shackle's phrase, "a new beginning" (Lachmann, 1986, p. 55), in principle wholly disengaged from all previous history. In this radical view, although it is conceded that people's choices are to be seen as rational responses to their perceived circumstances, it is insisted that these perceived circumstances are always, at least in part, the creation of their own mind (and thus by no means necessarily correspond to any actual circumstances). From such a position it is a short distance to the conviction that market outcomes are wholly unlikely ever systematically to manifest any equilibrating tendencies.

The modern Austrian version of subjectivism escapes these nihilistic conclusions by the injection of the entrepreneurial element. This element, although fully consistent with the subjectivist's insights into the autonomy of the human mind, enables us to rescue economic science from the abyss threatened by that radicalism which can discern no systematic continuity whatever in the course of human history.

Although subjectivism indeed affirms the autonomy of the human mind, our awareness of the entrepreneurial element in human action enables us to postulate a systematic linkage which shapes discoveries and actions into patterns that do tend correctly to reflect and anticipate those external phenomena relevant to successful action. In this fashion the modern Austrian version of subjectivism is able to explain and understand equilibrating market tendencies. In fact, as we have seen, it is not merely that this version of subjectivism permits such equilibrating tendencies, it is in fact the pivotal explanatory element which enables us to understand how, in a world without centralized direction, spontaneous social coordination can possibly emerge. This issue separating the modern Austrian version of subjectivism from the radical one deserves further exploration. This is especially the case in the light of some explicit criticisms raised by the radical school, against what we have termed the modern Austrian view.

RADICAL CRITIQUES AND MODERN AUSTRIAN DEFENCES

From the radical perspective the modern Austrian version of subjectivism is so moderate and diluted as to approach incoherence. Instead of being able to enjoy the best of both worlds (equilibrium theory and subjectivism), modern Austrian economics appears, from the radical perspective, to be shot through with crippling inner inconsistencies.

From the radical perspective, the options facing the social scientist are clear cut. Either one recognizes the autonomy of the human mind—involving the subjectivism, not only of human tastes and preferences, but also of human expectations and human interpretation of current events—or one does not. If human beings are not to be reduced to automatons whose choices are fully determined by existing circumstances (including tastes), then we must recognize the inherent indeterminacy of individual behaviour (and hence of market outcomes). It is all very well, the radical view would argue, to talk of successful entrepreneurial discovery. But the freedom of the human mind requires us, surely, to recognize the ubiquity of human and entrepreneurial error. Such recognition surely snaps, the argument runs, any linkages between initial circumstances and market outcomes, that might render equilibration a plausible possibility. Moreover the inherent unknowability of the future injects, in the radical view, yet an additional element of implausibility into the idea of market outcomes somehow coming into benign coordination with the "underlying realities" (see, for more detail on these radical criticisms of modern Austrian subjectivism, Kirzner, 1992, ch. 1).

After all, the argument runs, the relevant underlying realities presumably mean the future events upon which one wishes one's present decisions to impinge. But such future events are themselves strictly created by current decisions, so, that there is no independent existence at all to any realities to which human activities are to be adjusted. The future that one wishes to anticipate (in the course of one's decision-planning) is created by those selfsame decisions. To believe, as modern Austrian economics (together with mainstream economics) believes, that markets display systematic tendencies in which market outcomes tend correctly to fit in with an independently conceived future, is to surrender (as mainstream economics has surely already surrendered) all claims to consistent subjectivist recognition of the autonomy and freedom of the individual mind.

The modern Austrian version of subjectivism defends itself against these criticisms not by arguing the merits of moderation in subjectivism (as against a more consistent version of it), but by maintaining that a correctly conceived, utterly consistent version of subjectivism does indeed yield the conclusions of modern Austrian economics. Everyday human experience surely teaches us that human beings do successfully formulate decisions (and even multiperiod plans) in dealing with the vagaries of natural events and the uncertainties inherent in dynamic social intercourse. Neither the admitted unknowability of the future nor the admitted human propensity to err, nor any combination of the two, is able totally to frustrate human efforts to act rationally for the uncertain future. Humankind is not simply a helpless piece of flotsam buffeted by the hydrodynamics of social changes. Markets do display remarkable tendencies towards coordination. Our task as economists is not to explain how mistakes in decision-making may occur; such mistakes offer no mystery challenging our powers of explanation. Our task is to explain the observed tendencies to coordination. Modern Austrian economics, building on the subjectivist tradition from Menger to Mises and Hayek, finds this explanation not, as the radical subjectivists imagine, by compromising our commitment to subjectivist insights, but rather by deepening these insights. In the modern Austrian version of subjectivism, the idea of human entrepreneurial alertness is the analytical device that enables us to see how human creativity is in fact geared towards a tendency pointing to the discovery of opportunities that are in fact "waiting" to be discovered.

It is true that the future is created by current decisions. But it is equally true that that future is, from the perspective of the acting individual, something to be anticipated as if it were a datum of nature. Since each of the current decisions (which together generate the future course of events) is motivated and guided by entrepreneurial alertness, we can confidently assert that such alertness *is* able successfully to tend to link current decisions to the "underlying realities."

SUBJECTIVISM AND THE AUSTRIAN TRADITION

We saw earlier in this paper how Menger's subjectivist perspective enabled him to see how economic phenomena are the expression of consumer valuations operating to govern the prices and uses made of all consumer goods and productive resources. Throughout the history of the Austrian School it is this subjectivism, pioneered by Menger, that has served as the most prominent feature of the school.

This chapter has traced the varied fortunes of the Mengerian subjectivist legacy during the twentieth century. In particular we have argued that the key Mengerian insights find their preservation in that version of subjectivism that has informed and illuminated the modern revival of interest in Austrian economics. It is because alternative versions of the Mengerian subjectivist legacy seemed to have led either to an unacceptable modern neoclassical formalism on the one hand, or to an equally unacceptable radically subjectivist nihilism, on the other, that this modern revival of Austrian economics appears so promising.

REFERENCES

Hayek, F. A. (1949) *Individualism and Economic Order,* London: Routledge and Kegan Paul.

———— (1955) *The Counter-Revolution of Science: Studies on the Abuse of Reason,* Glencoe, IL: Free Press.

———— (1981) "Introduction," in Menger (1981). Originally published as the introduction to *Collected Works of Carl Menger,* London: London School of Economics, 1934.

Kirzner, I. M. (1973) *Competition and Entrepreneurship,* Chicago: University of Chicago Press.

———— (1979) *Perception, Opportunity and Profit,* Chicago: University of Chicago Press.

———— (1985) *Discovery and the Capitalist Process,* Chicago: University of Chicago Press.

———— (1989) *Discovery, Capitalism and Distributive Justice,* Oxford: Basil Blackwell.

———— (1992) *The Meaning of Market Process: Essays in the Development of Modern Austrian Economics,* London and New York: Routledge.

Lachmann, L. M. (1986) *The Market as an Economic Process,* Oxford: Basil Blackwell.

Menger, C. (1981) *Principles of Economics,* New York and London: New York University Press.

———— (1985) *Investigations into the Method of the Social Sciences with Special Reference to Economics,* trans. by F. J. Nock, New York: New York University Press; originally published in German in 1883.

Schumpeter, J. A. (1950) *Capitalism, Socialism and Democracy,* 3rd edn, New York: Harper and Row.

SUBJECTIVISM, FREEDOM AND ECONOMIC LAW

Let me open with some personal observations. I am profoundly grateful for the signal honor of being invited to deliver this inaugural memorial lecture in tribute to the late Professor Ludwig M. Lachmann. I must congratulate the Free Market Foundation and especially Mr. Leon Louw, together with the University of the Witwatersrand and my eminent good friend Dean Duncan Reekie, for their admirable vision and initiative in arranging this very special occasion. It is a particular pleasure to greet Mrs. Margot Lachmann here today. A distinguished student of human culture who has earned our deepest respect entirely in her own right, Margot is especially entitled to our applause today. It is she who gave Ludwig that lifetime of loyal, devoted support which enabled him to dedicate his own long and productive career to the cause of a more illuminating economic understanding, with such single-minded passion.

But my assignment today is not to eulogize Ludwig Lachmann. My assignment is to share with you some ideas on the foundations of economics—ideas which have emerged out of three decades of discussion and correspondence with Ludwig and which, I dare to hope, have benefited somewhat by my exposure to his utter intellectual honesty and to his luminous, uncompromising subjectivism. Many of you will of course recognize my indebtedness to Ludwig in a good deal of what I shall be arguing today. If at the same time you notice (as you can hardly fail to do) those points in my observations with which Ludwig himself might have expressed spirited disagreement, I feel confident that you will also agree with me, at least, that there could hardly be anything that could please Ludwig more than his being responsible for a lively, no-holds-barred intellectual fight-fest on the fundamentals of economic understanding.

LACHMANN AND THE CENTRALITY OF SUBJECTIVISM

Few will dispute the observation that the unifying thread running through Lachmann's social science was his radical subjectivism. It was radical subjectivism that Ludwig Lachmann deployed in order to deepen

From *The Driving Force of the Market: Essays in Austrian Economics* (New York and London: Routledge, 2000), 54–73. Reprinted by permission of John Wiley and Sons; the original source is the *South African Journal of Economics* 60, 1 (1992): 24–33.

our understanding of economic processes. And if one seeks to character-
ize the intellectual odyssey which made up Lachmann's scholarly career,
it seems fair to portray it as a consistent series of deepened, pioneering
extensions—the radicalization, if you will—of his own subjectivism.
And, we shall see, it is certain characteristic features of Lachmann's subjectivism which raise the problems with which we wish to grapple in this
lecture.

Lachmann was entirely unsatisfied by what he called "subjectivism
as the expression of human 'disposition'" (Lachmann, 1986, p. 55). It is
simply not enough to recognize that decisions made by consumers express the structures of their preferences. Such recognition for the role
of subjective tastes would be entirely compatible with the statement of
Pareto—a statement cited by Lachmann with disagreement so obviously
profound as to border on disbelief (Lachmann, 1977, pp. 56–248)—to the
effect that once the consumer has left us a picture of his indifference
map, we no longer need him at all (Pareto, 1927, p. 170), since, we then
already know exactly what he will decide to do. For Lachmann subjectivism represents, most importantly, "a manifestation of spontaneous action" (Lachmann, 1986). By this way of putting it, Lachmann meant to
draw attention to the power of the active human mind to frustrate any
pretensions by Paretian—or other—economists to predict, simply on the
basis of given scarcity constraints impinging on given preferences, what
action will in fact be taken.

Physical realities and constraints have, of course, enormously important consequences for economic outcomes. But the subjectivist must
insist that economic outcomes are not determined by any objective physical phenomena whatever. All the powerful influences exercised upon
human affairs by external phenomena are exercised strictly through the
intermediation of active human minds. Because of this process of intermediation, outcomes are simply not uniquely implied by external phenomena. What people do—the prices they offer to pay, the goods they
buy—depends on what they know, believe, and expect, i.e. on what Lachmann (somewhat boldly, perhaps) chose to call "mental acts" (Lachmann,
1977, p. 56). External phenomena certainly do promote discoveries, they
do shape expectations, and they do condition knowledge. But they do so
only in conjunction with the independent entrepreneurial conjectures of
active human minds. What people believe, expect and know is not determined by outside phenomena. What they do is therefore, indeed likely to

have been significantly affected by, even influenced by, physical phenomena, but is never determined by them. It may seem to the econometrician that demand for umbrellas is a function of rainfall. The subjectivist economist understands that the full interpretation of such econometric data must take into account the manner in which current rainfall affects people's expectations concerning future rainfall. For many purposes such a full interpretation may not contribute much that makes a difference; but for the most important objectives of economics such an interpretation matters a great deal indeed. So runs the subjectivist's statement of fundamental conviction.

It emerges, then, that a cardinal component of the subjectivist's position is the freedom which, he insists, characterizes human behavior. It is in this freedom that we see most starkly the difference between the subjectivist's view of the world and that of his mainstream economist colleagues. For the latter the decisions of market participants are not free (in the sense used here); they are determined by the data of the situation (including preferences). As Anthony de Jasay has recently remarked: "Choice 'caused' by the chooser's dispositions or preferences is the base hypothesis in all rational-choice theory. The hypothesis is used with particular rigour in economics" (de Jasay, 1991, p. 18). For the subjectivist, human action is, in this sense, "uncaused"; it is not determined by circumstances (even by the agent's own preferences). Heavy rainfall does not inexorably drive the consumer to buy an umbrella—although it may inspire him freely to choose to do so. Human behavior—and the economic phenomena which express this behavior—are, in the most important sense, disengaged from objective physical phenomena. There is no inexorable causal nexus running from the latter to the former. It is this freedom[1] (an expression of what Lachmann called "the autonomy of the human mind") which, at first glance, seems to raise the most serious difficulties for the very notion of economic regularities, let alone economic law (Lachmann, 1977, p. 248).

THE DIFFICULTIES RAISED BY SUBJECTIVIST FREEDOM

Economic science emerged as an attempt to understand what appeared to be the unmistakable regularities which are displayed by economic phenomena. For example, the observed tendency of costs and prices to approach each other was an important point of departure for classical economic theory. The entire history of economic thought can be seen as a series of endeavours more adequately and more satisfyingly to understand the economic laws which appear to govern the economic universe. Yet the subjectivism which has, ever since 1871, seemed so promising for the improvement of economic understanding, seems now to be pointing to the utter impossibility of economic law! Let us not forget that the "external phenomena" relevant to human action are largely made up of the actions of others (and of their consequences). Subjectivist freedom thus implies that, while my decision to buy an umbrella from you may well be inspired by your decision to offer to sell me one for a low price, my decision is nonetheless free; it is not the inevitable outcome of your decision. My decision incorporates my own expectations of future rainfall, and my own expectations concerning the possibility of a better bargain around the corner. These expectations are an expression of what I know (or think that I know) about my environment and, as Lachmann used to insist, "knowledge cannot be regarded as a function of anything else."[2] But if each individual decision is made under such conditions of freedom (of determining influence exercised by the decisions of others), how can we accept the very idea of economic regularities?

There is an irony here. Hayek's tribute to the contribution of subjectivism to economic science is well-known and often quoted: ". . . it is probably no exaggeration to say that every important advance in economic theory during the last hundred years was a further step in the consistent application of subjectivism" (Hayek, 1955, p. 31). But here we appear to have arrived at an almost diametrically opposed conclusion: the most consistent application of the notion of subjectivist freedom appears to sabotage every attempt by economic science to understand observed economic regularities.

The classical economists founded the notion of economic law squarely upon physical, even biological, regularities. The marginalist revolution (and particularly the work of Carl Menger) enabled economists to see how a recognition of the paramountcy of consumer demand pointed the way to a more satisfactory understanding of the coordination achieved by the market economy. Lionel Robbins took these Austrian subjectivist insights and, in his 1932 *Nature and Significance of Economic Science*, introduced them to shape most decisively the development of mainstream microeconomics during the second half of this century. But we now find ourselves confronted with the difficulty that the most consistent application of subjectivism appears to dissolve the very notion of economic law;

each decision is made independently, not only of the physical environment, but of the decisions of others. How can one salvage the possibility of economic regularities?

In what follows I shall attempt to show that subjectivist freedom of the decision is not only not fatal for the possibility of economic regularities but, in fact, is the indispensable ingredient necessary for attaining understanding of such regularities. Hayek's tribute to subjectivism can, we shall submit, be seen to be fully applicable to subjectivist freedom, after all. Let us first examine how mainstream microeconomics has, along Robbinsian lines, ostensibly reconciled a systematic theory of price with the freedom of individual decision making. We shall find that the inadequacies in this ostensible reconciliation point to the possibilities offered by a more consistent application of subjectivist insights.

MAINSTREAM MICROECONOMICS

Determinate market outcomes are achieved by mainstream microeconomics by means of two key devices. For simplicity we consider the pure exchange market, without production, consisting only of consumers exchanging given commodities at equilibrium prices. First, each consumer decision is seen as fully determined (within the constraining framework of resource limitations and given market prices) by that consumer's own preferences. The consumer freely exercises his own preferences. Second, all decisions are assumed to have somehow been (as Shackle has put it) pre-reconciled. Each and every decision is already somehow fully adjusted to the opportunities and constraints marked out by all other decisions in the system. It is seen as the central function of markets to ensure, somehow, such full mutual adjustment among decisions. So that determinate final market outcomes, viz., equilibrium market price and the consequent reshuffling of title to the initial endowments, emerge without having inflicted evident violence upon individual freedom. Each consumer has, after all, freely exercised his own preferences.

But even the briefest examination of this theoretical framework must convince us that it rests entirely upon the implicit denial of that freedom—that "manifestation of spontaneous action"—which we found central to Ludwig Lachmann's radical subjectivism. The first of the two devices (referred to in the preceding paragraph) is, of course, simply the Paretian device of accounting for market outcomes, not by reference to the consumer's own "mental acts," but instead by reference to the consumer's indifference map. Any freedom of the consumer to choose a market basket in a way that might permit him to err, to exercise imagination concerning, say future price changes, has been carefully eliminated. What the consumer is to buy is fully determined, independently of any subjective process of choice, by the circumstances (including, certainly, the consumer's own preference structure).

And the second of the above two devices is, of course, even more inconsistent with subjectivist freedom. The assumed pre-reconciliation of decisions postulates a set of supremely potent constraints, exercised by each decision over all others. Such a picture of the market seems, despite all the pre-reconciliation in the world, to be unable to be reconciled with the notion of each decision being free of determining influences exercised by other decisions. It is clear that mainstream microeconomics has achieved its theoretical account of the determination of market outcomes only by completely squeezing out subjectivist freedom from its field of vision.

It is true that mainstream microeconomics has not denied the consumer the prerogative of governing his decision by his own set of preferences. This is, indeed, the subjective element in the theory. But it is a strictly limited subjectivism, a subjectivism of "human disposition," not the Lachmannian subjectivism of active minds.

It is worth noticing that mainstream microeconomics has achieved determinate outcomes only by restricting its subjectivism to that level of explanation which precedes economic analysis itself. Consumer decisions are determined by (admittedly subjective) preferences. Once subjectivism has, à la Pareto, supplied us with the consumer's subjectively derived indifference map, the economic analysis then takes over in completely determinate fashion. There is nothing, in the explanation of the way an individual's decision is (given his subjective preferences) arrived at, that provides scope for human error, or human imagination (or, for that matter, any other subjectivist element). And the manner in which decisions are pre-reconciled in markets offers no scope for any human element whatever; pre-reconciliation is achieved simply by arbitrary assumption. An iron law is postulated that assures the simultaneous solution of all the Walrasian equations; pre-reconciliation is achieved by mathematics, not by human interaction. Neoclassical market equilibrium accounts for market regularities (a) by entirely eliminating the subjectivism of active minds, and (b) by admitting into consideration only that element of subjectivism (the subjectivism of human disposition) which can be excluded from the economic analysis itself.

We shall argue in what follows that an adequate understanding of how market regularities can occur, requires us to pay close attention to the subjectivism of active minds and, precisely for that reason, requires us to incorporate that subjectivism into the body, of our economic explanations. The systematic processes of the market are decisively shaped by the essentially human character, not only of the preferences to which consumer decisions are designed to cater, but also of those acts of the mind which form and inspire the component decision-steps in those processes. It can be useful to remind ourselves of what we mean when referring to the human character of action.

THE NATURE OF HUMAN ACTION

As Shackle has pointed out again and again, the decisions which constitute the analytical units in mainstream microeconomics are artificially structured in such a manner as to extrude from them virtually all those features which we associate with human choice. Economic theory has reduced "human action to such terms as could equally well apply to the behavior of inanimate objects" (Shackle, 1972, p. 443). The relevant objectives are presumed to be already given to the decision maker in a clear and definite ranking; there is no scope for agonizing over which of two options is to be valued more highly. The sacrifices needed to be made in order to achieve each given possible objective are presumed fully known; there is no scope for agonizing over what one is giving up in achieving any one objective. The decision has been boiled down to a strictly mathematical exercise; the solution to the constrained maximization problem to which decision making has been reduced is obtainable, given the information assumed to be already fully possessed, in purely mechanical fashion. What has been squeezed out of this picture, we have already seen, is the very possibility of human error, and all recognition of the radical (i.e. Knightian) uncertainty surrounding human choices—that uncertainty which (inevitably entailed by the future-oriented character of human action in an unpredictable world) is the circumstance switching on human resourcefulness and initiative, human dreams, hunches, human imagination and vision. If we are to reintroduce into economic analysis the essentially human character of choice, we must permit choice to be made under those conditions of radical uncertainty which defy any possibility of its effective elimination through the deployment of statistical probability theory. But it is here that we are confronted by the dilemma outlined earlier in this chapter. Surely the indeterminacy surrounding human choice thus seen in its full richness and complexity, the "freedom" which thus insulates human choice from any determining influence that might be exercised over it by external phenomena, renders human choice totally unfit to serve as a building block in the edifice of supra-individual, market regularities.

Human choice seen as embedded in the flux of radical uncertainty appears to be essentially open-ended. There simply are no constraints governing human imagination and human expectations. If a person is marooned on a small island surrounded by shark-infested, un-navigable waters, we know exactly where he will always be able to be found. But if part of those waters were suddenly to dry up, linking the island with the mainland, we have lost all basis for guessing his whereabouts: he could be anywhere. Uncertainty-bred removal of the constraints which circumscribe the decision in mainstream microeconomics seems to unchain choice to the point where action is entirely unexplained and in fact totally unexplainable. Or so it might seem upon initial reflection.

Careful consideration of the notion of human action, as developed especially by Ludwig von Mises, will perhaps convince us that the situation is rather more benignly complex. The situation confronting us is not, we shall argue, one in which human decisions are either fully determined (leaving no scope for the autonomy of the human mind) or totally unexplainable (leaving us with no hope for the understanding of market regularities). There is a third possibility, one which does recognize the autonomy of the human mind, the subjectivist freedom of the human decision, but which is nonetheless able to see how it is precisely the autonomous character of the human mind that can ensure a tendency towards actions which, in a special, subtle sense, do bear the imprint of the external circumstances. For Mises, human action is sparked by an inner autonomous motor which inspires appropriate regard to external circumstances. The external circumstances do not themselves constrain action, but action does nonetheless, and precisely because of the autonomous acts of the mind which inspire action, take external circumstances into account. The key to the matter lies in the notion of purposefulness which suffuses human action.

To say that human action is purposeful[3] is to say far more than (in fact, it may often be more accurate to insist that it is to say something quite different from the assertion) that each decision aims at the maximum fulfilment of given objectives, the greatest possible attainment of given ends. To say that human action is purposeful is to refer to the distinctively human attitude which pervades all wakeful, alert human existence. The purposefulness of human action refers to the circumstance that man is continually alive to changing conditions that may affect his prospects; it refers to man's continuous alertness to newly-noticed possibilities for removing what he believes to be unsatisfactory aspects of his situation. It refers indeed to the drive with which he pursues already-designated objectives; but it also refers to his readiness to recognize new objectives worthy of being adopted. It may indeed refer to the attitude which initiates the deliberate search for the information he knows that he will need for the attainment of his already-designated objectives; but it also refers to the attitude which inspires him to notice items of information the availability of which or the usefulness of which, had hitherto not been known to him (or, at any rate, kept in mind by him). To say that action is purposeful is to say that it is inspired by that restless activity of the human mind, that ceaseless exercise of the human imagination, that continual peering of the mind's eye into the foggy future—which are the characteristic watermarks of man's attitude to his human condition.

It is only through appreciation of this sense of the notion of human purposefulness that we can make sense of Mises's remarks linking action with the uncertainty which pervades the human condition. "That man acts and that the future is uncertain are by no means two independent matters. They are only two different modes of establishing one thing . . . If man knew the future, he would not have to choose and would not act. He would be like an automaton, reacting to stimuli without any will of his own."[4] To anyone trained in modern microeconomics, these remarks must sound strange indeed. In mainstream microeconomics man is seen as being able to choose precisely because he is assumed to know the relevant future; Mises sees choice as possible only because the future is unknown. The explanation, of course, lies in the two quite different notions of choice that are being referred to. Mainstream microeconomics deals with choice strictly in the sense in which a well-programmed computer can "choose" the optimum route through which to travel to a given destination. Mises is referring to genuinely human choice, for which human purposefulness (in the sense described in the preceding paragraph) is a necessary ingredient. It is of course obvious that in a world of complete certainty there can be no scope for that purposeful, alert attitude which in our world informs and suffuses choice. The very notion of action implies, therefore, that uncertainty which indeed characterizes our world. The very notion of the uncertainty of the future assures us that in such a world human beings will not be able to engage in the mechanical "choice" suitable to automata; they will perforce, because they are human beings, act. Elsewhere I have suggested (Kirzner, 1973, pp. 32–5) that the essential element present in Misesian human action which has been carefully excluded in mainstream microeconomics, should be recognized as the entrepreneurial element in human action. Just as Mises insisted on the uncertainty context of human action, so he insisted on the uncertainty context of entrepreneurship. "The term entrepreneur . . . means: acting man exclusively seen from the aspect of uncertainty inherent in every action" (Mises, 1949, p. 254). As we shall see, it is this entrepreneurial element in every action—that element which transforms mechanical decisions into human actions—which enables us to eat our cake and have it, to maintain the subjectivist freedom of the individual decision and yet understand the emergence of those powerful regularities which economic science has, for two hundred years and more, made it its business to explain.

OPEN-ENDEDNESS AND THE OVERCOMING OF UNCERTAINTY

It is the uncertainty which pervades our world which is responsible for that open-endedness of human action which sets it so sharply apart from the mechanical optimization which makes up the decision in mainstream microeconomics. The given ends-means framework which is the setting for the maximization exercises of mainstream microeconomics precludes the possibility of genuine choice because that very framework makes genuine choice unnecessary. The assumptions fed into the model ensure only one exit; these assumptions effectively close off any conceivable alternative exit. Lifting these constraints, relaxing these assumptions, therefore converts a closed model into an open-ended situation. But lifting these constraints does much more: it at once permits us to see the agent as a purposeful human being; we are at once permitted to introduce into our reasoning an element of explanation (reflecting a primordially important feature of human action) which the mainstream model of decision making prohibited us from deploying. That element of explanation is the theory of entrepreneurship, and the feature of human action to which this element of explanation relates is the human propensity—an "entrepreneurial" propensity to discover opportunities to improve one's situation. So that the step from the closed models of mainstream microeconomics to the open-ended world of subjectivist economics is not at all one which does no more than erase the only economic basis for accounting for market regularities. That step, while it indeed unavoidably entails profound scepticism for the determinacy purportedly achieved by those closed models, introduces, at the same time, a powerful new explanatory element into the scientific picture, precisely because that step permits consideration of a critically important element shaping real world events, viz. the element of entrepreneurial purposefulness. Hasty readers of Mises may, I have argued elsewhere, misunderstand his references to the uncertainty in which he insists that human action (and, especially, entrepreneurship) is embedded (Kirzner, 1982, ch. 12). They may conclude that, for Mises, what is important about uncertainty is that it obscures human vision and obstructs the way to efficient choice. They may therefore interpret Mises's emphasis on this uncertainty as an affirmation of the omnipresence of human entrepreneurial error. They may find it puzzling therefore that it should ever be argued that entrepreneurial behavior be seen as equilibrative. Surely that uncertainty, which for Mises is the essential element for entrepreneurial action, implies the inevitability of entrepreneurial error. With such error seen as an essential feature of entrepreneurial activity, how can we rest our explanation for an asserted universal equilibrating tendency upon the activity of the entrepreneur? (See also Loasby, 1989, pp. 161ff.)

But our observations in the preceding section on the meaning of the purposefulness which Mises sees as central to the human action concept, should help us see the fallacy in such a reading of Mises, and in such a line of questioning. What Mises meant to emphasize, in his insistence on the uncertainty context of human action in general, and of entrepreneurship in particular, was not the inevitability of error. Rather Mises wished to emphasize the distinctive character of that environment which calls forth the entrepreneurial element in each and every human agent. No one need deny that the uncertainty in which human action is embedded renders man prone to error. What Mises was underscoring, however, was that man's success in overcoming error—a success it would surely be a mistake totally to deny—arises out of his propensity to act, i.e. to act in a way which expresses his propensity to discover the existence of opportunities *despite* the acknowledged uncertainty of the future.

From this way of seeing matters it emerges that open-endedness does not at all mean that outcomes are simply random. Open-endedness means that man is free to choose for himself, that is, to determine for himself what he believes the relevant framework for decision to be. Precisely because he is so free to choose, in an environment in which virtually nothing is certain, we can be sure that his choices will be guided, informed and inspired by his purposefulness—by his entrepreneurial propensity to discern, amid the swirling fogs of the future, the outlines of the opportunities which in fact he faces.

SELF-INTEREST, RATIONALITY AND PURPOSEFULNESS: A BRIEF DIGRESSION

To drive home the important insight of the preceding section, it is worthwhile to digress briefly on the various assumptions introduced by different generations of economists in order to "nail down" human decisions in a way that permits us to account for market regularities. Critics of economic theory have traditionally focused on these assumptions as the targets of their ire. They have again and again challenged the conclusions of economics on the grounds of the alleged unrealism of these assumptions. The insight developed in the preceding section requires and permits a different—and, we suggest, a more convincing—line of defence for economic theory.

During much of the nineteenth century economics proceeded on the basis of a strict self-interest assumption. Economic theory was the domain of homo economicus (and his behavior was reliably predictable because the materialistic conception of economics was sufficiently dominant in the nineteenth century to permit the economist to know exactly where the economic interest of the agent lay). Economics has never quite shaken off the stigma of its early fling as the science of materialistic selfishness, and contemporary critics of economics still purport to find ammunition for their attacks in the selfishness charge.

Neoclassical economics distanced itself from the self-interest assumption by drawing attention to the notion of rationality, of efficient allocation of scarce resources, of constrained maximization—in regard to the attainment of whatever objectives one chose to postulate, altruistic as well as selfish. Critics of mainstream neoclassical economics must now focus their criticisms on the alleged unrealism of the assumed propensity of man to remain the cool, careful calculator, unswayed by passion, habit, impulse and error.

Thus the critics of economics (that is, those who indeed challenge the correctness of the view of economics ascribing powerful regularities to market systems) have focused on those various assumptions which economists have used to "pin down" what economic agents in fact decide to do. The insights of the preceding section offer a fresh foundation for understanding market regularities (that is, for drastically narrowing down the range of randomness governing individual behavior). The traditional criticisms of economics would seem, it may be suggested, to have far less relevance for economic theory so conceived (Kirzner, 1992, ch. 12). For we have seen that economic theory may be grounded, not in any assumed tropism pulling decision making unerringly toward the satisfaction of narrowly selfish goals, nor in any assumed model of constrained maximization assumed to govern behavior, but in the simple, universal propensity of man to be wakeful, alert and purposefully oriented towards the uncertainties of the future. The tendency of market outcomes to reflect, at least to some extent, the realities which surround the society of men, derives from the propensity of men shrewdly to size up these uncertainties and to act purposefully to discover and overcome error. That much research needs to be focused on understanding the scope and limits of this propensity need not be denied. That this propensity is indeed sufficient to support much of traditional microeconomic theory must, however, be emphatically affirmed. Let us turn to a brief statement of how this last claim can seriously be made.

ENTREPRENEURSHIP AND THE POSSIBILITY
OF SYSTEMATIC MARKET FORCES

We have drawn attention to the role of Misesian purposefulness in systematically overcoming uncertainty. Brief reflection should remind us that, indeed it is precisely upon the power of such purposefulness, that the central theorems of economics have, consciously or otherwise, traditionally depended. Consider the simple theorem that predicts a market tendency towards achieving a single price for a given good in a given market (usually associated with Jevons's Law of Indifference). This tendency obviously rests upon the economist's confidence in the speed and success with which entrepreneurs will pounce upon the pure profit opportunity created by any price discrepancies (which might initially be violating Jevons's Law). Now, a little reflection must surely convince us that economists' confidence in this powerful tendency supports not only their understanding of this tendency itself, but also their confidence in the tendency of costs and prices to converge, and their confidence in equilibrating tendencies in general, both in the context of the Marshallian single market and in that of the Walrasian system of interlinked markets. Economists typically spend very little time justifying their confidence in this basic tendency for pure profit opportunities to be competed away through arbitrage. And the reason for this is that, within the neoclassical paradigm, the possibility of pure profit itself is something of an embarrassing paradox. The neoclassical assumption of perfect knowledge is, as is well known (certainly ever since Knight's *Risk, Uncertainty and Profit*), simply inconsistent with the possibility of pure profit. So that neoclassical economists must either be hard-boiled about it and insist that their models simply preclude such possibilities (that is, they insist on equilibrium theory while explicitly refusing, on positivist methodological grounds, to see the need for justifying the equilibrium assumption at all), or they must attribute pure profit to sudden unexpected changes in underlying conditions and postulate (without too much elaboration) that "of course" the profit possibilities so generated will rapidly lead to their own equilibrating destruction.

But the rapid self-elimination of opportunities for pure profit is not at all something to be taken for granted as obvious. After all, if an opportunity that exists at a given moment in time has not yet been perceived (and its very existence proves that to have been the case, because to perceive an opportunity for pure profit must be assumed immediately to inspire a move to grasp it), then it is not obvious at all how that opportunity will come to be spontaneously perceived at any subsequent moment in time. After all, if the opportunity has indeed been totally unperceived that means that market participants have been unaware of the worthwhileness of opportunities to search for the pure profit possibilities we are discussing. Clearly our universal reliance on the powerful market forces, which tend to eliminate pure profit opportunities, rests on our confidence in the entrepreneurial propensities of market participants. Such entrepreneurial propensities are precisely those which Mises associated with the general purposefulness of human action in the face of uncertainty.

MARKET PROCESSES AND THE SPREAD OF KNOWLEDGE

The central thrust of the preceding sections can be driven home by a re-statement in terms of processes of change in knowledge. Subjectivists of all stripes will agree that changes in economic outcomes must express changes in human knowledge. It is only as they systematically modify the knowledge (including expectations regarding the future) possessed by market participants that we can understand how exogenous changes in physical circumstances (for example) can generate systematic changes in market prices, allocation of resources, and so forth.

Yet it is not at all obvious how such changes in knowledge and ex-pectations can be systematically generated—or, rather, it ceases to be ob-vious as soon as we abandon the implicit assumption that changes in external circumstances are somehow instantaneously and automatically mapped by corresponding changes in man's knowledge. (Once again, de-liberate search activity cannot be relied upon to explain such changes in knowledge—because the relevant question is how do men know what dif-ferent items of information they must now search for, and how can they know that different ways of searching are now worthwhile, and so on. Af-ter all, yesterday's deliberate plans for search were based on an obsolete outline-picture of the world. Today we should, in the light of objectively changed conditions, see that outline-picture quite differently. But how do the changed conditions in fact achieve this changed outline-picture in men's minds?)

We are inevitably driven to the insight that it is man's entrepreneurial propensity upon which we must rely for our reasonable confidence that changes in external circumstances do tend, sooner or later, to come to be noticed by entrepreneurial market participants. And, as pointed out, it is upon this tendency for systematic changes in human knowledge to occur, that economic theory necessarily relies for its most basic, and its most far-reaching conclusions.

SUBJECTIVIST FREEDOM ONCE AGAIN

This chapter began with a discussion of what we have called "subjectivist freedom." We saw how a consistent subjectivist perspective requires us to see human action as undetermined by objective external circumstances (including the circumstances consisting of the actions of other market participants). That statement led us to articulate a serious problem, that of reconciling recognition of subjectivist freedom with the very possibility of understanding economic regularities.

Our discussion has permitted us to find the solution to this problem. Not only have we seen how an open-ended perspective on human decision making—one which sees such decision making as not constrained by the contours of single-exit models—can be consistent with economic regularities. We have in fact seen how it is only by reference to such open-ended concepts of decision making, concepts which offer full scope to subjectivist freedom, that we can begin to appreciate the power and the reach of the entrepreneurial element in individual human action and in market entrepreneurship. Hayek's remarks concerning the contributions of subjectivism to advances in economic understanding turn out to be fully applicable also to the contribution offered by recognition of subjectivist freedom.

SUBJECTIVIST FREEDOM AND FREE MARKETS

We have emphasized the special meaning we have assigned to the term subjectivist freedom. Subjectivist freedom refers not to any institutional arrangements permitting substantive liberties to the individual market participant, but strictly to the absence of determining control over human behavior exercised by external circumstances. Yet it would be disingenuous for us to fail to note certain important points of contact between the kind of freedom referred to in the concept of free markets, and the subjectivist freedom which we have been discussing. It turns out that the extent to which we can rely on the purposefulness unleashed by subjectivist freedom is not unrelated to the scope for substantive liberties permitted by the institutional context.

Subjectivist freedom inspires purposefulness. But purposefulness can inspire human action to discern the outline of available opportunities only where there is the prospect of an actual opportunity to achieve a desired objective. Where the desired objectives (which an "opportunity" indicates to be in principle available) may not in fact be achieved (even though their availability may have been noticed) due to some externally imposed institutional constraint (for example, a law restricting price increases, or an excess profit tax, or a law prohibiting the production of some specific product)—then we have no grounds for assuming that any kind of "purposefulness" can be depended upon to generate relevant discovery. An uncertain world is a world in which profitable opportunities (as yet unperceived) are likely to exist; it is a world in which as yet unidentified opportunities provide scope for open-ended variety of decision-making, a scope which we have identified as subjectivist freedom; and it is, finally, a world in which the institutional freedom to enjoy discovered opportunities can in fact spark the discovery potential which we have identified as entrepreneurship. As we have seen, it is the latter circumstance which justifies the confidence which economists have in the tendencies of markets to identify—and thus eliminate—opportunities for pure profits.

It is the circumstance that entrepreneurial purposefulness cannot be relied upon unless pure profits are permitted to be enjoyed, that underlay the Austrian critique of the possibility of socialist economic calculation. Government officials whose status, by definition, precludes their being able personally to profit from their commercial discoveries, cannot be depended upon to achieve through planning, or through bureaucratically setting nonmarket "prices" to stimulate effective market activities, those discoveries the generation of which constitutes the real contribution of free markets.

THE ECONOMICS OF SUBJECTIVISM: CRITICISM FROM TWO DIRECTIONS

We can now appreciate why it is that subjectivist economics (as it has emerged, for example, as a result of the Austrian tradition in economic thought) faces attacks from two opposite directions.[5] On the one hand mainstream neoclassical critics are likely to wonder why we have to go through all this subjectivist talk concerning the asserted "freedom" of human action. If, when we come down to the bottom-line entrepreneurship (or whatever) can be relied upon to move markets towards equilibrium, then why may we not, for modelling purposes, operate with equilibrium models exclusively—that is, why may we not use models which behave as if external phenomena independently constrain economic behavior and thus generate economic regularities?

At one level of discussion the subjectivist may be prepared to concede a certain validity to this criticism. For certain purposes it is indeed not necessary to explore the manner in which outcomes emerge as a result of the spontaneous, free choices of market participants; it is sufficient to focus on our degree of confidence that those choices will tend to discover the best relevant options in fact available. But at the deeper level of discussion no such concessions need be made by the subjectivist. At this deeper level the proper response to this kind of mainstream criticism lies in the area of economic methodology; it rests upon an approach to economics which seeks, not replicable predictions, not econometric "explanation" in terms of statistical correlation, but essentialist understanding of actual social phenomena in the manner in which they occur.[6] For this latter approach equilibrium models offer no help at all. They simply assert the outcome; they offer no explanation for its plausible attainment.

But there is a line of criticism of the subjectivist economics which we have outlined in this paper, which proceeds from the diametrically opposite methodological direction (from that of mainstream economics). Such ultra-subjectivist criticism objects, not to our emphasis upon the subjectivist freedom of individual decision making, but to our insistence that such freedom is entirely consistent with (in fact necessary for) the emergence of systematic microeconomic forces. The position taken by these critics is likely to emphasize the possibilities for entrepreneurial error and, in particular, the possibility that interacting entrepreneurial errors may magnify the scope for and likelihood of entrepreneurial errors. (This, for example, is what Keynes was referring to in his comparing the stock market to a casino.)

The proper response to this kind of criticism must lie in further clarifying and articulating the arguments in this paper which have supported the notion of a systematic, all-pervasive human propensity to discover those errors of others which manifest themselves in pure profit opportunities. We must never permit our understanding of human freedom—the subjectivist variety—to obscure our understanding of how freedom inspires human purposefulness.

Markets do work. They work so obviously well that our scientific curiosity is aroused to seek understanding of the counter-intuitive phenomenon of this success. What we have argued here is that the achievement of a deepened appreciation for the nature and implications of subjectivism—an objective which Ludwig Lachmann himself pursued with such steadfast tenacity and with such sparkling brilliance—can here, as elsewhere, offer a most illuminating contribution towards enhanced economic understanding.

NOTES

This chapter was presented as a paper at the University of the Witwatersrand on August 19, 1991, as the inaugural Ludwig Lachmann Memorial Lecture, sponsored jointly by the University of the Witwatersrand and the Free Market Foundation of

Southern Africa. Research support by the Sarah Scaife Foundation is gratefully acknowledged. The author is also grateful to Professor Mario Rizzo for helpful discussion during the preparation of the paper, and to members of the Austrian Economics Colloquium at New York University for useful comments on an earlier draft. Only the author is responsible for errors in the chapter.

1. It should be obvious that the term *freedom* used here does not relate to philosophical issues having to do with free will and the like. The term here refers strictly to the absence of any determining influence upon human behavior that might be exercised by external phenomena. The subjectivist's foe is not so much philosophical determinism as psychological behaviorism.

2. Lachmann (1977, p. 92). Although Lachmann never, to my knowledge, made reference to it, it must have given him great pleasure indeed that Shackle—whom Lachmann admired as the master-subjectivist—chose this sentence (together with several others from the same review by Lachmann of a book of Shackle's) to be placed at the head of Shackle's *magnum opus*, *Epistemics and Economics* (1972).

3. As is well known, Mises used the term "rational" as synonymous with "purposeful." On this see Fraser (1937, p. 37); Robbins (1935, p. 93). For an extensive discussion of Misesian human action and its "purposefulness," see Kirzner (1960, ch. 7).

4. Mises (1949, p. 105). Compare also the famous observation by Knight (1921, p. 294): "Consciousness would never have developed if the environment of living organisms were perfectly uniform and monotonous, conformable to mechanical laws. In such a world organisms would be automata."

5. For further discussion of some of the issues raised in this section see also Kirzner (1985, ch. 1; 1992, ch. 1).

6. For further discussion on this issue see Mäki (1990).

REFERENCES

Fraser, L. M. (1937) *Economic Thought and Language. A Critique of Some Fundamental Economic Concepts*, London: A. & C. Black.

Hayek, F. A. (1955) *The Counter-Revolution of Science*, Glencoe, IL: The Free Press.

de Jasay, A. (1991) *Choice, Contract, Consent: A Restatement of Liberalism*, London: Institute of Economic Affairs.

Kirzner, I. M. (1960) *The Economic Point of View*, Princeton, NJ: Van Nostrand.

——— (1973) *Competition and Entrepreneurship*, Chicago: University of Chicago Press.

——— (1982) *Method, Process and Austrian Economics, Essays in Honor of Ludwig von Mises*, Lexington, MA: D. C. Heath.

——— (1985) *Discovery and the Capitalist Process*, Chicago: University of Chicago Press.

——— (1992) *The Meaning of Market Process. Essays in the Development of Modern Austrian Economics*, London and New York: Routledge.

Knight, F. H. (1921) *Risk, Uncertainty and Profit*, Boston, MA: Houghton Mifflin.

Lachmann, L. M. (1986) *The Market as an Economic Process*, Oxford: Basil Blackwell.

—— (1977) *Capital, Expectation, and the Market Process,* Kansas City: Sheed, Andrews and McMeel.

Loasby, B. J. (1989) *The Mind and Method of the Economist. A Critical Appraisal of Major Economists in the Twentieth Century,* Aldershot: Edward Elgar.

Mäki, U. (1990) "Mengerian economics in realist perspective," in B. Caldwell (ed.) *Carl Menger and his Legacy in Economics,* Durham, NC: Duke University Press.

Mises, L. von (1949) *Human Action. A Treatise on Economics,* London: William Hodge & Co. Ltd.

Pareto, V. (1927) *Manuel d'Economie Politique,* 2nd edn, Paris.

Robbins, L. (1935) *The Nature and Significance of Economic Science,* 2nd edn, London: Macmillan.

Shackle, G. L. S. (1972) *Epistemics and Economics,* Cambridge: Cambridge University Press.

ANOTHER LOOK AT THE SUBJECTIVISM OF COSTS

The insight that the cost associated with an item must reflect all the opportunities sacrificed in order to obtain it, has long been fundamental for economists. This opportunity cost doctrine (perhaps the earliest statement of which was made in an 1876 paper by Wieser) is one of the contributions of the Austrian School which has come to be fully absorbed into the contemporary neo-classical orthodoxy.[1] Since Professor Buchanan's incisive treatment of the entire subject, however, economists have learned to appreciate the subtlety of the opportunity cost concept, once its subjectivist implications have been fully drawn, and to recognize the pitfalls which await those who wield the opportunity cost notion without awareness of these implications.[2] A number of contributions to the literature have further explored various aspects of the subjectivism of opportunity costs and have drawn our attention to additional important and valuable insights.[3] This paper seeks to tidy up some remaining issues that appear, perhaps, to warrant further clarification. In attempting this task we will have to review some very elementary and obvious ideas. The need for some tidying up arises from the apparent ease with which ideas are lost sight of as soon as economists move beyond the most elementary of contexts.

COSTS AND COSTS

Let us first review a number of admittedly related, but nonetheless quite distinct, concepts for which the term "cost" might be (and often has been) applied. (Of course the term "cost" has also been used with other meanings as well, but present purposes do not require our attention to more usages than those listed here.) It will be convenient to employ an example introduced by Alchian, in which a homeowner builds a swimming pool; we are inquiring into the cost of the building of the pool.[4]

One concern in seeking the "cost" of the pool may be to establish the array of disadvantages that result from building the swimming pool. Presumably the attendant reduction in the homeowner's bank balance would be one of the disadvantages and thus a component in cost (in this

From *Subjectivism, Intelligibility, and Economic Understanding,* ed. Israel M. Kirzner (New York: NYU Press, 1986), 140–56. Reprinted by permission of NYU Press.

sense). But other disadvantages would have to be included as well, e.g., the "nuisance of noisy, disobedient neighborhood children and uninvited guests."[5] If cost is to be understood in terms of "disadvantages," it will clearly be necessary to distinguish between the sum of the disadvantages that accrue to the homeowner himself (the "private cost" of building the pool) from the disadvantages that may accrue to others (e.g., the nuisance to neighbors of noisy visitors to the pool, invited or not). Or one may seek somehow to assess the sum of disadvantages to everybody (the "social cost").[6]

A different focus of concern may inspire the search for the swimming pool's "cost." One may wish to know what alternative goods that might otherwise have been forthcoming have been precluded through the building of the swimming pool. Here one must consider not so much the disadvantages associated directly with the pool (money subtracted from cash holdings, noise, etc.) as the alternative goods (which may have *their* own disadvantages) that would have been possible if the pool was not constructed. Thus the homeowner might have purchased a car instead of the pool. The pool has "cost" him the car.

This notion of cost is often considered to be an opportunity cost notion, since it refers to the alternative opportunity that the swimming pool has precluded. However, in order to distinguish it from the subjective version of opportunity cost (to be discussed below), we will call this present notion of cost the "objective opportunity cost" notion. It is objective in that the cost of the pool is taken to be a definite good (in this case a car) that might have been enjoyed had the pool not been built. What "might have been enjoyed" in the present context is understood as being a matter of *fact,* objectively determinable, quite apart from anyone's judgments or expectations. It is, for example, held to be an objective fact that the $10,000 expended for the pool, could have (under given factual market conditions) purchased a car.

It should be noticed that the car is the private (objective) opportunity cost of the swimming pool in that it refers to what the homeowner might have *acquired* instead of the swimming pool. But someone might be interested in the objective opportunity of the pool in a different sense. Someone might ask about the alternative goods which might have been *produced* instead of the swimming pool. (If the homeowner built the pool with his own labor, tools and materials this cost would of course also be the private cost of the pool.) One may ask, in the situation in which the homeowner had the pool built by a contractor (who hired labor and tools, and bought the materials), what alternative output might these inputs have produced—possibly in other industries altogether. Suppose they could have produced a summer cottage (which, let us say, our homeowner has absolutely no interest in using at all). Then it might be held that the (objective) opportunity cost of the pool is the summer cottage. The cottage is the potential output "displaced" by the pool. Since our homeowner never did himself possess these physical resources, and since, moreover, he has no interest whatever in the cottage, this cost notion is clearly not the private cost to him of his pool. It would presumably be considered a "social opportunity cost" in that the total output obtained by adding together all the goods and services produced in a society with its available resources, *including* the pool, might have been a different one in that, instead of the pool, it might have contained one more summer cottage. This is the objective social opportunity cost of the pool in that the capability of the labor, tools, and materials (that produced the pool) to have produced the cottage instead is viewed as a matter of objective fact (given the physical requirements for the production of the pool and the cottage respectively).

The final concern which may inspire attention to the cost of building the swimming pool, may be to understand *why the homeowner in fact decided to build the pool.* We know that, in considering whether or not to build the pool, the homeowner was aware that building the pool must entail some sacrifices on his part. Were these sacrifices too great, the homeowner would, it is clear, have reluctantly decided against the pool. To explain economic phenomena, arising as they do out of individual decisions, it is necessary, for each decision taken, to be aware that the relevant sacrifices to the decision maker were considered worthwhile by him. To acquire a swimming pool (to follow Alchian's example again) called for a decision not to buy a car. Only the homeowner himself, however, can know how likely it is that a car *would,* in fact, have been the alternative enjoyed (if the pool were out of reach); only he can know how intense a sacrifice the "loss" of the car means to him. The cost of the pool to the homeowner, then, represents *his assessment at the moment of his decision regarding the pool, of what he would be giving up* in order to acquire it. The emphasis (in this *subjective* opportunity cost notion) is upon the moment of decision, and upon the way in which the decision maker himself sees the alternative opportunity which *he* must sacrifice.

The subjectivity of this notion of opportunity cost flows, of course, directly from its exclusive relevance to the decision. Economists learned long ago that demand behavior cannot be understood without probing beyond the physical objects purchased by the consumer, to the prospective utility which these objects represent for him. In exactly the same way the subjective opportunity cost concept permits us to recognize that costs help explain economic behavior not because costs represent definite objects "displaced," but because they represent perceived utility prospects deliberately sacrificed.

ON THE COSTS OF WIVES AND CHILDREN

A clear understanding of the differences between these various cost concepts can help elucidate points that have sometimes occasioned confusion.

The Noisy Neighborhood Children

Alchian is one writer who has emphasized the sharp difference between the disadvantages of, or the undesirable attributes inherent in a swimming pool, and its opportunity cost. The decision maker must choose among events. Each event is an amalgam of "goods and bads." The opportunity cost of the chosen event is the next most highly valued event—not the undesirable attributes of the chosen event. The nuisance of noisy neighborhood children, Alchian emphasizes, is an undesirable attribute of the pool. It is not part of its opportunity cost. Our discussion may shed a somewhat different light on the matter.

If the idea of the opportunity cost is understood in its subjective version, it may be possible, surely, to find an opportunity-cost-counterpart for the disadvantages inherent in a chosen event. If a homeowner is choosing between building a swimming pool and purchasing a car, then it is very likely that the noisy neighborhood children that will be attracted by the pool enter very definitely into his cost calculations; they may well affect the decision taken. The options considered by the homeowner are, after all, whether to enjoy a car, together with a peaceful backyard, or whether to enjoy the swimming pool, *without* such a peaceful backyard (because of the noisy children). Thus, in choosing the pool, the homeowner is consciously sacrificing the peace and quiet which he recognizes will be destroyed by the noisy children. From the subjective point of view any disadvantage associated with the chosen event (and not with its rejected alternative) represents the sacrifice of the corresponding advantage (or at least the absence of disadvantage) contained in the rejected alternative.[7] (Of course, if a given disadvantage is common both to the adopted option and to its alternative, it cannot enter into the opportunity cost of the adopted option.)

In insisting that for the opportunity cost concept the noisy children represent only one of the undesirable attributes of the pool, not part of its cost, Alchian appears to be understanding the notion of opportunity cost in objective terms. From this point of view the availability of one chosen object may be seen as displacing another definite object. The latter is the cost of the former. In this view each object is seen as an amalgam of desirable and undesirable attributes. In order to perceive that the adoption of the undesirable attributes of one option entails a felt sacrifice (of the absence of these attributes in the alternative option), it seems necessary to emphasize, not displaced physical output, but perceived prospects deliberately sacrificed.

The Expensive Wife

In 1969 no less serious a scholarly journal than the *Journal of Political Economy* published a semihumorous "Note on the Opportunity Cost of Marriage" by Gary North. This note was remarkable not so much for the very obvious fallacy it contains (which it is very likely that the author deliberately introduced as part of the attempted merriment) as for the fact that several of the subsequent serious comments it elicited utterly failed to take notice of the fallacy.[8] North considered the situation of the man who contemplates marriage to a highly educated woman able to earn a high salary on the professional labor market. Taking it for granted that, after marriage, the wife will give up outside job opportunities and concentrate entirely on running the household, North refers to her shockingly high opportunity costs. A man of modest means, North argues, should never consider courting a woman of such talents; she is simply too costly. "The best kind of wife, from the point of view of contemporary economics, is obviously an uneducated woman . . . [for whom] a man . . . forfeits a small opportunity cost in her lost salary. . . ."

North's article drew comments from several economists, one of them George Stigler.[9] Stigler accepted without question North's analysis to the effect that the opportunity cost of marrying the educated woman is a high one. His criticism of North's conclusion was confined—apparently altogether seriously—entirely to pointing out that if the wife in question indeed stays at home as housekeeper, this demonstrates that the minimum estimate of her revenue equivalent as housekeeper must outweigh the high cost of the forgone professional income. But this clearly concedes the obvious fallacy in North's tongue-in-cheek story which incorrectly counts the forgone professional income as the *opportunity cost of the decision to marry the educated woman* rather than her uneducated sister. Before this marriage decision the prospective groom had no alternative prospect whatever of enjoying the woman's high professional income; his decision to marry her involved no sacrifice by him of her income at all (even if it is understood from the start that marriage calls for her staying at home). To be sure, once the two have married, a *subsequent* decision that she stay at home carries with it the cost of her forgone income. But this is irrelevant to North's injunction to the would-be groom to marry the uneducated girl in order to avoid high costs. Again, if it is understood that marriage necessarily involves forsaking outside employment, then the educated girl's decision to marry carries with it a cost *to her* of the lost professional income. But this is again irrelevant to North's matrimonial advice to the fellow.

That so eminent an economist as Stigler should have failed to point all this out appears to suggest an extreme version of the objective approach to the notion of opportunity cost. Such a version apparently divorces the notion of opportunity cost entirely from the context of the decision. Instead of considering the costs deliberately assumed at the moment of a particular decision, this version focuses on that which has been displaced as a result of a given state of affairs. In this fashion, apparently, it is somehow conceivable to see the educated wife in the kitchen as bearing a cost tag on which is inscribed the professional salary which she might have commanded in an alternative state of affairs. To marry her rather than her uneducated sister is to assume a high-cost option rather than a low-cost one.

That the subjective version of the opportunity cost doctrine is invulnerable to seduction by such a fallacy must surely be counted as one of its merits.

ON THE SUBJECTIVITY OF COSTS

There are several sources for our emphasis upon the subjectivity of opportunity cost (in the context in which cost helps us understand decisions taken). It will be helpful to spell these out. Let us consider a case in which two homeowners in two different (but similar) towns decide to build similar swimming pools in their backyards. To the outside observer it may appear that the two face similar sets of circumstances, that they are called upon to make similar sacrifices. In short, the two pools are built at "equal cost." The subjectivist, however, cannot accept this view.

First, while the situation which the outside observer perceives in each case as facing the homeowner appears identical with that which confronts the second homeowner, we have no assurance that this identity exists in anyone's perception other than that of the observer. An outside observer may presume that the prospect of noisy children from the neighborhood, which faces each of the prospective pool owners, is taken into account by each of them correctly and equally. But in fact it is possible that one homeowner forgets altogether to consider this undesirable attribute of the prospective pool. In other words, two decision makers may "see" different things despite the fact that they really confront the same objective situation. The costs which enter into the respective decisions can clearly in no sense be said to be equal.

Second, a somewhat different (although closely related) source for the incorrectness of any conclusion by the outside observer that the two homeowners face equal costs is provided by our understanding of the role of entrepreneurship in decision making. Even if two decision makers do see present realities in identical fashion, there is no reason to assume that they will assess future prospects equally. In one sense the preceding case (in which one homeowner forgot about the prospect of a noisy backyard) represents such an entrepreneurial lapse. A clearer example of the importance of the entrepreneurial elements is perhaps provided by the case where the two homeowners each carefully take account of the prospective disadvantage of the noisy children but reach different conclusions concerning its likelihood. Perhaps one homeowner predicts more accurately than the second what other future neighborhood attractions are likely to "compete" with a backyard pool. Both homeowners see present circumstances identically. But they see the future differently. The respective costs of the pool are as different as the two assessments of the future.

Third, another circumstance renders it an error to conclude that the cost of a pool is the same for each of the homeowners. Even if the two arrive at exactly the same predictions concerning the noise to be expected in their respective backyards, they may attach different degrees of significance to this prospective disadvantage. For one homeowner a noisy background may be perceived as a minor irritant; for the second it may loom as a major discomfort.

Finally, our discussion thus far in this section might suggest that the subjectivity of opportunity costs merely makes it impossible *as a practical matter* to rank costs faced by different decision makers. This would be a serious misunderstanding of the position being taken. The truth surely is that costs, as understood in the subjective version, enter into decisions in a strictly private manner. To rank the costs faced by different decision makers is as conceptually impossible a task as is that of comparing utilities interpersonally. (In fact, of course, these two tasks are merely variants of a single impossible undertaking.) Both costs and utilities enter into decisions in a private fashion. They are essentially without meaning except within the context of the private decision.

SUBJECTIVE COSTS, OBJECTIVE COSTS AND EQUILIBRIUM PRICES

The foregoing has important implications for an often-discussed question. Can the private money outlays made by an entrepreneur in the course of producing output serve as a correct, objective measure of the entrepreneur's subjective opportunity costs of production?

Some recent contributions to the literature on the subjectivity of costs have discussed how, under specified conditions (chief among which being the equilibrium state, and the absence of nonpecuniary motivations) money outlays do provide an objective representation of subjective costs.[10] This position reflects the line of reasoning lucidly articulated by Professor Baumol in his 1970 review of Buchanan's book.[11] Baumol's exposition deserves verbatim quotation.

> There surely is a wide variety of circumstances in which the objective cost data do constitute a reasonable approximation to the subjective opportunity costs. This is brought out clearly by the famous argument of Adam Smith, about which Buchanan builds much of his discussion: "If . . . it usually costs twice the labor to kill a beaver which it costs to kill a deer, one beaver should naturally exchange for or be worth two deer." This is plausible even if cost is interpreted as subjective opportunity cost because in Smith's economy hunting is carried on more or less continuously. Assuming that hunting is not done for pleasure, if the objective cost of beaver—the payment to the hunter—were less

than twice as high as that of a deer, more hunters would turn to deer slaying and away from beaver trapping until the market costs (prices) were modified to reflect the relative outlay of time involved. The relative marginal valuations of beaver and deer meat by each and every consumer would then also be driven to the same two-to-one ratio, so that to each person the subjective opportunity cost of a pound of deer flesh would be the same, and would be represented correctly by the objective relative cost figure.[12]

For Baumol, then, the result of the market process is that for all consumers "the subjective opportunity cost of a pound of deer flesh would be the same" (since each consumer would face—and would have adjusted the margins of consumption to—the same one-to-two ratio between deer and beaver flesh prices). Also, this common subjective deer flesh cost would be correctly represented by the objective relative cost (of hunting deer as compared to that of hunting beaver). Or, as Buchanan sums it up, "marginal opportunity cost, measured in the numeraire, is equal for all suppliers."[13]

Now, there is nothing in these discussions described above to which exception can be taken. It does, however, appear important to emphasize the limited sense in which it is correct to describe money outlays as constituting "objective costs," either in the sense of somehow translating subjective, private, interpretations and valuations, into interpersonally visible, comparable and measurable terms, or in the sense of being publicly observable cost *to society* (rather than merely a common representation of distinct *private* sacrifices). Let us take up these limitations in turn.

Comparing Costs Interpersonally

It would, for many economists, doubtless be highly desirable to be able to map the private, subjective costs perceived by different decision makers upon an external and interpersonally valid scale. It is tempting, but of course quite wrong, to believe that money outlays—even under equilibrium conditions and without nonpecuniary distractions—constitute such a mapping.

In equilibrium, output and consumption decisions with respect to pairs of products have been adjusted to bring both marginal rates of substitution and of transformation into equality with relative prices for each consumer and producer. It may even be loosely claimed that for each consumer a dollar's worth of each commodity at the margin provides the marginal utility of one dollar. In this special sense, then, it is not incorrect to say that both utilities and subjective costs are the "same" for all consumers. But all this does not, of course, entitle us to view a dollar as an objective, interpersonally valid yardstick of utility. For you, as for me, a marginal dollar's worth of bread provides approximately the same utility as does a dollar. This does not mean that you and I attach equal "significance," in any absolute sense of the word, to the given physical quantity of bread. It is certainly highly important to understand how, under equilibrium conditions, *rankings* at the margin are, for all market participants, brought into uniformity. But this does not imply that private, subjective appraisals have been rendered publicly visible.

Quite similarly the subjectivity of costs has not been magically suspended merely by the circumstance that, both for you and for me, a pound of deer flesh can be acquired only at the same dollar outlay. What I believe that I must sacrifice for deer flesh is a mental picture which I have of possible future enjoyments, a picture which is inaccessible to anyone else. There is no straightforward meaning that can be attached to the question whether or not this picture is the same as that which for you constitutes the subjective cost of similar deer flesh. And this is not affected by the feeling that *each* of us may have that the sacrificed prospect is identical in significance with that which would be made possible by the expenditure of a marginal dollar.

Now one can readily understand a tendency to shrug off this kind of purism. For you, as for me, the sacrifice called for in order to enjoy a unit of deer flesh is a given quantity of beaver. Then, surely it is the case, it may be objected with some impatience, that for you the opportunity cost of deer *is* the same as it is for me. You must give up exactly what I must give up. A prospective marginal unit of beaver may be associated with a private picture for you; it may be associated with an equally private prospective picture for me. But since for each of us these (admittedly incommensurable) pictures are mental representations of the same physical object (a given quantity of beaver), it may seem unfruitful pedantry to insist on reserving the term "opportunity cost" for the incommensurable subjective mental representations of a given commodity sacrificed, rather than for the objective commodity itself. And if a given outlay of money might have purchased that commodity (both for you and for me), why should that sum of money not be recognized as the objective measure of the common opportunity cost to each of us of what we buy with that outlay?

The recent writers on subjective costs (cited above) have emphasized the unrealism of the equilibrium construct as thoroughly undermining the suitability of money outlays for service as such an objective measure of opportunity cost. Here we wish to draw attention to one aspect of equilibrium which is particularly important for understanding the unsuitability of money outlays for such service. In equilibrium analysis it is taken for granted that, while you and I may differ about the significance of a given objective prospect, we are nonetheless disagreeing about what we both recognize as being the *same* object. In other words, the state of equilibrium is one in which all market participants correctly perceive that which is objectively perceivable. It is precisely this aspect of equilibrium to which we wish to draw critical attention.

As discussed in an earlier section, the subjectivity of opportunity costs derives, in part, from the circumstances that different individuals perceive different things even when they are looking at the same object. If two individuals were always to see the given object (or prospect) that is before them correctly, then we might indeed wish to replace discussion about differing prospective utilities to be sacrificed by reference to the identical object (the prospective sacrifice of which is at issue). But wherever we wish to take into account the extent to which decisions reflect highly personal views not only concerning the significance of the facts before one's face, but also concerning the very facts themselves, we dare not talk of sacrificed *objects* apart from the private *perceptions* of these objects. A given amount of money does not, except under highly artificial assumptions, represent the same purchase possibilities to two individuals exploring the same supermarket. It is certainly unhelpful to focus on analytical models in which such artificial assumptions have been made, to an extent that permits us to overlook the crucial difference between the following statements. You and I have expended equal amounts of money. You and I have sacrificed the prospective utilities which we respectively attach to the given sum of money. The statements are simply not completely interchangeable statements. There may, it is true, be imaginable sets of circumstances under which some might be content to use the first statement as a workable (and more easily manageable) substitute for the second. Our point is that, if the cost notion is to serve as an *explanation* of why a person made the decision he did, it will not do to invoke a

statement such as that made in the first statement, as such short explanation (in place of the more complete second statement) unless we can rely
on the assured, complete awareness of the objective facts that enter into
the first. Most economists would agree that such complete awareness is
likely to be achieved, in general, only through learning process which involve decisions based on *faulty* awareness. If *these* decisions are to be explained, as they surely can and must be, on the basis of relevant costs, we
dare not confine discussions of cost to contexts in which the possibility of
faulty (or otherwise idiosyncratic) awareness of facts has been assumed
away. The use of money outlays provides no justification for so confining
the discussion.

Money Outlays as Measuring Costs to Society

The use of money outlays to serve as objective measures of cost is often suggested in order to assess the "social cost" of a particular undertaking. It is useful to emphasize that, strictly speaking, such attempts can
have nothing at all to do with the subjectivist notion of opportunity cost.
The subjective notion of the term "cost" is necessarily always private. It has no
meaning outside the context of a decision. All decisions are made by individuals; hence all costs (in this usage) are private costs. While decisions
may be made that affect society, or even be made on behalf of society,
they are nevertheless made by individuals (whether as private citizens,
voters, public officials, or members of governing groups) and hence involve only private costs, that is, sacrifices which the decision maker sees
himself to be making. (Of course a public official may consider the effect
of a course of action upon the public, but such considerations enter into
his decision, after all, only to the extent that *he* considers them to be important.) For us to be able to talk of the (subjective) *social* opportunity cost
of a decision, it would be necessary to imagine society *as a whole* making
decisions. In any but a metaphorical sense a society simply cannot make
decisions. Hence, there can be no notion of social cost (in the sense of a
subjective opportunity cost).[14]

One may indeed wish to discuss the alternative volume of goods that
might have been forthcoming in a society had resources been allocated
for purposes other than those in fact pursued. It may seem not inappropriate to describe these goods as the social cost of the project pursued.
And, if money outlays might have commanded such a volume of goods, it
seems natural to see these outlays as being but the monetary expression

of this social cost. But the truth is that for no individual entrepreneur can this volume of goods be described as the subjective opportunity cost of his decision to acquire the resources for the purposes pursued. If these alternative goods are described as social cost, this can only be in a sense for which no actual decision can have been relevant. If such social cost is held to be an opportunity cost, this can only be in a nonsubjectivist meaning of this term. Money outlays may, under assumed conditions of equilibrium, measure this quantity of alternative goods that might have been produced. But to use such outlays as a measure of social cost cannot, *even though these outlays are made by individuals,* succeed in erasing the conceptual gulf that separates the objective notion of social cost from the subjective, private, notion of opportunity cost. Even under equilibrium conditions the money outlays of individual entrepreneurs cannot at the same time represent both private and social "costs"; money outlays may indeed be taken to represent alternative outputs (and hence social cost [in the objective sense discussed above]), but private (subjective) opportunity costs are not these alternative outputs, and certainly not these money outlays. They are the *significance* of the perceived purchases forgone by these outlays.

We may put the matter quite briefly. Money outlays for a particular project, are, of course, objective. They may, under specified conditions, be held to represent the objective opportunity costs to society of that project. But money outlays cannot serve as an objective counterpart for any *subjective* notion of social cost simply because, in strict terms, the notion of a subjective social cost is without meaning.[15]

One may, as noted, wish to use the term "cost" in an objective sense, or, with Professor Buchanan and the Austrians, one may wish to reserve the term to refer only to subjective sacrifices. If it is the latter usage which is being followed, then money outlays are simply not, in and of themselves, costs; they certainly do not translate subjective costs into objective costs.

CHOICE, HYPOTHETICAL CHOICE, AND SOCIAL COST

We may in fact go further in our contention that money outlays cannot provide an objective translation of subjective opportunity costs. Thus far our discussion has left unchallenged at least the insight that money outlays may be seen as an objective expression of *social* opportunity cost. We merely pointed out that the latter term must itself then be used to refer to costs in an objective, decision-irrelevant, sense. But in fact, we will now argue, there are grounds for the assertion that the term social cost, as widely used, does indeed imply a true opportunity cost in a decision context (and thus ultimately in a quasi-subjective sense), albeit in very limited and special terms. So that, we will point out, if money outlays are indeed held to measure social costs, we shall have to reinterpret these outlays as costs in a less than completely objective sense. All this may appear to be quite confusing and paradoxical and indeed to involve an abrupt about-face from our earlier insistence that social cost can under no circumstances be recognized as a cost in the sense of the subjective opportunity cost. These matters do deserve elucidation.

Until now we have recognized (among the various meanings different economists have attached to the term "cost") objective as well as subjective opportunity cost interpretations. One might well question the felicity of using the term "cost" to denote the objective disadvantages or objective output losses in fact imposed on society by the construction of a swimming pool, whether or not these disadvantages were taken into account prospectively by the homeowner. But we did not question the possible interest and importance attached to the volume of such disadvantages or losses. Whether or not we wished to refer to the sum of such disadvantages or losses as the cost of the swimming pool, we recognized that it might well be important, for normative purposes, to take cognizance of these disadvantages or forgone social outputs even if the homeowner himself did not do so. We wish now to argue, however, that, in referring to such disadvantages or forgone alternative social outputs as "costs," economists are, in fact, whether they are completely aware of it or not, implicitly treating these disadvantages and lost outputs *in the context of hypothetical decisions.*

We maintain, that is, that all the cost concepts we have considered do ultimately depend upon the subjective opportunity cost notion (which we have endorsed as the only version capable of rendering individual decisions intelligible). Even the apparently objective notion of displaced social output and the like *are treated as cost only because one is imagining a decision through which these alternative advantages are deliberately being sacrificed.*

If the cost of a particular process of production is being discussed, this is presumably because the worthwhileness of the project is under examination. For the decision maker responsible for the project this is of course a matter of obvious and immediate relevance (and is the reason why we have emphasized the role of cost in explaining decisions). For those other than the decision maker himself, consideration of the cost of a project is presumably taken in order to make a judgment on its worthwhileness, either from the point of view of the decision maker himself (i.e., a judgment by another of whether or not the decision maker made a wise decision) or from the point of view of "society" (e.g., whether the project's full "cost" to society is being taken into account). These judgments may be either prospective or retrospective, but they are all judgments concerning efficiency. Such judgments, then, answer the following kinds of question: "*Should* this project be undertaken, or are its expected benefits outweighed by the costs?" "Should this project have been undertaken, or were its expected benefits outweighed by the costs?" These questions are questions about decisions, either actual decisions or hypothetical decisions.[16] In reviewing hypothetical decisions the reviewer may imagine himself to be responsible only for himself ("If *I* were the prospective producer. . . ."), or for society at large ("If *I* were in charge. . . ."). However, the reviewer may imagine a decision "by society" (regardless of whether he is aware of the strictly metaphorical character of "decisions by society") whether or not to permit a private entrepreneur to decide to initiate the project.

Into all these hypothetical decisions, then, costs enter in exactly the same way as they do into actual decisions by individuals. The objective social costs of a project enter into such hypothetical decisions in the following way. Let us imagine that a privately built swimming pool increases the noisiness of a neighborhood (a matter by which, let us say, the homeowner himself is unaffected). Then an economist may argue that, after taking the externalities imposed upon neighbors fully into account, the social cost of the pool renders its construction a mistake, from the point of view of society. This means that the economist is making the judgment that if "society" were choosing whether or not to have the pool (or whether or not to permit the homeowner to build the pool), a negative decision would be in order, since relevant costs are held to outweigh relevant benefits. But all this means that the so-called "objective costs" to society of the pool, are being imagined to be taken into account by a hypothetical decision maker. As such, such costs must be imagined to be *perceived* and evaluated by this hypothetical decision maker. As a result, these objective costs turn out to be at least quasi-subjective, after all.

Now we have indeed argued throughout this paper that *actual* decisions are made only by individuals, not by "society." It is for this reason that we have insisted that "social costs" (as something apart from private decision making) cannot be true subjective opportunity costs. We certainly still maintain this position. Nonetheless our present discussion is designed to emphasize that such social costs, while indeed not true subjective opportunity costs in the straightforward sense, can be imagined to be meaningful only in the context of *imagined* decisions, possibly by altogether *imaginary* decision makers. The cost notion, even in its apparently objective versions, ultimately expresses an implicit subjectivism.

While, for purposes of such discussions of social efficiency, economists may be indulging in questionably legitimate stretches of their imagination, we must understand them as after all implicitly treating costs as quasi-subjective.[17] It follows, as stated earlier, that while money outlays may be used to measure "social cost" under relevant equilibrium conditions, the ultimate subjectivity that is inherent in the cost notion, cannot even then be thoroughly exorcised.

Let us sum up our position. In explaining actual decisions the only costs that are relevant are private, subjective perceptions of required sacrifices. Conversely, the use of cost in judging the actual efficiency (to relevant decision makers) of particular projects, can refer only to subjective costs as they appear to these decision makers. For costs in this true sense, attempts to find objective measures or counterparts—whether in terms of money outlays or anything else—to subjective costs, are doomed to failure. Moreover, we have found, the subjective element is so deeply engrained in the notion of cost, that even truly objective versions of cost turn out ultimately to reflect an implicit quasi-subjectivism. Notions of social cost are, as has been amply demonstrated in the recent literature, totally illegitimate in the strict context of subjective cost. We have found that, in addition, such ostensibly objective notions of cost turn out to conceal a quasi-subjective element, after all.

NOTES

1. T. W. Hutchison, *A Review of Economic Doctrines, 1870–1929* (Oxford: Clarendon Press, 1953), p. 156.

2. J. M. Buchanan, *Cost and Choice* (Chicago: Markham, 1969). The numerous debts which the writing of this paper owes to Buchanan's discussion will be apparent to every reader of that book. A recent paper offering an excellent new exposition of similar insights is J. Wiseman, "Costs and Decisions," in *Contemporary Economic Analysis,* eds. D. A. Currie and W. Peters (London: Croom Helm, 1980), vol. II.

3. S. C. Littlechild, "The Problem of Social Cost," in *New Directions in Austrian Economics,* ed. L. Sparado (Kansas City: Sheed Andrews & McMeel, 1978); E. C. Pasour, Jr.,

"Cost and Choice—Austrian vs. Conventional Views," *Journal of Libertarian Studies* (Winter, 1978); E. C. Pasour, Jr., "Cost of Production: A Defensible Basis for Agricultural Price Supports?" *American Journal of Agricultural Economics* (May, 1980); K. I. Vaughn, "Does it Matter That Costs are Subjective?" *Southern Economic Journal* (March, 1980).

4. A. A. Alchian, "Cost," in *Encyclopedia of the Social Sciences* (New York: Macmillan, 1969), vol. III (also in *Economic Forces at Work: Selected Works by Armen A. Alchian* [Indianapolis: Liberty Fund, 1977], pp. 404ff.) Page references are to *Encyclopedia*.

5. Alchian, op. cit., p. 404.

6. Of course such attempts may raise serious questions concerning the very meaning of such a sum.

7. Let the advantages of the adopted and the rejected options be represented by A, C, respectively; and let the disadvantages of the adopted and rejected options be represented by B, D, respectively. Then one may say that the net utility of the adopted alternative is A-B, and its cost is C-D (with the latter term not including reference to B at all, confirming Alchian's position). However, it seems entirely in order to say that in choosing the first option the decision maker is embracing the utility A plus the "freedom from disadvantage D," and that the sacrifices called for are made up of the forgone utility C plus "freedom from disadvantage B." It must be readily conceded that such accounting considerations may sometimes appear arbitrary and even forced. If I choose to sit on a hard park bench rather than on the soft grass, it may seem artificial to say that the hardness of the seat enters into the cost of my decision (in the form of the sacrificed softness of the grass). It certainly may seem more natural to say that the hardness of the bench merely reduces its utility. But it should be emphasized that this is not because disadvantages cannot in fact be represented as associated sacrifices, but because they may under given circumstances not be perceived as such. Where such perception is not lacking, the point being made in the text comes back into full relevance.

8. This does not apply to the insightful comment by Madelyn L. Kaflogis, "Marriage Customs and Opportunity Costs" *Journal of Political Economy* (March/April, 1970), pp. 421–3.

9. "Opportunity Cost of Marriage: Comment" *Journal of Political Economy* (September/October, 1969) p. 863.

10. Vaughn, op. cit.; Pasour, op. cit.

11. See, for a discussion of Baumol, Vaughn, op. cit., pp. 709ff.

12. W. J. Baumol, "Review of *Cost and Choice*," *Journal of Economic Literature* (December, 1970), p. 1210.

13. J. Buchanan, op. cit., p. 85.

14. See however the final section of this paper for a somewhat different way of stating this.

15. See the following section for a discussion in terms not so strict.

16. See Littlechild, op. cit., p. 85, for a discussion of the role of hypothetical choices.

17. For example, there may be problems with the internal consistency of such imagined choice situations.

PHILIP WICKSTEED: THE BRITISH AUSTRIAN

"Wicksteed's place in the history of economic thought is beside the place occupied by Jevons and the Austrians."[1] Ever since this profoundly insightful 1932 comment by Lionel Robbins, Philip Wicksteed has, at least doctrinally, been identified with the Austrian tradition. Perhaps for this very reason, however, we should, at the outset of a discussion of the Austrian character of Wicksteed's work, emphasize that, whatever the strength of Wicksteed's Austrian doctrinal credentials, he was not a member of the Austrian School in the usual sense. This British contemporary of Menger, Böhm-Bawerk, and Wieser appears to have had no direct contact or correspondence with any of them. His biography,[2] which provides detailed descriptions of Wicksteed's trips abroad, makes no mention of his ever having visited Vienna. His work seems to have made no direct impact on the work of his Austrian contemporaries.[3] He, in turn, while certainly mentioning their work,[4] seems not to have drawn any of his main ideas from them.[5]

From 15 *Great Austrian Economists*, ed. Randall G. Holcombe (Auburn, Ala.: Ludwig von Mises Institute, 1999): 101–12. Reprinted by permission of the Ludwig von Mises Institute.

1. Lionel Robbins, Introduction to Philip H. Wicksteed, *The Common Sense of Political Economy and Selected Papers and Reviews on Economic Theory*, Lionel Robbins, ed. (London: Routledge and Kegan Paul, [1910] 1933), p. xv.

2. C. H. Herford, *Philip Wicksteed: His Life and Work* (London and Toronto: J. M. Dent, 1931).

3. It is, however, of some interest that Joseph Schumpeter, then a twenty-three-year-old brilliant young Austrian economist, made a point of visiting for "an hour's chat" at Wicksteed's home in 1906. On that occasion, Schumpeter reports, Wicksteed's personality "radiated upon me," leaving an impression of "repose that owed nothing to callousness, . . . benevolence that was not weakness, . . . simplicity that went so well with . . . refinement, . . . unassuming modesty that did not lack dignity." Joseph A. Schumpeter, *History of Economic Analysis* (New York: Oxford University Press, 1954), p. 831. Robbins, in his Introduction to Wicksteed's *The Common Sense of Political Economy* (p. viii), credits Wicksteed, *The Alphabet of Economic Science* (London: Macmillan, 1888), with introducing the term "marginal utility" as a translation of the Austrian *Grenz-nutzen*.

4. See, e.g., Wicksteed, *The Common Sense of Political Economy*, vol. 1, p. 2, and vol. 2, pp. 765, 808, 812.

5. In a 1926 paper, Hayek apparently held that Wicksteed—who devoted much of his own work to the theory of distribution—had paid little if any attention to "the

The elements in Wicksteed's work which we shall identify as "Austrian" were, it is well-recognized, the outcome of his own careful elaboration of the insights he discovered in the work of that other British "Austrian," William Stanley Jevons. Nor does Wicksteed's work seem to have had seminal impact on the second generation of Austrians, although it is to its economics that Wicksteed's own work is closest.[6] Late in his life Mises refers to Wicksteed's "great treatise"[7] but it would certainly be an exaggeration to contend that Mises's own system drew its central ideas from Wicksteed, rather than from Menger and Böhm-Bawerk.

Moreover, while, as we shall see, there is in Wicksteed's work a considerable affinity with the Austrians in regard to the scope, character, and content of economic analysis, this affinity hardly extends to the free-market ideological perspective often held to be inextricably linked with the Austrian tradition. Where the Austrians have fairly consistently been foremost among the economic critics of socialism, Wicksteed was deeply sympathetic to it.[8] If, despite all of this, Wicksteed is yet regarded by

---

principles of imputation developed by the Austrian School." See F. A. Hayek, *Money, Capital, and Fluctuations: Early Essays*, Roy McCloughry, ed. (Chicago: University of Chicago Press, 1984), p. 43. At one point, Wicksteed credits the generation of economists who followed Jevons—mentioning particularly those "in Austria and in America"—with expanding on the "universal application of the theory of margins." The statement here in the text should, moreover, also be modified by noting that Robbins refers to "influences which shaped Wicksteed's thought" as including "Jevons and the earlier Austrians." See Wicksteed, *The Common Sense of Political Economy*, vol. 2, p. 812.

6. An admittedly incomplete survey of Austrian work during the 1920s has revealed few references to Wicksteed. This absence was particularly noticeable in Hans Mayer's important 1932 paper, "The Cognitive Value of Functional Theories of Price," in *Classics in Austrian Economics: A Sampling in the History of a Tradition*, Israel M. Kirzner, ed. (London: William Pickering, 1994), vol. 2, pp. 55–168.

7. Ludwig von Mises, *The Ultimate Foundation of Economic Science: An Essay on Method* (Princeton, N.J.: D. Van Nostrand, 1962), p. 78.

8. Ian Steedman concluded his article "Wicksteed, Philip Henry," in *The New Palgrave: A Dictionary of Economics*, John Eatwell, Murray Milgate, and Peter Newman, eds., 4 vols. (New York: Macmillan, 1987), p. 919, by stating that Wicksteed's *The Common Sense of Political Economy* is a "brilliant demonstration of a writer who . . . was friendly to the socialist and labor movements of his time, and who was sometimes a sharp critic of the market system, could yet be a purist of marginal theory." Robbins (Introduction to Wicksteed, *The Common Sense of Political Economy*, p. vi), reports that "all his life" Wicksteed "retained a sympathy for the idea of land nationalization."

late-twentieth-century Austrians as a distinctly kindred spirit,[9] this must be attributed not to any strong personal links between Wicksteed and his Austrian contemporaries, nor to any shared political or ideological perspectives, but, far more narrowly, to a common set of doctrinal insights. These insights, contrary to the thrust of the Marshallian economics dominant at the time Wicksteed was writing, clearly and starkly recognized the profoundly *revolutionary* character of the marginal-utility emphasis introduced into economics during the 1870s. The story of Wicksteed as an Austrian must revolve around these doctrinal insights.

THE WICKSTEED STORY

Born in 1844, the son of a Unitarian clergyman, Wicksteed was educated at University College, London, and Manchester New College, from 1861 to 1867, when he received his master's degree, with a gold medal in classics.[10] Following his father into the Unitarian ministry in 1867, Wicksteed embarked on an extraordinarily broad range of scholarly and theological explorations. His theological and ethical writings continued long after he left the pulpit (in 1897), and appear to have been the initial point of departure for a number of his other fields of scholarly inquiry. These included, in particular, his deep interest in Dante scholarship, an interest which not only produced a remarkable list of publications, but which built Wicksteed's reputation as one of the foremost medievalists of his time. It was Wicksteed's theologically-driven interest in and concern for the ethics of modern commercial society, with its disturbing inequalities of wealth and

---

Despite all this, it must be emphasized that Wicksteed's message to the would-be social reformer was consistently that of the trained neoclassical economist. Referring to the "economic forces" which "are persistent and need no tending," Wicksteed reminds "the social reformer" that if "we can harness [these economic forces] they will pull for us without further trouble on our part, and if we undertake to oppose or control them we must count the cost" (p. 158).

9. Murray Rothbard cites Wicksteed many times in *Man, Economy, and State: A Treatise on Economic Principles* (Auburn, Ala.: Ludwig von Mises Institute, 1993). When the present writer sought to present an Austrian restatement of price theory in the early 1960s, he found himself turning again and again to Wicksteed as a guiding source. See Israel M. Kirzner, *Market Theory and the Price System* (Princeton, N.J.: D. Van Nostrand, 1963).

10. Herford, *Philip Wicksteed*, p. 25.

income, which appear to have led him into his economic studies, following on his reading of Henry George's 1879 *Progress and Poverty*.[11]

Perhaps it was the circumstance that economics entered into Wicksteed's field of scholarly vision in his mid-forties, and as only one of a number of areas of his interest—most of them to which he was committed for years before he began his economics—which led Schumpeter to remark that Wicksteed "stood somewhat outside of the economics profession."[12] Yet, within a few years, Wicksteed published a significant economic work of his own,[13] carefully expounding on the theory he learned from Jevons, and became a lecturer on economics for the University Extension Lectures.[14] In 1894, Wicksteed published his celebrated *An Essay on the Co-ordination of the Laws of Distribution,* in which he sought to prove mathematically that a distributive system which rewarded factory owners according to marginal productivity would exhaust the total product produced. But it was his 1910 *The Common Sense of Political Economy* which most comprehensively presents Wicksteed's economic system, and which expresses most clearly and emphatically those insights which today's Austrians find most congenial. Important elements of this Austrian side of Wicksteed's work were concisely presented in his well-known 1913 Presidential Address to Section F of the British Association, published in *Economic Journal,* March 1914, under the title "The Scope and Method of Political Economy in the Light of the 'Marginal' Theory of Value and Distribution." Apart from participation in a 1922 *Economica* symposium, Wicksteed published nothing further on economics during the last dozen years of his life, which ended in 1927. What was it in Wicksteed's economics which later Austrians have found most similar to their own tradition?

11. See Herford, *Philip Wicksteed,* p. 197. George's book led Wicksteed to discover Jevons's book, a work which was to exercise the greatest influence on Wicksteed's own economic thought. See William Stanley Jevons, *The Theory of Political Economy* (London: Macmillan, 1871).

12. Schumpeter, *History of Economic Analysis,* p. 831.

13. Wicksteed, *The Alphabet of Economic Science.*

14. This was a kind of adult-education program initiated in Great Britain in the 1870s to extend "the teaching of the universities, to serve up some of the crumbs from the university tables, in a portable and nutritious form, for some of the multitude who had no chance of sitting there." See Herford, *Philip Wicksteed,* p. 90.

WICKSTEED THE AUSTRIAN

Lionel Robbins's assessment of Wicksteed as an Austrian was not only insightful of Wicksteed's contribution to marginalist economics, it also expressed Robbins's own understanding of the history of modern economic thought. It was no accident that the Preface to Robbins's own enormously influential *An Essay on the Nature and Significance of Economic Science* (1932) concludes with an acknowledgment of his "especial indebtedness to the works of Professor Ludwig von Mises and to *The Common Sense of Political Economy* of the late Philip Wicksteed."[15] Robbins, at least in 1932, saw Wicksteed as a pioneer in that line of post-1879 economic writing, which clearly and cleanly directed economic thought in a direction differing drastically from that taken by classical economic thought. It was in this that Robbins identified Wicksteed's common ground with the Austrians (and particularly with Mises). It was an interpretation of modern economics which sharply disagreed with the perspective of Alfred Marshall, so dominant in British economics.

> The main stream of economic speculation in [Britain] in the last forty years has come via Marshall from the classics. . . . In intention at any rate Marshall's position was essentially revisionist. He came not to destroy, but—as he thought—to fulfil the work of the classics. Wicksteed, on the other hand, was one of those who, with Jevons and Menger, thought . . . that complete reconstruction was necessary. He was not a revisionist, but a revolutionary.[16]

In what follows, we shall identify several distinct components of Wicksteed's revolutionary approach to economic understanding.[17] Each of these components bears a strong Austrian flavor, and stems arguably

15. Lionel C. Robbins, *An Essay on the Nature and Significance of Economic Science,* 2nd ed. (London: Macmillan, 1935), p. 16.

16. Robbins, Introduction to Wicksteed, *The Common Sense of Political Economy,* pp. xvf). Stigler describes Wicksteed as one of the only two "important English economists of the period between 1870 and the World War who explicitly abandoned the classical tradition." See George J. Stigler, *Production and Distribution Theories: The Formative Period* (New York: Macmillan, 1941), pp. 38–39ff. The other economist to whom Stigler is here referring is William Smart, the translator of Böhm-Bawerk and Wieser.

17. It should be noted that Wicksteed consistently refrained from claiming originality for his ideas. He saw himself as expounding and elaborating on the economics he learned from Jevons.

from Wicksteed's subjectivist stance in economic thinking. We shall focus (a) on Wicksteed's emphasis on a subjectivist understanding of the
concept of cost; (b) on Wicksteed's rejection of the classical view of economic analysis as concerned narrowly with the phenomena of material
wealth (and with a model of *homo oeconomicus* intent on nothing but the
gain of material wealth); and (c) on Wicksteed's (admittedly limited but
nonetheless significant) concern with the *process* of market equilibration (rather than exclusively with the attained equilibrium state itself).
We may venture the conjecture that, in regard to these three aspects of
Wicksteed's Austrianism, it was the first which seems to have most impressed Robbins, the second which perhaps most impressed Mises, and
the third which may be of greatest interest to modern Austrians, the disciples of Mises and Hayek. Space constraints preclude any but an outline
discussion of each of these three Austrian aspects of Wicksteed's work.

WICKSTEED AND THE SUBJECTIVISM OF COST

It was in regard to the role of costs in the theory of economic value that
Wicksteed saw himself as most clearly departing from the Marshallian
orthodoxy of his British contemporaries. He saw that orthodoxy paying lip-service to the marginal-utility theory introduced by Jevons, but
refusing to recognize the full implications of this theory for the final
rejection of the classical cost theory of value. "The school of economists
of which Professor Marshall is the illustrious head," Wicksteed wrote
in 1905,

> may be regarded from the point of view of the thorough-going Jevo-
> nian as a school of apologists. It accepts . . . the Jevonian principles,
> but declares that, so far from being revolutionary, they merely sup-
> plement, clarify, and elucidate the theories they profess to destroy. To
> scholars of this school, the admission into the science of the renovated
> study of consumption leaves the study of production comparatively
> unaffected. As a determining factor of normal prices, cost of produc-
> tion is coordinate with the schedule of demands.[18]

In other words, Wicksteed rebelled against a view of production activity
which sees it as a matter of strictly technical relationships, entirely distinct
from the marginal-utility considerations governing consumption activity.

18. Wicksteed, *The Common Sense of Political Economy*, vol. 2, p. 812.

It was the confusion arising from this Marshallian view which was responsible for the residual classical idea that market price is in some sense the outcome of a balancing of an (objective) cost of production with (subjective) marginal utility. In Wicksteed's own strongly-held opinion, the Jevonian view is an emphatically different one:

> In no case can the cost of production have any direct influence upon the price of a commodity, if the commodity has been produced and the cost has been incurred; but in every case in which the cost of production has not yet been incurred, the manufacturer makes an estimate of the alternatives still open to him before determining whether, and in what quantities, the commodity shall be produced; and the stream of supply thus determined on fixes the marginal value and the price. *The only sense, then, in which cost of production can affect the value of one thing is the sense in which it is itself the value of another thing. Thus what has been variously termed utility, ophelemity, or desiredness, is the sole and ultimate determinant of all exchange values.*[19]

For Wicksteed, the only sense in which cost plays a role in the explanation of the market price is that in which cost is the anticipated value of a prospective alternative which is, at the moment of production decision, being rejected in favor of what it is decided to produce.

It is this view of Wicksteed which led Professor James Buchanan to write that the

> opportunity-cost conception was explicitly developed by the Austrians, by the American, H. J. Davenport, and the principle could scarcely have occupied a more central place than it assumed in P. H. Wicksteed's *Common Sense of Political Economy.*[20]

---

19. Wicksteed, ibid., vol. 1, p. 391 (italics added). Wicksteed, in his celebrated 1913 paper ("The Scope and Method of Political Economy in Light of the 'Marginal' Theory of Value and Distribution," *Economic Journal,* 1914), pursued this insight so far as to establish one of his best-known and most provocative analytical insights, viz. that there is, in reality, no such thing as an independent "supply curve." The supply curve is merely part of what Wicksteed called the "total demand curve" which includes the schedule of quantities of a commodity which existing holders of that commodity will wish to hold for their own consumption, at different prices.

20. James M. Buchanan, in *L.S.E. Essays on Cost,* James M. Buchanan and G. F. Thirlby, eds. (London: London School of Economics and Political Science, 1973), p. 14.

As Buchanan has emphasized,[21] Wicksteed's work "was a major formative influence on the cost theory that emerged in the late 1920s and early 1930s at the London School of Economics [LSE]." Certainly Robbins's own recognition of the Austrian School during these years, and his own intellectual leadership at the LSE at this time must have helped cement the perception of intellectual affinity linking Wicksteed with the Austrian School.

WICKSTEED AND THE SCOPE OF ECONOMICS

Wicksteed devoted many pages of his *Common Sense* to the elucidation of the meaning of the adjective "economic." And his final major restatement of his overall perspective bore the title "The Scope and Method of Political Economy in the Light of the 'Marginal' Theory of Value and Distribution."[22] Here, again, we find Wicksteed pursuing the radical implications of the Jevonian revolution, and being led inevitably to the rejection of classical views on the scope of economics. It is utterly incoherent, Wicksteed insisted again and again, to view the pursuit of material wealth as constituting a uniquely distinct field for economic inquiry; it is both arbitrary and analytically unhelpful, to say the least, to see the conclusions of economic science as dependent upon the dominance of selfish motives (as identified with the classical *homo oeconomicus*).

It is here that we find Wicksteed treading the same path as the Austrians, and, in particular as Ludwig von Mises. Both Wicksteed and Mises insisted on the *universal* application of the conclusions which flow from our understanding of human purposefulness and rationality in the making of decisions. "We habitually talk," Wicksteed wrote,

> of a man gaining some object "at the price of honor"; or say to some one who contemplates an action which would alienate his friends, "Oh yes! Of course you can do it, if you choose to pay the price," "Price," then, in the narrower sense of "the money for which a material thing, a service,

21. See James M. Buchanan, *Cost and Choice: An Inquiry in Economic Theory* (Chicago: Markham Publishing, 1969), p. 17; also Buchanan and Thirlby, *L.S.E. Essays on Cost*, p. 14. For the extent to which Buchanan believes that Wicksteed attained Buchanan's own theoretical understanding of cost, see Buchanan, *Cost and Choice*, p. 17.

22. This was also part of his 1913 Presidential Address to Section F of the British Association.

or a privilege can be obtained," is simply a special case of "price" in the wider sense of "the terms on which alternatives are offered to us."[23]

"Sensitive people," Mises wrote,

> may be pained to have to choose between the ideal and the material. But that . . . is in the nature of things. For even where we can make judgments of value without money computations, we cannot avoid this choice. Both isolated man and socialist communities would have to do likewise, and truly sensitive natures will never find it painful. Called upon to choose between bread and honor, they will never be at a loss how to act. If honor cannot be eaten, eating can at least be forgone for honor.[24]

It is no accident that when, in 1933, Mises first comprehensively laid out his view of economics as simply a branch of a "universally valid science of human action,"[25] and argued that the "laws of catallactics that economics expounds are valid for every exchange regardless of whether those involved in it have acted wisely or unwisely or whether they were actuated by economic or non-economic motives,"[26] he referred, in a footnote, to the page in Wicksteed from which we have cited the passage quoted above.

For Mises, the exclusion of altruistic motives from economics is arbitrary and based on misunderstanding. What drives human behavior is simply human purposefulness. "What a man does is always aimed at an improvement of his own state of satisfaction." Only in this sense can we accurately understand

> an action directly aiming at the improvement of other people's conditions. . . . The actor considers it as more satisfactory for himself to

23. Wicksteed, 1933, p. 28. It is noteworthy that this page is cited approvingly by Ludwig von Mises, in *Epistemological Problems of Economics*, George Reisman, trans. (Princeton, N.J.: D. Van Nostrand, 1960), p. 34.

24. Ludwig von Mises, *Socialism: An Economic and Sociological Analysis* (London: Jonathan Cape, 1936), p. 116. In this early (the original German edition was published in 1922) expression of Mises's rejection of any sharp line separating the economic from the non-economic, Mises does not cite Wicksteed.

25. Mises, *Epistemological Problems*, p. 12.

26. Ibid., p. 34.

make other people eat than to eat himself. His uneasiness is caused by the awareness of the fact that other people are in want.[27]

Wicksteed elaborated on this same insight in his insistence that the "proposal to exclude 'benevolent' or 'altruistic' motives from consideration in the study of Economics is . . . wholly irrelevant and beside the mark." The common Austrian foundational tenet is the primacy of human *purposefulness*, seen far more broadly than as the expression of egoistic, selfish greed. As Robbins recognized,[28] it is considerations such as the dependency of economic phenomena upon "purposive action" which enables us adequately to dismiss the "oft-reiterated accusation that Economics assumes a world of economic men concerned only with money-making and self-interest." Clearly, what Wicksteed and the Austrians were doing was consistently and subjectivistically redirecting the focus of economic analysis away from the material *objects* of classical inquiry, to the implications of individual human choices and decisions.

WICKSTEED AND THE MARKET PROCESS

"A market," Wicksteed wrote,

> is the machinery by which those on whose scales of preference any commodity is relatively high are brought into communication with those on whose scale it is relatively low, in order that exchanges may take place to mutual satisfaction until equilibrium is established. But this process will always and necessarily occupy time.[29]

No doubt modern Austrians will be able to find a number of points on which to quibble with Wicksteed's careful and elaborate discussion[30] of how markets tend toward the equilibrium to which he is here referring.

---

27. Ludwig von Mises, *Human Action: A Treatise on Economics,* Scholar's Edition (Auburn, Ala.: Ludwig von Mises Institute, [1949] 1998), p. 243.

28. Robbins, *Nature and Significance,* pp. 93ff. Robbins cites Mises in regard to the purposefulness of "rational" behavior. Robbins noted the parallelism between Wicksteed and Mises in this regard (see his Introduction to Wicksteed, *The Common Sense of Political Economy,* p. xxiii). Arguably it was this insight which inspired the central ideas in Robbins's first edition of *Nature and Significance.*

29. Wicksteed, *The Common Sense of Political Economy,* vol. 1, p. 236.

30. Ibid., pp. 219–29.

What is important, however, for our assessment of Wicksteed's Austrianism is his explicit recognition of the market as the framework within which a time-consuming equilibrating *process* is occurring—a process during which market participants are gradually "brought into communication" with each other—rather than as the social instrument in which initially assumed perfect mutual knowledge is instantaneously translated into an array of equilibrium prices and quantities.

Robbins perceptively drew attention to this aspect of Wicksteed's work.

> Wicksteed's approach is by no means the same as Pareto's. His analysis of the conditions of equilibrium is much less an end in it self, much more a tool with which to explain the tendencies of any given situation. He was much more concerned with economic phenomena as a process in time, much less with its momentary end-products.[31]

Admittedly, Wicksteed was not unique among the great neoclassical economists in seeing the market as a competitive *process*. Robbins's above-cited observation refers to a contrast with Pareto, from whom Wicksteed had otherwise learned a good deal. But outside the Walrasian school, an understanding of the competitive process was not as rare as late-twentieth-century portrayals of neoclassical economics may seem to imply.[32] Yet, one will surely find few early-twentieth-century discussions in which the details of the competitive market process (in the course of which errors come to be corrected, and mutual knowledge is *derived* rather than initially assumed) are as carefully worked out as they are in Wicksteed. Here we see Wicksteed, in Austrian fashion, seeing the decisions of market participants not as the implications of equilibrium conditions somehow assumed already to exist, but as the initiating causes for (and stages in) the process of equilibration itself.

In conclusion, perhaps the sense in which Wicksteed can best be seen as Austrian is captured in Mises's remarks on the distinguishing features of the economist. "The economist," he wrote,

> deals with matters that are present and operative in every man. . . . What distinguishes [the economist] from other people is not the

31. Robbins, Introduction to Wicksteed, *The Common Sense of Political Economy*, vol. 1, p. xix.

32. On this, see the important work of Frank M. Machovec, *Perfect Competition and the Transformation of Economics* (London: Routledge, 1995).

esoteric opportunity to deal with some special material not accessible to others, but the way he looks upon things and discovers in them aspects which other people fail to notice. It was this that Philip Wicksteed had in mind when he chose for his great treatise a motto from Goethe's *Faust:* Human life—everybody lives it, but only to a few is it known.[33]

SELECTED READINGS

Buchanan, James M. 1969. *Cost and Choice: An Inquiry in Economic Theory.* Chicago: Markham Publishing.

Buchanan, James M., and G. F. Thirlby, eds. 1973. *L.S.E. Essays on Cost.* London: London School of Economics and Political Science.

Hayek, F. A. 1984. *Money, Capital, and Fluctuations: Early Essays.* Roy McCloughry, ed. Chicago: University of Chicago Press.

Herford, C. H. 1931. *Philip Wicksteed: His Life and Work.* London and Toronto: J. M. Dent.

Jevons, William Stanley. 1871. *The Theory of Political Economy.* London and New York: Macmillan.

Kirzner, Israel M. 1963. *Market Theory and the Price System.* Princeton, N.J.: D. Van Nostrand.

Machovec, Frank M. 1995. *Perfect Competition and the Transformation of Economics.* London and New York: Routledge.

Mayer, Hans. 1932. *The Cognitive Value of Functional Theories of Price.* (German original in H. Mayer, ed. *Die Wirtschaftstheorie der Gegenwart.* Vienna. 1932. Vol. 2.) English translation in *Classics in Austrian Economics: A Sampling in the History of a Tradition.* Israel M. Kirzner, ed. London: William Pickering. 1994. Vol. 2. pp. 55–168.

Mises, Ludwig von. [1922] 1936. *Socialism: An Economic and Sociological Analysis.* London: Jonathan Cape. Translated from the second German edition, 1932.

———. [1933] 1960. *Epistemological Problems of Economics.* Translated from the German by George Reisman. Princeton: D. Van Nostrand.

———. [1949] 1998. *Human Action: A Treatise on Economics,* Scholar's Edition. Auburn, Ala.: Ludwig von Mises Institute.

———. 1962. *The Ultimate Foundation of Economic Science: An Essay on Method.* Princeton, N.J.: D. Van Nostrand.

Robbins, Lionel C. [1932] 1935. An Essay on the Nature and Significance of Economic Science. 2nd ed. London: Macmillan.

Rothbard, Murray N. 1962. *Man, Economy, and State: A Treatise on Economic Principles.* 2 Vols. Princeton, N.J.: D. Van Nostrand.

33. Mises, *The Ultimate Foundation of Economic Science*, p. 78.

Schumpeter, Joseph A. 1954. *History of Economic Analysis*. New York: Oxford University Press.

Steedman, Ian. 1987. "Wicksteed, Philip Henry." *The New Palgrave: A Dictionary of Economics*. John Eatwell, Murray Milgate, and Peter Newman eds. 4 Vols. New York: Macmillan.

Stigler, George J. 1941. *Production and Distribution Theories: The Formative Period*. New York: Macmillan.

Wicksteed, Philip H. 1888. *The Alphabet of Economic Science*. London: Macmillan.

———. 1933. *The Common Sense of Political Economy and Selected Papers and Reviews on Economic Theory*. Lionel Robbins, Introduction and editor. London: Routledge and Kegan Paul.

ROUNDABOUTNESS, OPPORTUNITY, AND AUSTRIAN ECONOMICS

In recent decades, the term "Austrian economics" has somehow come to denote two quite distinct segments of economic reasoning. On the one hand, the term has come to refer narrowly to Austrian capital-and-interest theory, particularly as it has developed from its roots in the work of Eugen von Böhm-Bawerk.[1] On the other hand, it has come to refer to the tradition focussing on competitive-entrepreneurial market *processes* (rather than on states of market equilibrium).[2]

These segments of economic reasoning appear on initial examination to be genuinely independent of each other. It is true that to recognise that the production process which involves capital takes place over time is not at all the same thing as recognising the dynamically competitive character of market processes. And, conversely, to understand the way competitive entrepreneurial activity may generate equilibrating (or other) tendencies, through time, is by no means to recognise the implications of the fact that production takes place over time. All this is no doubt partly responsible for a degree of confusion in doctrinal nomenclature. The description "Austrian economist" is not always an unambiguous label. The purpose of this essay is to argue that in at least one important respect *both* of these apparently independent segments of economic reasoning do reflect a common point of departure. Moreover, to see this connection may throw a helpful light on certain aspects of these two segments. I shall first review each of these segments separately.

From *The Unfinished Agenda: Essays on the Political Economy of Government Policy in Honour of Arthur Seldon*, ed. Martin J. Anderson (London: Institute of Economic Affairs, 1986), 93–103. Reprinted by permission of the Institute of Economic Affairs.

1. For example, J. R. Hicks, *Capital and Time: A Neo-Austrian Theory*, Clarendon Press, Oxford, 1973; and Malte Faber, *Introduction to Modern Austrian Capital Theory*, Springer, Heidelberg, 1979.

2. For example, Gerald P. O'Driscoll and Mario J. Rizzo, *The Economics of Time and Ignorance*, Basil Blackwell, Oxford, 1985, and my *Competition and Entrepreneurship*, University of Chicago Press, Chicago, 1973.

CAPITAL-AND-INTEREST THEORY:
THE IMPLICATIONS OF "ROUNDABOUTNESS"

Ever since Böhm-Bawerk, Austrian capital-and-interest theory has re-
volved around the concept of "roundaboutness." This insight—that
production takes time—focusses attention on intertemporal allocation
of resources, on intertemporal rates of exchange, and on the structure
over time of the stock of capital in the economy. Because the passage of
time permits us to witness the successive initiation of time-consuming
processes of production (and their subsequent successive completions), a
cross-section of production activities at a given date will reveal a wide array of processes of production arrested at different stages towards completion, embodying stocks of resources invested already for a wide array of
lengths of past time. In the market, exchanges are constantly being made
that involve the sale of current services of resources (intended to be used
to generate future output), the sale of "half-baked cakes" (intended to be
used to generate future "fully-baked cakes"), and the sale of finished products (intended to obviate the necessity of engaging in time-consuming
production effort). Moreover, the sums paid in such market transactions
are often themselves the proceeds of intertemporal exchanges, particularly
of short- or long-term borrowing transactions. Thus the entire array of
spot and intertemporal prices, including the various money and "own"-
rates of interest,[3] is inseparably bound up with the complex arrays of time-
consuming processes of production. These prices reflect, therefore, the
interplay of economic decision-making at different times by producers,
resource-owners and consumers, and thus express awareness of the physical productivities of different kinds and degrees of "roundaboutness," as
well as the time-preferences of the various market participants.

It will be helpful to refer to the following model of a simple economy
which involves rudimentary time-consuming processes of production.
Consider a "steady-state" economy[4] in which, each year, current employment combines with (free) land to produce, one year later, 1,000 units of

3. "'Own'-rates of interest" is a technical term that refers, for example, to the number of future apples obtainable for current apples—that is, the commodity is defined
in terms of itself, rather than in money values.

4. That is, an economy in which there is no growth, so that everything continues as
before, from one year to the next.

wheat. This production process requires that each year 700 units of wheat are used for seed and wages to workers. During each year these 700 units of wheat are "advanced" by capitalists/producers who are repaid, or repay themselves, at harvest time. Out of the entire 1,000 units of gross wheat output available at harvest time 700 units constitute repayment of principal, replenishing the 700-unit stock of circulating wheat capital, and the remaining 300 units are surplus, or profit, or interest revenue, enjoyed by the capitalists/producers. And so it goes on year after year.

A non-Austrian perspective might see this economy in a way which overlooks the time-dimension in production, arguing that the annual output is sufficient both to cover the annual 700 wage costs and to yield the annual surplus of 300. In 1986, 1,000 units are produced: of these, 700 units correspond to the quantity used for seed and wages in 1986, 300 are 1986 profits or surplus. And so it goes on year after year.

But from the Austrian perspective this economy is seen as one in which, each year, capitalists/producers and workers engage in multi-period planning and may participate in exchanges over time. Workers (and owners of seed) sell current labour and seed to producers for 700 units of wheat. (They thus refrain from using their seed and their labour themselves—with available land—to obtain the 1,000 units of wheat available a year from now.) Producers/capitalists draw on their stock of 700 units of wheat to buy the labour and seed currently available, in order to obtain 1,000 units of wheat a year from now. The 300-unit surplus is thus seen as implicit interest earned by producers/capitalists on their one-year investment (of 700 units of circulating wheat capital). Presumably, if current labour had been used in processes of production shorter than one full year (so that wheat output would have been available, say, in six months), annual output would have been smaller, expressing a smaller surplus (or "implicit" interest revenue earned by the capitalists). The time-length of the production process being used presumably reflects, then, first, the producers'/capitalists' awareness of alternative physical outputs to be expected from production processes involving different lengths of time, and, second, the structure of their time preferences. Longer or "lengthier" processes of production might, perhaps, have yielded a somewhat larger output of wheat, but the additional cost in "waiting" was judged too burdensome; shorter processes would have avoided waiting a full year (for loan repayment and for receipt of interest revenue) but would have provided too small a volume of annual output.

Clearly there is nothing in this Austrian analysis that, on the face of it, invokes insights concerning market processes, imperfect knowledge and entrepreneurial discovery. If we were to assume universal perfect knowledge, of both current and future conditions, the Austrian perspective on the intertemporal decisions and intertemporal market relationships involved in the model would nonetheless still be valid. The 300 units of profit in our model are not at all to be seen as profit in the pure-entrepreneurial-profit sense. Even if all potential gains from intertemporal trade are already fully perceived and firmly grasped, these 300 units of surplus will continue to be received by the capitalists/producers, given the time-preferences assumed in the model and the productivity of roundaboutness. Apparently this segment of Austrian economic analysis neither depends on nor provides support for those other Austrian insights into the competitive-entrepreneurial character of market process.

I shall nonetheless argue below that Austrian capital-and-interest analyses do dovetail significantly and illuminatingly with Austrian insights on the market process. Let us now briefly review these latter ideas.

AUSTRIAN MARKET PROCESS THEORY: THE AFTERMATH OF OPPORTUNITY

Building particularly on the work of Mises and Hayek (but thereby reviving insights more or less common to Austrians ever since Menger), modern Austrian economics has emphasised the significance of market *processes*. Where contemporary neo-classical or mainstream economists have seen the market, almost exclusively, as a social engine yielding instantaneously achieved states of equilibrium (in the context of alternative given conditions of supply and of demand), modern Austrians see the market as a systematic but *open-ended* process of competitive-entrepreneurial decisions executed on qualities and quantities of output, methods of production, and bids and offers on the prices of inputs and outputs.

A key insight embodied in this modern Austrian perspective concerns the role of the *hitherto unperceived opportunity*. In mainstream economics (and particularly general equilibrium analysis), the notion of an unperceived opportunity is either completely excluded, or is treated in a manner which in reality defines such opportunities out of existence. For Austrians, on the other hand, it is the systematic sequence of discoveries concerning hitherto unperceived opportunities which constitutes the market process. It is the anticipated gain (the pure profit) from such discoveries that provides the entrepreneurial incentive which "drives" or inspires this market process.

Mainstream economics, especially mainstream microeconomics, assumes, in effect, that all objectively existing opportunities for pure gain are *instantaneously* perceived and grasped. The notion of an unperceived opportunity is thus excluded. Each opportunity is at once extinguished; at all times opportunities for pure gain are therefore absent. *Apparently* unexploited opportunities for gain observed in the market are explained away by reference to the costs of obtaining the relevant information: the gain, it is argued, is more than offset by the costs. In other words, in this mainstream view, the ignorance responsible for ungrasped gain is never *complete* ignorance: that is, it is always the case that agents at least know what knowledge they lack, and where and at what cost such a lack can be made good. From this mainstream perspective, therefore, learning processes are deliberate, and proceed at a deliberate pace governed by the calculated comparison of the costs and benefits of learning. Market processes are never, contends the mainstream, sparked by the spontaneous imagination of alert or daring entrepreneurs; they consist, rather, in perfectly co-ordinated executions of plans that are, at each and every instant, fully optimal in the light of relevant costs and benefits. Clearly then, in this view, there is never a question of equilibrating or non-equilibrating market processes—*since the market is,* at each and every instant of time, *already in the relevant state of equilibrium.*

Austrian analysis, by contrast, sees the market quite differently. The decisions being made in markets on any given date are likely to express genuine error; that is, on that date the decisions being made happen (from the perspective of the fictitious "omniscient observer") to be not the best available to the decision-makers *in the light of the information costlessly available to them.* Possibilities for the capture of pure gain arise, indeed, out of the unexploited opportunities overlooked in the course of these error-laden decisions. These gains were not grasped, not because it was not worthwhile (because of the costs of acquiring knowledge) to learn how to obtain them, but because market participants had no inkling they were available (perhaps because of ignorance of how to set about finding out whether such gains exist, or how to grasp them).

THE EPISTEMOLOGY OF GAIN

Further, in this modern Austrian view, the perennial existence of hitherto unexploited opportunities for pure gain itself offers a powerful incentive, inspiring entrepreneurial discovery of these opportunities, provided that potential entrepreneurial entry is not arbitrarily obstructed. Competitive entry by alert, imaginative entrepreneurs thus constitutes a sequence of steps inspired, at each turn, by the prospect of pure gain. Such a sequence of discoveries may constitute, in turn, any one of several aspects of the market process and may correspond to the "gale winds of creative destruction" identified by Schumpeter. Here what is discovered are technological possibilities that were, it is evident in retrospect, simply "waiting to be noticed" by daring, imaginative entrepreneurs. But such a sequence of discoveries may also constitute the competitive process whereby the market price of a product is competed down towards its lowest cost of production. Or it may constitute the competitive process whereby the market converges on the specific desired attributes of given classes of products. Here we witness no grand revolutions in technology or organisation but instead a series of competitive moves in which entrepreneurs implement their hunches about how far as yet untried prices or product qualities offer opportunities for pure gain.

These Austrian insights into the character of the market process seem to hold no apparent relevance for issues involving capital-and-interest theory. It is true that the market process is a process of learning through time. But the sense in which time is significant for the market process is, at least analytically, distinct from the sense in which time enters into the Austrian analysis on capital-and-interest questions. Here its importance is that production which uses capital involves intertemporal decision-making. Time enters into the analysis of market processes because such processes unfold through time as sequences of episodes of learning—even where no intertemporal decisions are under consideration at all.[5]

It is, of course, true that real-world entrepreneurs are likely to be capitalists. (A number of writers have roundly criticised the analytical

5. Of course, the market process refers also to processes of learning that are related to intertemporal decisions; moreover, the phenomenon of the market process itself generates complicating opportunities for intertemporal speculation. But even if all such intertemporal considerations were to be absent, the essential character of the market process through time would remain.

isolation of the pure entrepreneur.[6] My views on this issue have been ex-pressed elsewhere.[7]) But the circumstance that real-world decisions that are related to capital-and-interest theory are likely at the same time to make relevant the theory of the competitive-entrepreneurial market pro-cess (and *vice-versa*) does not of itself reveal any common point of depar-ture for these two segments of theory. I nonetheless still hope to show that such a common starting-point can be identified, and that such an identi-fication can throw a useful light on both segments of Austrian thought.

SUBJECTIVISM AND THE ECONOMICS OF UNDERVALUATION

Both of these segments of theory rely crucially on the notion of *under-valuation* as a driving force in economic decision-making; and the pos-sibility of such a driving force itself depends heavily on the *subjectivism* that has always been central to Austrian analysis. Acceptance of these as-sertions not only draws the two segments together; it also illuminates our understanding of the real-world decisions that are the subjects of these two separate bodies of analysis.

That the Austrian understanding of the market process reveals its driving force to be undervaluation follows from recognition of the *en-trepreneurial* character of that process. Each entrepreneurial step in this process consists of an action inspired by the prospect of pure entrepre-neurial profit. But that profit occurs only where the market yields two distinct market values for the same item. Whether one is concerned with pure arbitrage profit (with the speculative profit won by buying low and subsequently selling high), or with profit won by the producer inspired to undertake production of an item that consumers discover to be im-mensely interesting—profit results from the market permitting the en-trepreneur to acquire something at a lower price than that at which the market itself is willing to buy the very same item (or items produced from it). In other words, entrepreneurial profit occurs when an entrepre-neur has become alert to the existence of an undervalued item available on the market. Such undervaluation is relative to the "true" value which the entrepreneur knows (or believes he knows), or thinks he can create. It

---

6. For example, Murray N. Rothbard, "Professor Hébert on Entrepreneurship," *Journal of Libertarian Studies,* Vol. VII, No. 2, Fall 1985, pp. 282–284.

7. *Perception, Opportunity and Profit,* University of Chicago Press, Chicago, 1979, Chapter 6.

is the alertness of the entrepreneur to this difference between the market value and the "true" value of an item, that spurs entrepreneurial reallocation of the item from lower to higher, more optimal, uses.

The phenomenon of perceived undervaluation can be understood only in terms of subjectivist insights. Undervaluation occurs as a result of failure by market participants to recognise the true (that is, potential) value of an item. Awareness of such undervaluation requires that someone, some alert entrepreneur, interpret the world differently (more accurately) than the rest of the market has interpreted it. Values are not determined by objective conditions but by subjective interpretations and by subjective hunches about them. Economic progress, to the extent that it is driven by entrepreneurial discovery and innovation, is inspired by the differences in valuations generated by such interpretations and hunches.

It may not be equally apparent that Austrian insights on capital-and-interest issues similarly involve perceived undervaluation. Consider what occurs when a capitalist advances resources to allow an entrepreneur to command the services of current inputs in order to achieve output which will be available only in the future. The owners of these current inputs make their input services available at a (low) price which reflects their own (higher) time-preferences. (They apply a high rate of discount in arriving at their present valuations of the future output their services can produce.) The entrepreneurs, on the other hand, recognise that, for capitalists (whose time-preferences are lower), the value of these current input services is much higher. For capitalists, using the lower rate of discount, the present value of the future output is much higher than it is for the owners of current input services. It is the difference between the low value (placed on anticipated output by current input owners) and the high value (placed on that same output by capitalists) that inspires the producers' decision to engage in roundabout methods of production. From the perspective that discounts the future less sharply, the higher value is the "truer" value of these input services; thus their lower current market price represents an undervaluation. It is the subjectivist perspective, of course, that accounts for such differing valuations of the same future output. To see how it is indeed the perceived "undervaluation" that drives the capitalistic production process, consider the simple model of the time-consuming production of wheat discussed above. In that model 700 units of wheat were advanced each year to yield 1,000 units one year later.

Now, in a closed and static "Crusoe" economy (with Crusoe "advancing" 700 units of wheat to support his efforts this year, resulting in 1,000 units of wheat available a year later) no such undervaluation would be apparent. Crusoe prefers 1,000 future units to 700 present units; that is all. What "drives" his steady pattern of investment is simply the productivity of round-aboutness. (His time preferences determine the margin at which additional roundaboutness is no longer seen as attractive.) But in a market economy the initiation of roundabout methods of production calls for the purchase of current input services and their commitment to the production of future, rather than for more immediately forthcoming, output. What inspires such commitment is the perception by producers of a difference in the valuations placed on future output by input owners and capitalists, respectively.

To be sure, Austrians are not predisposed to refer to the lower present (high-time-preference) valuations placed on future output as representing "undervaluation." From the subjectivist perspective a lower time-preference is no more "true" than a high time-preference; the high present values that reflect a lower time-preference are no more "correct" than the lower present values that express a high time-preference. Different persons value given future receipts differently; each valuation is as valid as any other. Nonetheless, when the future arrives and becomes the present, the previously diverse valuations converge until all valuations support those made earlier by the least "impatient" among the market participants. To be sure, these upwardly-revised valuations (on the part of the more "impatient" market participants) are not really revisions at all; the new valuations are made at a different time from, and are hence not commensurable with, the earlier valuations. Nevertheless, there surely is a sense in which a market participant treats his present valuation of a presently available good as more "truthful" than his earlier valuations in anticipation of that availability. In this limited (perhaps metaphorical) sense, we may say that what drives the adoption of more physically productive, roundabout methods of production is the "undervaluation" of future outputs on the part of owners of current input services (as judged by those whose time-preferences render them less impatient).

ENTREPRENEURIAL CAPITAL-USING DECISIONS

Entrepreneurs assemble resources to produce products. In a capital-using world, the outputs emerge only at some date later than that on which the original resources are assembled. Economic progress occurs when current resources are applied, in appropriately roundabout methods of production, towards the production of output, the value to consumers of which has been generally underestimated. The Austrians see market agitation as being inspired by the drive for gains generated by subjectivistically-based diversity in valuations. Where such agitation places resources in the hands of entrepreneurs who more correctly anticipate future conditions, where it inspires the diversion of resources away from more immediate enjoyments in favour of (what from the perspective of the future will appear as) the more valuable future outputs, this agitation will be seen to have constituted economic progress. The view of the classical economists who somehow failed to distinguish between pure interest and pure entrepreneurial profit (as components of the total share of output received by the classical capitalist class) is seen to have a certain plausibility, precisely from the Austrian perspective. There *is* a significant sense in which the classical profit expresses a single economic entity—and it is Austrian subjectivism (paradoxically so central to subsequent analytical distinctions within that classical profit entity) that throws light on that singleness.

THE EMERGENCE OF
ENTREPRENEURSHIP THEORY

CLASSICAL ECONOMICS AND
THE ENTREPRENEURIAL ROLE

One of the better-known aspects of the theoretical system known as classical economics is that it suffered from a failure to identify the entrepreneurial role separately from the role of the capitalist. In the classical system the capitalist received profits, and there was little understanding that the latter "confused and garbled concept"[1] is in fact to be seen as a complex of analytically separate items. One writer has sweepingly, but not inaccurately, observed that "until the last quarter of the nineteenth century economists in Britain had only the vaguest conceptions of the undertaker's function."[2]

This failure to recognize the entrepreneurial role does call for explanation. As we shall see, the figure of the entrepreneur was fairly well recognized in the eighteenth-century world of commerce. Moreover, in other earlier and contemporary systems of economic thought the function of the entrepreneur was identified and, indeed, even emphasized. Why then, one must ask, did the English classical economists construct their system in a fashion that so completely submerged the entrepreneurial function, jumbling it so unhelpfully with that of the capitalist? The purpose of this chapter is not so much to offer a new answer to this question as to report on a search of the literature for recognition of the difficulty and for the alternative explanations that have been offered.

THE ENTREPRENEUR IN EIGHTEENTH-CENTURY
ENGLISH COMMERCE

Scholars researching the history of entrepreneurship have traced early references to the entrepreneurial role in eighteenth-century commercial literature. As we shall notice, French writings show perhaps more widespread awareness of the entrepreneur than do eighteenth-century English authors. But the research has nonetheless turned up enough references

From *Perception, Opportunity, and Profit: Studies in the Theory of Entrepreneurship* (Chicago and London: University of Chicago Press, 1979), 37–52. © 1979 by the University of Chicago. Reprinted by permission.

Presented at a session of the meetings of the History of Economics Society, held at Cambridge, Massachusetts, May 1975.

to convince us that the entrepreneurial figure was by no means unnoticed in England. As early as 1697, we find the term "projector" used by Daniel Defoe in the sense of someone rather similar to Schumpeter's "creative" entrepreneur.[3] Postlethwayt's *Universal Dictionary of Trade and Commerce* (London, 1751–55) uses the term "honest projector" to include both the inventor and the creative entrepreneur as contrasted with "idle, roguish and enthusiastical projectors" whose activities reflect "whim and knavery."[4] Hoselitz, noting a 1705 usage of the term "projector" to refer to Sir Walter Raleigh in his capacity of discoverer and colonizer, remarks that the term had an "invidious flavor and was applied to either fraudulent or highly speculative enterprisers."[5] The term "undertaker" had its origins in sixteenth-century usage to refer to contractors, and in particular to government contractors. Gradually, it came to be used synonymously with projector, serving as the English counterpart of the French entrepreneur. By the middle of the eighteenth century, an undertaker was simply a big businessman or an ordinary businessman. However, Hoselitz discovered, "by the time of Postlethwayt and Smith the more general meaning to the word tended to become obsolete and only the special meaning of an arranger of funerals survived. The undertaker in English economics was replaced by the capitalist who only toward the end of the nineteenth century again gave way to the entrepreneur."[6] Smith himself did use both projector and undertaker. By undertaker he apparently meant primarily capitalist. The price of output, Smith argued, must cover not only the cost of labor and materials, but also something "for the profits of the undertaker of the work who hazards his stock in this adventure."[7] At one place Smith discusses the higher wages that must be offered to attract workers when "a projector attempts to establish a new manufacture."[8] And he remarks, in this regard, that the "establishment of any new manufacture, of any new branch of commerce, or of any new practice in agriculture, is always a speculation, from which the projector promises himself extraordinary profits."[9]

THE ENTREPRENEUR IN EIGHTEENTH-CENTURY FRANCE

Recognition of the entrepreneurial role was even clearer in eighteenth-century France. Although it was once thought that J. B. Say in 1803 was the first to use the term entrepreneur, it is now well known that the term was familiar to French economists from Cantillon to Turgot to Quesnay. Hoselitz has discovered a whole series of French writings indicating that the term was used in France as early as the Middle Ages in the sense of *actor* (with apparant special reference to warlike action). In particular, the entrepreneur was in charge of large-scale construction projects such as cathedrals, bearing no risks but simply carrying the task forward until resources were exhausted. By the seventeenth century the term was used to designate the risk bearer, typically "a person who entered into a contractual relationship with the government for the performance of a service or the supply of goods. The price at which the contract was valued was fixed and the entrepreneur bore the risks of profit and loss from the bargain."[10] During the eighteenth century, the French writers on economic matters used the term in a variety of senses. In 1729 Belidor, like Cantillon in 1725,[11] used entrepreneur to mean risk bearer. For Quesnay, an entrepreneur is, less colorfully, "simply a tenant farmer who rents property at a fixed rent and produces a given output with given factors at given prices." On the other hand, for Beaudeau (1767) and Turgot, the risk-bearing aspect of the entrepreneur is again emphasized with attention also to his ownership, planning, organizing, and supervising.[12] In addition, the entrepreneur appears to have typically been wealthy. One turn-of-the-century American profit theorist has interpreted the physiocratic surplus theory as reflecting recognition of enterprise as the dominant productive factor.[13]

ADAM SMITH AND THE ENTREPRENEUR

There is a certain ambiguity in the literature concerning whether Smith failed completely to identify the entrepreneurial role separately from the role of the capitalist. We have already seen, of course, that on occasion Smith made passing reference to the undertaker[14] and the projector. And one writer has claimed that Smith took the next step (beyond the position of the physiocrats) in differentiating the function of the entrepreneur.[15] Knight has pointed out that Smith and his followers "recognized that profits even normally contain an element which is not interest on capital. Remuneration for the work and care of supervising the business was always distinguished. Reference was also made to risk, but in the sense of risk of loss of capital, which does not clearly distinguish profit from interest."[16] Despite Smith's indirect references to the entrepreneurial role, therefore, his discussion of profits on stock tended to confuse any possible distinction between the pure interest of the capitalist and the pure profit of the entrepreneur.[17] Although Smith explicitly recognizes that gross profit on stock leaves the producer with a net profit after he pays interest to the lenders of the capital,[18] it is made quite clear that profits on stock are "regulated altogether by the value of the stock employed, and are greater or smaller in proportion to the extent of this stock."[19] Whatever the "labour of inspection and direction" the producer may himself furnish, profits "bear no proportion to the quantity, the hardship, or the ingenuity of this supposed labor."[20] Thus, Smith led the way for the general classical approach to the distribution question, in which no separate share of output is recognized as accruing to a separate function of entrepreneurship. In fact, one modern writer has considered Smith's treatment of profit as "the income of the capitalist entrepreneur" to be worthy of applause. He criticizes those writers from Say on who have "with all the resources of excessively atomistic analysis, dismembered Smith's basic idea."[21]

On the other hand, this "basic idea" of Smith was criticized in the years following publication of the *The Wealth of Nations*. Redlich[22] has drawn attention to an open polemic letter written to Smith by Jeremy Bentham, in which Smith is accused of not seeing the importance of the projector (used in the sense of creative entrepreneur). J. B. Say was explicit in criticizing Smith for having involved himself in great difficulty by not separating the profits of the entrepreneur from the profits of his capital.[23] And Blaug has drawn attention to several British economists of the early nineteenth century who did more or less accurately distinguish entrepreneurial profit.[24]

Our problem therefore emerges fairly clearly. Eighteenth-century writers on commercial affairs, including Smith himself, both in England and France, recognized the entrepreneurial figure. At least in France, the economists had already emphasized a distinct entrepreneurial role in production. And yet Smith and his followers failed to make the necessary analytic distinction between the profits captured by the pure entrepreneur and the profits on capital itself. Instead, the classical economists were led to search for a theory of distribution in which a single entity, profit, was perceived as accruing to a single factor class, capital. Some explanation is surely called for to account for what, from a present perspective, appears as an analytic blunder. The need for explanation is greater by virtue of the circumstance that the concepts needed for a more careful treatment were, as we have noticed, so obviously at hand. Before canvassing the literature for attempts to provide this explanation, I shall digress briefly to notice the way Smith treated one particular type of entrepreneur.

THE INDEPENDENT WORKER

We have seen how the entrepreneurial role came, in Smith's system, to be seen as inseparable from the role of the capitalist. It is worth noting that Smith was in fact not prepared to recognize a separate entrepreneurial role even where it manifested itself quite apart from any capitalist function. "In some parts of Scotland," Smith reported,[25] "a few poor people make a trade of gathering, along the seashore, those little variegated stones commonly known by the name of Scotch Pebbles. The price which is paid to them by the stonecutter is altogether the wages of their labor; neither rent nor profit make any part of it."

Since these gatherers of pebbles require no capital for their operations, since their pebbles come from ownerless land and are free goods, Smith can discover no elements of profit or rent in the market value of the pebbles when delivered to the stonecutter. It did not occur to Smith that the pebble gatherers may be exercising entrepreneurship. And this despite Smith's belief, noticed by Cannan,[26] that no worker would accept a master unless he were unable to set himself up as an "independent workman."

Half a century before Smith, Cantillon had explicitly drawn attention to the role of "Undertakers of their own Labour who need no Capital to establish themselves, like Journeyman artisans, Copper-smiths, Needle-women, Chimney Sweeps, Water Carriers" and to "Undertakers of their own labour in Art and Science, like Painters, Physicians, Lawyers, etc."[27] It makes no difference to the entrepreneurial role, Cantillon points out, "whether (Undertakers) set up with a capital to conduct their enterprise, or are Undertakers of their own labour without capital."[28] When Smith considers the high profits made by apothecaries on the drugs they sell, higher than the prevailing rate of profit on capital, he is quick to point out the special skills of the apothecaries which may account for a high implicit wage, but fails to consider the possibility that an apothecary may be treated in Cantillon's terminology as an undertaker of his own labor.[29]

Smith's treatment of the independent worker confirms that, in spite of his insight into the entrepreneurial role, he was unable to perceive it in isolation from the role of capitalist or laborer with which the entrepreneurial role comes packaged in the real world. It is for an explanation of this failure that we turn to the literature.

SOME REMARKS ON THE LITERATURE

It would not be correct to say that the literature of the history of thought has ignored this problem. In fact, as we shall see, the literature yields a surprising number of explanations for the failure of classical economics to accord the entrepreneurial element its due. But, it must be observed, the literature has hardly treated the problem as a serious one calling for careful research. Many of the explanations seem to have been suggested quite casually, as if they were almost self-evident. And the surprising number of explanations to be found appear, in part, to arise precisely out of this casualness with which they were offered. The possibility of alternative explanations was apparently not seriously entertained, nor was any search made in the literature for such alternatives. The result has been that the different explanations to be found in the various writings on classical economics are neither carefully developed nor offered with awareness of competing interpretations.

In what follows, the different attempts at explanation and interpretation are grouped around several leading themes that seem to repeat themselves again and again.

Explanations in Terms of Current Business Practice

Probably the most popular explanation for the classical neglect of the role of the entrepreneur is one that depends on the pattern of business organization characteristic of the classical period. As long ago as 1855, Mangoldt sought the explanation for the insistence of the French economists following Say on separating profit from interest in the "different character of typical French industry, and the greater relative importance of the manager's personality in it relatively to the capital sector."[30] Both Schumpeter[31] and Hoselitz[32] have suggested that Say's own insistence on separating the entrepreneurial function from that of the capitalist was related to his personal experience in and knowledge of the entrepreneurial role, which the other classical economists lacked.

There exist two somewhat different emphases in the explanation in terms of contemporary business practice. It is pointed out that in Smith's time the entrepreneurial role was, in practice, generally merged with that of the capitalist. Some writers, like Blaug, emphasize that entrepreneurship typically involved the entrepreneur's own capital.[33] "Until the 'railway mania' of the 1840's, trading on the stock exchange was largely confined to government bonds and public utility stocks. The domestic capital

market was poorly organized and virtually all new industrial investment was financed out of undistributed profits. There was, consequently, little basis in practice for considering the investment function
independently of the level of saving. Without distorting reality, it was
possible to think of the active entrepreneur as identical with the inactive investor of capital."[34] Schumpeter similarly saw the distinction
between the entrepreneur and the capitalist facilitated during the second half of the nineteenth century "by the fact that changing methods
of business finance produced a rapidly increasing number of instances
in which capitalists were no entrepreneurs and entrepreneurs were no
capitalists."[35]

Other writers emphasize the related circumstance that, during the
classical period, the corporate form of business organization, in which the
capitalist role of stockholders is sharply distinguished from the decision-
making role of managers, was not yet widely prevalent.[36]

In this regard, it is of interest to notice that one historian of thought
has emphasized an almost precisely opposite chain of causation. The
failure of the British classical economists to identify a separate entrepreneurial profit has been related by Haney not to the relative absence of
the joint-stock company, but to its relative frequency. Contrasting Hermann's treatment of undertaker's gains with that of the British economists, Haney writes of this being "an interesting illustration of the close
relation between the industrial environment and economic thought."[37]
In England the growing importance of joint-stock companies controlling
large commercial and industrial concerns meant that a considerable class
was receiving an income other than rent or wages, which suggested the
idea of profits as a return on business capital. On the other hand, in Ger-
many, industry was carried on in smaller units with the handicraftsman
using his own relatively small capital, being his own manager and businessman. "Thus the function of the business undertaker—as the Germans called the entrepreneur or enterpriser—was relatively more dominant than in England."[38]

Explanation in Terms of the Wage-Fund Theory

An interesting explanation of the classical schema was advanced by
Edwin Cannan, reflecting his own view of entrepreneurship as a particular kind of labor and of entrepreneurial profit as a kind of wage. The
classical economists, Cannan argued, were unable to realize this because
they were trapped by the wage-fund theory. This theory, Cannan explains,

denied that wages are derived from output, maintaining instead that they are advanced from the capital of employers. The classical economists, therefore, could not possibly make wages "include income received by undertakers not by way of advance but as a consequence of the success of their undertakings." It was only when "at last the wage-fund theory of wages expired" that "the way was open for the classification of the earnings of undertakers' labour along with that of other kinds of labour."[39]

In Cannan's opinion, Marshall's view of entrepreneurial profit as "earnings of management" was the natural consequence of this liberation from the wage-fund theory.[40] According to this view, the classical economists had every reason to distinguish the entrepreneurial role from the role of the capitalist. What prevented them from properly treating this role as a special category of labor was that they could not see wages as income derived from labor. They "denied that the produce had anything to do with the level of earnings except in so far as, conjoined with saving or accumulations, it affected the magnitude of the capital devoted to the payment of wages."[41] Although, therefore, entrepreneurial labor may indeed be reflected in the size of the volume of output, entrepreneurial profit could not be explained by the classical economists as wages reflecting that entrepreneurial productivity. On the other hand, entrepreneurial profit could not, clearly, be seen, as other wages were held to be, as advanced out of capital, since the entrepreneurs were themselves the capitalists. The consequence was that while the "English economists of the first three-quarters of the nineteenth century" were prepared "to throw out of 'profits of capital' all that the undertaker gets in consequence of his personal activity rather than his possession of capital," they "threw it into the air instead of finding a place for it in their treatment of income derived from labour."[42]

Explanation as a Deliberate Theoretical Effort

Several writers seem to have viewed the suppression of the entrepreneurial role in classical economics not as an analytical lapse calling for excuse, but as arising from a deliberate, and at least partly meritorious, theoretical advance. In this view, Adam Smith was consciously reacting against the earlier ways of seeing the productive process. "Before Smith . . . ," Meek has observed, "'profit' had usually been regarded either as a mere synonym for 'gain,' or as a sort of superior wage or as a surplus over cost whose level varied (as Stewart put it) 'according to circumstances.'

With one bold stroke Smith cut through the difficulties involved in these earlier approaches to the problem. He postulated profit as the income of the class of employers of labor . . . he argued that competition would tend to reduce this profit to 'an ordinary or average rate' on the capital employed."[43] Many years ago, Hawley saw Smith as reacting against physiocratic errors. The physiocrats, Hawley explained, are entitled to the credit of recognizing enterprise as the dominant productive factor. But they erred in thinking that "because enterprise was dominant the other productive factors existed only for its benefit, and that the community was prosperous in the proportion in which the 'surplus' was enhanced at the expense of wages and interest."[44] Hawley sees Smith and his followers as properly revolting against this but as falling, consequently, into the opposite error of "practically ignoring enterprise."

Explanation in Terms of Emphasis on Labor

Some writers have attributed the classical neglect of entrepreneurship to the dominance, in the classical paradigm, of labor. Schumpeter wrote that natural-law preconceptions were to blame for Smith's emphasizing the role of labor "to the exclusion of the productive function of designing the plan according to which this labor is being applied."[45] As a result, the role of the businessman came to be reduced to that of advancing capital.

This interpretation of Schumpeter is to be contrasted with that of Cannan, cited earlier. For Cannan, the contribution of the entrepreneur is seen as a special kind of labor. Smith, according to Cannan, saw this too but was prevented by the wage-fund theory from pursuing the necessary implications. For Schumpeter, on the other hand, the entrepreneurial contribution is to be sharply distinguished from that of labor, and it was the classical preoccupation with labor, therefore, that prevented perception of the entrepreneurial function.

Kuenne, in a few short sentences, has adumbrated an explanation for the classical submersion of the entrepreneur that, while pointing to the dominance of the labor and, generally, cost of production theory of value, is somewhat different from the explanations both of Cannan and of Schumpeter. The classical theories of value, Kuenne asserts, "tempted theorists to resolve capital goods into their labor or primary factor content"[46] and thus to merge the capitalist with an entrepreneur whose contribution could be explained as labor of superintendence.

Explanation in Terms of Emphasis on Capital

In sharp contrast to explanations that stress the classical emphasis on labor must be classed a recent explanation that depends on a postulated central role in classical thought for capital. Eagly has recently sought to present the classical economists as, like the physiocrats, placing capital at the center of the stage. As a result of this pivotal role, the capitalist came to be seen as the dominant decision maker in the system. He is seen as setting labor into motion. Laborers and landlords are assigned negligible roles as decision makers compared with the capitalists, who control, allocate, and accumulate capital. As a consequence, what we now identify as the purely entrepreneurial function was perceived as inseparably bound up in the capitalist function. It was not until the classical paradigm was replaced by the Walrasian and other neoclassical ways of looking at the economic system that entrepreneurs could emerge as analytical figures in their own right. Their emergence was possible only because the new paradigm reduced the capitalist to one who merely owns stock, on an equal footing with laborers and landowners.[47]

Did the Classics View Production as Automatic?

Eagly's interpretation of the classical economists as treating the capitalist as the *dominant decision maker* in the system contrasts with alternative views of the classical system in yet another respect. A number of writers have treated the classical neglect of entrepreneurship as reflecting an approach that sees production as being *an automatic process not calling for active decision making at all*. If one accepts this interpretation of classical thinking, then one has, it can be argued, in effect a new explanation of the absence of the entrepreneur from the classical system. In this explanation, the entrepreneurial role is missing from the classical system because the classical economists did not assign any central importance to the decision-making element in the production process. The economic regularities they believed they saw did not depend on any such decision-making element. Therefore, their analysis did not have to encompass the entrepreneur.

Most emphatic in regard to the automaticity of the classical production process was Schumpeter. Schumpeter, writing of the Ricardians and of Senior, remarks that they "almost accomplished what I have described as an impossible feat, namely, the exclusion of the figure of the entrepreneur completely. For them—as well as for Marx—the business process runs substantially by itself, the one thing needful to make it run being an adequate supply of capital."[48] Of Smith's view of the economic process, Schumpeter has remarked that a reader of Smith is "bound to get an impression to the effect that this process runs on by itself."[49]

We have seen that, for Eagly, the dominance of the capitalist in the classical schema does *not* mean that active decision making is absent from the system, merely that such decision making is located within the capitalist function. Blaug appears to be thinking similarly when he writes of the classical perspective as making it "possible to think of the active entrepreneur as identical with the inactive investor of capital."[50] Cannan's view seems to be slightly more complicated.

In some passages Cannan might, on a superficial reading, appear to attribute to the classical economists, as do Eagly and Blaug, a view of the capitalist role that includes active decision making. Thus Cannan writes of the displacement, in late nineteenth-century economics, of capital from the "triad of productive requisites." This would not, he comments, have been of much importance if capital had not, in the classical system, been "represented as the most active element in the triad. As it is, the change is immense. No longer is capital supposed to decide whether industry shall be set in motion or not, and whether it shall flow into this or that channel when it is set in motion. Capital takes its proper place as an inanimate stock of goods and machinery. . . . The power of 'managing' industry is attributed not to the mute and inanimate capital, nor even to the owners of the capital, but to the 'entrepreneurs.'"[51]

Here Cannan might be understood as seeing the classical production process not as automatic but as one in which the decision initiatives derive from capital and its owners.[52] On the other hand, Cannan's references to a classical view of decision making as contrasted with mute, inanimate capital may be significant. It may be said with truth, Cannan argued at one point, "that it is the capitalists or owners of the capital who for the most part take the 'initiative' in industrial enterprise, and so in a way 'put labor into motion.' But it certainly is not the capital itself, a mere mute mass of objects, which puts industry into motion."[53] Here Cannan appears to be implying that the classical economists had a view of production in which it is indeed automatic in the sense that all direction flows from the "mere mute mass" of capital itself. Again, in the passage cited above (in which Cannan remarks on the displacement of capital from the classical triad) Cannan goes on to remark that even the entrepreneurs who, now that the dominance of capital has been broken, are seen as managing industry, "can only direct industry into particular channels by virtue of their intelligent anticipation of the orders of the consumers, whose demands they have to satisfy on pain of bankruptcy."[54]

It thus seems more accurate to read Cannan as charging the classical economists, as we have seen Schumpeter do, with an automatic view of the process of production. This automaticity is to be understood, however, as being closely related to the classical neglect of demand as an active force directing production. Whereas modern economics, in Cannan's view, sees the pattern of the allocation of resources directed by entrepreneurs responding to dictates of consumer demand, the classical vision saw production as somehow automatically determined by the availability of stock, of labor, and of land. According to this interpretation of Cannan, his references to capital as, in the classical system, deciding whether and how to set industry into motion, should not be understood as emphasizing the capitalist as being, for the classical economists, the active decision maker. Rather Cannan, in these passages, is underlining the awkwardness of a view that sees production, which Cannan himself sees to be obviously the result of active entrepreneurial decision, as flowing *without* anyone being assigned the specific role of decision making, just as if the decisions were made by themselves.

What emerges from this reading of Cannan, then, is a possible explanation for the classical neglect of the entrepreneur. This interpretation ascribes to the classical economists a view of production that, because it had little recognition of the sovereign role of demand, saw it as automatic and therefore in no need of the entrepreneurial role that anticipates consumer wishes. Cannan himself seems not to have considered this interpretation. Nonetheless, such an interpretation may have some merit.

Explanation in Terms of Long-run and Equilibrium Emphasis

Running through several discussions of the weakness of classical economics on profit theory and on the entrepreneurial role is at least a hint of yet another explanation. This one accounts for the classical failure to emphasize the entrepreneur by referring to the classical failure to distinguish carefully between long-run, normal equilibrium states of affairs and real-world market conditions. Knight was the most explicit of these writers. In seeking to explain the earlier weaknesses in profit theory, Knight wrote: "A further source of confusion was the indefiniteness of the conception and use of the ideas of natural and market prices in the minds of the early writers. Only recently . . . has the analysis of long-time normal prices by Marshall and of the 'static state' by Clark and Schumpeter begun to give to economists a clearer notion of what is really involved in 'natural' or normal conditions. To the earlier classical writers this obscurity hid the fundamental difference between the total income of the capitalist manager and contract interest."[55]

Cole appears to have had a similar explanation in mind when, in discussing Ricardo's failure to follow Cantillon and Say in distinguishing the entrepreneur, he blames Ricardo's emphasis on long-run conditions and on static analysis as distracting attention from short-run forces that produce change. Such an explanation may perhaps be supported from Adam Smith's discussion of speculators' profits. "The speculative merchant," Smith observes, "exercises no one regular, established, or well-known branch of business. He is a corn merchant this year, and a wine merchant the next, and a sugar, tobacco, or tea merchant the year after. He enters into every trade when he foresees that it is likely to be more than commonly profitable. . . . His profits and losses . . . bear no regular proportion to those of any one established and well-known branch of business. A bold adventurer may sometimes acquire a considerable fortune by two or three speculations."[56] Smith explains very carefully that the general tendency for wage and profit rates to be equal throughout the market may be thwarted by unusual events such as wartime conscription of sailors that forces up wages of merchant sailors, or a public mourning that raises the price of black cloth, and that in new industries wages and profits may be above normal. It is not difficult, then, to perceive that Smith's view of the normal long-run tendencies in production can afford to ignore the bold new adventurous speculator-projector. The circumstance that post-Walrasian emphasis on equilibrium has, in our times, led to the role of the entrepreneur being virtually expunged from economics, lends further plausibility to this explanation.

Earlier in this chapter, we noticed that eighteenth-century English usage distinguished between the "honest projector" and the "idle, roguish, and enthusiastical projectors" whose activities reflect "whim and knavery." Without knavery, the ordinary course of commerce tends to preclude above-normal profit. The more permanent forces of the market tend to eliminate temporary sources of entrepreneurial gain. Permanent gains flow from the ownership of capital; temporary gains unrelated to the size of capital stock can be ignored as either temporary or the fruit of knavery. The classical unconcern with the entrepreneur therefore need not be criticized at all; it can be perceived as the altogether consistent implication of classical attention to the more powerful, permanent, and enduring forces in the economic system.

NOTES

1. L. Mises, *Human Action* (New Haven: Yale University Press, 1949), p. 532.

2. M. Dobb, *Capitalist Enterprise and Social Progress* (London: Routledge and Sons, 1925), p. 17.

3. F. Redlich, "The Origin of the Concepts of 'Entrepreneur' and 'Creative Entrepreneur,'" *Explorations in Entrepreneurial History* 1, no. 2 (February 1949): 3 ff.

4. Ibid.

5. B. F. Hoselitz, "The Early History of Entrepreneurial Theory," *Explorations in Entrepreneurial History* 3, no. 4 (April 1951): 196 n.

6. Mill did use the term undertaker (*Principles of Political Economy*, Ashley ed. [London, 1909], p. 406), but he regretted the unfamiliarity of the term and the unavailability of a counterpart for the French entrepreneur. Cannan remarked that Mill was probably writing with Say's criticism of the lack in English of a "name for the *entrepreneur d'industrie*" in mind. Cannan believed Say was "ignorant or forgetful of the word 'undertaker'" (E. Cannan, *A Review of Economic Theory*, London, 1929, p. 308). See also Hoselitz, "Early History of Entrepreneurial Theory," p. 200 n.

7. A. Smith, *The Wealth of Nations*, Cannan ed. (New York: Modern Library, 1937), p. 48. Hoselitz ("Early History of Entrepreneurial Theory," p. 204) cites Smith's use of the phrase "undertaker of a great manufacture" in *Wealth of Nations*, p. 438.

8. A. Smith, *Wealth of Nations*, p. 114.

9. Ibid., p. 115. On p. 339 Smith contrasts "prodigals and projectors" with "sober people."

10. Hoselitz, "Early History of Entrepreneurial Theory," pp. 194 ff.

11. Redlich has remarked that with Cantillon "the word entrepreneur first assumed the role of a technical term" ("Origin of the Concepts," p. 2).

12. See Hoselitz, "Early History of Entrepreneurial Theory," pp. 198 ff., 207, 210. See also C. A. Tuttle, "The Entrepreneur Function in Economic Literature," *Journal of Political Economy* 35, no. 4 (August 1927): 503–4.

13. F. B. Hawley, *Enterprise and the Productive Process* (New York: Putnam, 1907), pp. 153 ff., 340 f.

14. Tuttle, "Entrepreneur Function," thus appears incorrect in asserting the contrary.

15. Ibid.

16. F. H. Knight, *Risk, Uncertainty and Profit* (New York: Houghton Mifflin, 1921), p. 24; see also M. Blaug, *Economic Theory in Retrospect,* 1st ed. (Homewood, Ill.: Irwin, 1962) p. 86 n.

17. In a recent paper Nathan Rosenberg expressed his surprise at discovering that *Wealth of Nations*—"a book that shook the world by recommending a maximum degree of freedom for business enterprise"—assigns no major role to the entrepreneur (N. Rosenberg, "Adam Smith on Profits: Paradox Lost and Regained," *Journal of Political Economy* [November/December 1974], p. 1177).

18. Smith, *Wealth of Nations,* pp. 52, 97.

19. Ibid., p. 48.

20. Ibid.

21. J. Marchal, "The Construction of a New Theory of Profit," *American Economic Review* 41, no. 4 (September 1951): 549. For a sharply different appraisal of Smith, exculpating him from the "post-Smith classical treatment of interest as identical with profits," see J. W. Conard, *An Introduction to the Theory of Interest* (Berkeley: University of California Press, 1959), p. 12.

22. Redlich, "Origin of the Concepts," p. 7.

23. J. B. Say, *Traité d'économie politique,* 6th ed. (Paris: Guillaumin, impression of 1876), p. 84 n (cited by Cannan, *Review of Economic Theory,* p. 308).

24. M. Blaug, *Ricardian Economics: A Historical Study* (New Haven: Yale University Press, 1958), pp. 153 ff.

25. Smith, *Wealth of Nations,* p. 51.

26. E. Cannan, *A History of the Theories of Production and Distribution in English Political Economy from 1776 to 1848,* 3d ed. (London, 1917), pp. 201 ff.

27. R. Cantillon, *Essai sur la nature du commerce en general,* ed. with an English translation, etc., by H. Higgs (London: Royal Economic Society, 1931), p. 53.

28. Ibid., p. 55.

29. Note that Cannan, in commenting on Cantillon's discussion of the independent worker, writes that "ordinary people in Cantillon's times and ours would not say he made a profit unless he had to pay out money" for the materials needed for production (E. Cannan, *A Review of Economic Theory* [London, 1929], p. 303).

30. Knight, *Risk, Uncertainty and Profit,* p. 25.

31. J. A. Schumpeter, "Economic Theory and Entrepreneurial History," in *Explorations in Enterprise,* ed. H. G. Aitken (Cambridge: Harvard University Press, 1965), p. 46.

32. Hoselitz, "Early History of Entrepreneurial Theory," p. 212.

33. "The concept of profit in the eighteenth century was complicated by the fact that capitalist and manager-entrepreneur were, so often, the one person" (R. M. Hartwell, "Business Management in England during the Period of Early Industrialization: Inducements and Obstacles," in *The Industrial Revolution,* ed. R. M. Hartwell [New York: Barnes and Noble, 1970]). See also N. Rosenberg, "Adam Smith on Profits," p. 1177.

34. M. Blaug, *Ricardian Economics*, pp. 153 ff.

35. Schumpeter, "Economic Theory and Entrepreneurial History," p. 48. See also Tuttle, "Entrepreneur Function," pp. 507–8; Knight, *Risk, Uncertainty and Profit*, p. 23.

36. Sidney Sherwood, "The Function of the Undertaker," *Yale Review* 6 (November 1897): 244; Hawley, *Enterprise and the Productive Process*, p. 10.

37. L. Haney, *History of Economic Thought*, 4th ed. (New York: Macmillan, 1949), p. 563.

38. Ibid., p. 564. For further comments on the relation between the classical economists' notions concerning capital and the business environment of their day, see J. R. Hicks, "Capital Controversies: Ancient and Modern," *American Economic Review* 64 (May 1974): 310. It is of further interest to note, in passing, that the view that explains classical neglect of the entrepreneur by reference to the infrequency of joint-stock firms, contrasts, as well, with the thrust of the Galbraithian view that the mature corporate form of business organization is responsible for the eclipse of the entrepreneur in contemporary capitalism (J. K. Galbraith, *The New Industrial State* [New York: Houghton Mifflin, 1967], chap. 8).

39. Cannan, *Review of Economic Theory*, p. 309.

40. Ibid., p. 310.

41. Ibid., p. 356.

42. Ibid., p. 309.

43. R. L. Meek, "The Physiocratic Concept of Profit," *Economica*, vol. 26 (February 1959); reprinted in *The Economics of Physiocracy* (Cambridge: Harvard University Press, 1963), p. 297. Meek notes that Smith "was careful to distinguish profit from wages of management."

44. Hawley, *Enterprise and the Productive Process*, pp. 153 ff.; see also pp. 340 ff.

45. Schumpeter, "Economic Theory and Entrepreneurial History," p. 47.

46. R. E. Kuenne, *Eugen von Böhm-Bawerk*, Columbia Essays on Great Economists, no. 2 (London and New York: Columbia University Press, 1971), p. 2.

47. R. V. Eagly, *The Structure of Classical Economic Theory* (New York: Oxford University Press, 1974), chap. 8.

48. J. A. Schumpeter, *History of Economic Analysis* (New York: Oxford University Press, 1954), p. 556.

49. Schumpeter, "Economic Theory and Entrepreneurial History," p. 47.

50. Blaug, *Ricardian Economics*, p. 154.

51. Cannan, *History of the Theories of Production and Distribution*, p. 398.

52. See also ibid., pp. 313 ff., where Cannan refers to entrepreneur as displacing the capitalist as the most active element in economic theory.

53. Ibid., p. 119.

54. Ibid., p. 398.

55. Knight, *Risk, Uncertainty and Profit*, pp. 23 ff.

56. Smith, *Wealth of Nations*, p. 114.

During the past two hundred years of history of economic thought, four separate stages can be distinguished in respect to the significance economists attach to the entrepreneurial role in the market economy.

As is well known, the classical economists (with some notable exceptions such as J. B. Say, who continued the French tradition begun by Cantillon) did not recognize an entrepreneurial function distinct from that of the capitalist. For the classical economists "profit" meant the income share received by the capitalist, with no attempt made to distinguish pure interest separately from (what we would today call) pure entrepreneurial profit.[1] In the classical schema, they sought to understand the important characteristics of the capitalist economy within a framework that ignored the entrepreneurial role.

In the decades following the marginalist revolution, a vigorous literature emerged in which the entrepreneurial role was thoroughly discussed. During the 1880s and subsequently, entrepreneurship and entrepreneurial profit were the subject of doctoral dissertations and journal articles,[2] including contributions by some leading neoclassical theorists. An American economist prominent at the turn of the century, F. B. Hawley, made this topic his lifework. And of course the second decade of the present century saw the fully elaborated theories of entrepreneurship developed by Schumpeter and by Knight. The first half-century of neoclassical ascendancy was a period in which the entrepreneurial role was identified and its subtleties and elusiveness thoroughly, if perhaps not quite definitively, explored.

But the half-century that began about 1920, a half-century during which modern microeconomic theory attained a significantly higher standard of sophistication, saw economists paying scarcely any attention at all to analyzing the ways entrepreneurial activity affects the course of events in markets. To cite an often-quoted observation of Professor Baumol, the entrepreneur "virtually disappeared from the theoretical literature."[3]

From *Discovery and the Capitalist Process* (Chicago and London: University of Chicago Press, 1985), 1–14. © 1985 by the University of Chicago. Reprinted by permission.

The fourth stage to be identified has thus far endured for only a very few years—perhaps the session devoted to the entrepreneur in the December 1967 meetings of the American Economic Association can be taken as its beginning. During these past few years economists have rediscovered the entrepreneur, and the topic has been explored in conferences and books (including one book devoted to a history of economic thought on entrepreneurship).[4] Whether this flurry of activity has produced significant advances in economic understanding may not be universally agreed on, but certainly it must be recognized that the earlier modern tradition of neglect for the entrepreneurial role has, during this current stage, been decisively broken.

This opening chapter has two principal objectives. The first is to suggest an explanation for the rather surprising neglect of the entrepreneurial role during the half-century following 1920 and for the no less mysterious reappearance, in recent years, of the entrepreneur among the dramatis personae recognized by economic theory. The second, related objective will be to proceed, from the suggestions advanced in fulfilling the first objective, to consider some of the difficulties that surround contemporary attempts to reintegrate the entrepreneurial role into economic understanding. In a number of ways the ideas developed in this chapter will serve as a foundation for much that I will elaborate upon later.

THE APPEARANCE AND THE DISAPPEARANCE
OF THE ENTREPRENEURIAL ROLE

That the marginalist revolution brought in its train an awareness of the need for separate attention to the entrepreneur is not surprising. It was in the course of this revolution that economists came to view factor incomes no longer as shares of national output but as the revenues received in return for the sale, at market prices, of productive services (valued by the purchasing factor employers for their incremental contribution to output). As this way of seeing factor incomes was more thoroughly developed, it was only natural that the pure profits won by the energetic, daring, innovative entrepreneur were perceived to constitute an altogether different economic category. Pure profits, it came to be seen, are what remain after *all* factors of production have received their appropriate marginal-productivity rewards, rewards sufficient to elicit all the resource effort needed to deliver the relevant output. It was recognition of this circumstance that spurred economists at that time to search for what it was that entrepreneurs did that was not covered by the neoclassical marginalist view of production. It was here that economists debated the significance of change, of innovation, or of uncertainty.

But this very recognition by economists that entrepreneurial activity resists the marginalist's mode of analysis eventually caused the banishment of such activity from the theorist's purview. Such banishment had already been foreshadowed in Walras's treatment, where the entrepreneur was permitted neither to win any profits nor to suffer any losses. It is plausible to argue that as economic theory became more sophisticated, as marginal analysis and market equilibrium theory came to be more carefully and more fully articulated, the entrepreneur receded more and more from theoretical view. This seems to have been the result of two mutually reinforcing (if perhaps not wholly consistent) attitudes.

First, it seems probable that theorists came to see it as something like an analytical *virtue* to abstract from entrepreneurship. After all, it is the theorist's task to pierce the superficial veil of ever changing daily events in order to grasp the enduring underlying regularities upon which these ephemeral events are superimposed. An understanding of markets, the neoclassical economists came to believe, requires us to focus on the sets of optimizing decisions that can all be simultaneously accommodated. To the extent that at a given time entrepreneurial daring and innovation generate activities that cannot be so accommodated, they constitute phenomena that *obstruct* theoretical vision of that underlying equilibrium set of potential activities that is alone fully consistent with the basic data, consumer tastes, resource constraints, and available technology. From this perspective the theorist sees it as his responsibility *not* to permit his attention to be diverted (by concern with the theory-defying vagaries of adventurous, original entrepreneurs) from the deeper systematic regularities that lie waiting to be discerned.

Second, as the equilibrium perspective of neoclassical microeconomics became more and more dominant during this period, and particularly as Walrasian modes of thinking came to pervade that microeconomics since the 1930s, it became fashionable to treat the real world as if it were indeed close to equilibrium at all times. In other words, the neoclassical theorist fell, in effect, into the habit of considering markets to be fully coordinated, with entrepreneurs making neither profits nor losses (just as in the Walrasian system). From this point of view any apparent discrepancies between the real world and equilibrium conditions are more likely to be held to reflect complete adjustment to some overlooked real circumstances (overlooked, that is, by the applied theorist in his identification of the relevant conditions for equilibrium) than to be seen as evidence of disequilibrium. Once again the result was to withdraw analytical attention from phenomena that could not be fitted into the equilibrium mold.

THE REDISCOVERY OF THE ENTREPRENEUR

The two attitudes just identified as plausibly responsible for the failure of modern microeconomics since the 1920s to grapple with the entrepreneurial role seem to correspond to two separate reasons that possibly have contributed to the current rediscovery of that role by economists.

With the economics of general equilibrium fully developed by the 1970s, it was perhaps understandable that theorists began to turn their attention to facts that did not fit easily into the equilibrium mold. While it might have appeared an analytical virtue in earlier times to avoid concentrating on such entrepreneurially generated elements, it now became something of a theoretical challenge to do so. With general equilibrium theory considered settled territory, the analytical frontiers were seen, at least by some economists, to be situated in terrain characterized by entrepreneurial discovery, innovation, and bold speculation under uncertainty. The very irrelevance, for such activities, of traditional microeconomic tools only enhanced the challenge these frontiers offered to economic theory.

And again, other economists, growing impatient with the patently implausible assumption that the world is at all times in the neighborhood of equilibrium, began to focus their analytical curiosity on phenomena (such as entrepreneurial activity) that seem most blatantly to give the lie to that assumption. For such economists the technical sophistication that had characterized modern microeconomic theory came to be seen less as advanced virtuosity than as arid, formal exercises with less and less relevance for the real world. The study of entrepreneurship seemed called for not so much to extend the corpus of economic theory beyond its existing equilibrium scope as to come to grips with what began to appear as the glaring irrelevance of the corpus of received theory for the phenomena of the market around us.

We shall discover that these various insights hold some significance for the specific ways contemporary economists have variously sought to reintegrate the role of the entrepreneur into economic understanding. Let us pause to reflect on the many activities we associate with entrepreneurial behavior and upon what distinctive characteristics we may perhaps perceive as common to all of them.

ENTREPRENEURIAL ACTIVITIES AND THE ESSENCE OF ENTREPRENEURSHIP

The kinds of activities we associate with entrepreneurial vision and energy are varied and numerous. They include, certainly, forming new business ventures; introducing new products; initiating new techniques of production; altering prices (offers or bids) to meet or to forestall competitors; striking out in new territory to identify new markets for one's product; identifying new sources of finance; and streamlining internal patterns of organization.

What is remarkable is that economists have, over the past two and a half centuries, reached such a variety of conflicting conclusions concerning the essential character of such entrepreneurial activities.[5] For some writers entrepreneurial activities are simply a special kind of labor; for others what is distinctive about them is their innovative character, their ability to disrupt the status quo; for yet others it is their *speculative* aspect (i.e., their taking a position with respect to the *uncertain* future). Some economists saw the entrepreneur as *middleman,* as *arbitrageur;* others saw him as *leader;* others as *employer.* Some theorists found the essence of entrepreneurship in its *coordinating,* "gap-filling" role; others found it in the entrepreneur's deployment of superior *information.*

I have, over a number of years, found it useful to recognize the central role played by *alertness* of the entrepreneur. What is entrepreneurial about the activities listed at the beginning of this section is, in this view, that each reflects the decision maker's belief that he has discovered possibilities that both he and his actual or potential competitors had hitherto not seen. Such discoveries may reflect alertness to changed conditions or to overlooked possibilities. Scope for such alertness is afforded not only by unexploited opportunities offered by existing conditions but also, and especially so, by those to be created by future conditions. (In regard to opportunities to be created by future conditions, of course, "alertness" refers not to the ability to see what exists, but to the necessarily speculative ability to "see" into the future. In particular, such metaphorical "alertness" may consist in the vision to *create* something in the future.[6] The crucial element in behavior expressing entrepreneurial alertness is that it expresses the decision maker's ability spontaneously to transcend an existing framework of perceived opportunities.

We turn now to observe how this "alertness" perspective on entrepreneurial behavior represents a "middle way" between two alternative ("extreme") modes of treating such behavior that have been discussed in the contemporary literature.

TWO EXTREME VIEWS

The two "extreme" views that have been discussed point in diametrically opposite directions. The one view sees the entrepreneur as responding systematically and frictionlessly to the conditions of the market, with pure entrepreneurial profit the smoothly corresponding reward that these market conditions require and make possible. From this perspective entrepreneurship is "called forth" systematically, if not quite predictably, by these market conditions. I will call this (for reasons to be made apparent shortly) the "neoclassical" view of the entrepreneur. The second view sees entrepreneurship not as *responding to* external market conditions, but as independently and spontaneously *injecting* new elements *into* those conditions, in a manner totally unpredictable from and wholly undetermined by existing circumstances. The "neoclassical" view is exemplified by the work of T. W. Schultz; the opposite extreme view is associated with the work of G. L. S. Shackle.

Schultz's view sees the entrepreneur[7] as performing a needed service in the market—the service of reallocating resources under conditions of disequilibrium. This service is valuable in definite ways, and there is therefore a demand curve for it. The ability to provide this service ("the ability to deal with disequilibria") is scarce, and there is a supply curve with respect to it. This service therefore tends to command a market price that is, in principle, implied by the relevant supply and demand conditions. Notice that the quantity and varieties of entrepreneurial services performed, and also the size of pure profit, are "determined" by these given supply and demand conditions. The level of pure entrepreneurial profit seems to be adjusted through market competition, in this view, so as to bring the supply of and the demand for entrepreneurial ability into mutual coordination. At any given time, in other words, the "right" quantity of entrepreneurial services is forthcoming, that is, the "right" quantity of the service of dealing with disequilibria is at all times being appropriately deployed. Clearly the direction this Schultzian view of entrepreneurship is pointing is one in which full coordination, in the relevant sense, is *always* maintained by the market. The market is always generating the correct volume of services needed to correct incorrect decisions. This direction, one fears, is likely to lead to a neoclassical world whose full and continuous equilibrium necessarily leaves the entrepreneur no scope whatever for spontaneous innovative activity. This neoclassical approach has, it seems, merely squeezed the real-world entrepreneur back into the neoclassical full-equilibrium box.

The alternative extreme approach, which I have associated with the work of G. L. S. Shackle, reflects a general impatience with neoclassical microeconomic theory and especially with the notion of individual choice that that theory employs. So far from being prepared to let the activities of the entrepreneur be subsumed under (indeed swallowed up by) the equilibrium calculus of supply and demand, Shackle's approach, in effect, sees the validity of the latter calculus as seriously compromised by the *universality* of what others might call entrepreneurial choice. Where the notion of choice employed in equilibrium theory sees decisions as determinate, mechanically generated by calculative reason operating upon the given objective conditions and the given preferences that make up the environment, Shackle emphasizes that choice is an "originative and imaginative art,"[8] in no sense an automatic response to given circumstances. The critique of received microeconomic theory implied in this perspective on choice recognizes that the systematic results of microeconomic theory depend upon our ability to abstract from the troublesome entrepreneurial, "originative" elements in the real world. But whereas this may have led earlier theorists to ignore these troublesome elements, and thus to neglect the role of the entrepreneur almost entirely it has led Shackle to quite different conclusions. For Shackle it is precisely these troublesome "entrepreneurial" features of human decision making that we *cannot,* in good conscience, filter out of our explanations. Thus this refusal to compress entrepreneurship within the equilibrium constraints of supply and demand theory has led not to the identification of a range of phenomena for which received microeconomic theory holds little relevance, but to serious questioning of the usefulness of that theory as a whole. Human choice is originative, "entrepreneurially" injecting new knowledge, new expectations, new imaginings, new dreams, into the existing situation. We must, Shackle therefore argues, reject the ambitious claims made by neoclassical economics to provide explanations of market phenomena that depend wholly on equilibrium configurations of maximizing decisions.

Clearly, these views of Schultz and of Shackle are radically different approaches to entrepreneurship. The neoclassical approach (represented by Schultz) in effect brings us back to a world of full equilibrium, a world in which the volume and the value of entrepreneurial activity are responses to and are determined by the given underlying cost and utility functions. The alternative approach (which I have associated with Shackle) in effect deploys the originative aspects of entrepreneurship to rebel vigorously against the relevance of any theoretical construction, such as equilibrium theory, that sees market phenomena as determinate, inexorable market responses to the preferences and constraints characterizing the given situation. The neoclassical view implies exclusion of all true novelty and surprise from our explanations; the alternative view points to the exclusion of explanations other than those that run in terms of the novelty, spontaneity, and intrinsic unpredictability of human choices. The view expressed in this book is at sharp variance with *both* of these extreme views concerning entrepreneurship.

The sections that follow seek to show how the "alertness" view of entrepreneurship mentioned earlier in this chapter enables us to adopt a middle course, avoiding the extreme features of each of the approaches I have outlined above.[9]

ENTREPRENEURIAL ALERTNESS AND THE BEST OF BOTH WORLDS

The approaches outlined in the preceding section offered us clear-cut and, indeed, seemingly inescapable options. Either we abstract from "originative" entrepreneurial activities or we discard our claims to render the world intelligible by reference to equilibrium configurations of maximizing decisions. Either we ignore the entrepreneur or we jettison the received theory of price. (It will be observed that a sense of these stark options underlay the rationalization provided earlier for the failure of microeconomists after 1920 to discuss the entrepreneur and his role.) My position in this book is that this statement of the choice facing the economic theorist is quite misleading. I claim, indeed, that the "alertness" view of entrepreneurship enables us to have the best of both worlds: we *can* incorporate entrepreneurship into the analysis without surrendering the heart of microeconomic theory. But even this statement of my position does not quite do it justice. I claim, more accurately, that *only* by incorporating entrepreneurship into microeconomic theory can the core of that theory be salvaged.

My "alertness" view of the entrepreneurial role rejects the thesis that if we attribute genuine novelty to the entrepreneur, we must necessarily treat entrepreneurially generated market events as not related to earlier market events in any systematic way. The genuine novelty I attribute to the entrepreneur consists in his spontaneous *discovery* of the opportunities marked out by earlier market conditions (or by future market conditions as they would be in the absence of his own actions). It is the opportunity for pure profit that those market conditions made possible that switches on the alertness of potential entrepreneurs, generating entrepreneurial discovery.

My view of the role of entrepreneurial discovery rejects, further, the thesis that recognition of entrepreneurial activities obscures the relevance of equilibrium configurations or that such relevance can be preserved only by compressing entrepreneurial activities, too, into the equilibrium mold. I hold, on the contrary, that entrepreneurial discoveries are the steps through which any possible tendency toward market equilibrium must proceed. So, far from being confusing "noise" masking the more enduring equilibrium relationships (reflecting underlying data), entrepreneurial activities make up, in my view, the process of mutual discovery by which alone we can imagine equilibrium ever to be approached.[10]

Another way of stating the position that underlies the remaining chapters of this book is as follows. I must reject the view that requires us to hold *either* that agents already possess relevant items of knowledge (with this option including, as a special case, possession by agents not of the relevant items of knowledge themselves, but rather, and altogether equivalently, their possession of knowledge of how to search for and obtain those relevant items of knowledge) *or* not only that agents are grossly ignorant at any given time, but also that they must, except as a matter of sheerest luck, necessarily continue to remain ignorant of the relevant items of knowledge. I maintain, rather, that human alertness at all times furnishes agents with the propensity to discover information that will be useful to them. Without resorting to any assumption of systematic, deliberate search, and without our relying on sheer luck, I postulate a continuous discovery process—an entrepreneurial discovery process—that, in the absence of external changes in underlying conditions, fuels a tendency toward equilibrium.

My position certainly does not admit a theory of price that is based upon the offensive assumption that market participants, at all times, have within their grasp full knowledge concerning relevant market data (including the decisions of other participants). Such an assumption is, in effect, embedded in the neoclassical position that sees entrepreneurship as a perceived ability to correct the allocation of misapplied resources. For processes of corrective reallocation so conceived, no genuine discovery is required at all. Such processes involve merely the systematic and inevitable following through of all the implications of knowledge already possessed at the very first moment. For me, to conceive of market processes in this way is indeed to attempt to understand markets with *no* role assigned to the creative entrepreneur.

But on the other hand, I also refuse to fall into the seductive trap offered by the opposite extreme. That extreme is to assume that because the knowledge possessed by market participants at any given moment is certainly likely to be supremely inadequate for the achievement of any kind of social optimum, we must see that ignorance as—except as a matter of sheer luck—an indelible feature of the situation. To adopt this extreme is to give up any notion of systematic market processes for which equilibrative tendencies might be relevant.

My view, therefore, sees initial market ignorance indeed as an inescapable feature of the human condition in a world of change, but also as subject to continual erosion as a result not of sheer luck, but of profit-inspired spurts of entrepreneurial discovery. Precisely because market decisions at a given time are based in large part on mutual ignorance (as well as on ignorance of physically available opportunities), the configuration of market prices is likely to offer pure profit opportunities for those able to discover where existing decisions were in fact mistaken. Here lies the source for any equilibrating tendencies that markets display.

THE ECONOMICS OF ENTREPRENEURSHIP
AND THE SCOPE OF ECONOMICS

Much of what I have argued in this chapter, and will argue in subsequent chapters, can be stated in the form of a comment on the scope of economic science. At least since Robbins's *Nature and Significance of Economic Science* (1932), the scope of economics has been perceived, in mainstream economics, to coincide with that aspect of human affairs that can be described in terms of optimizing decision making. From this perspective, economic theory tended to be confined to the study of phenomena that are consistent with the assumption that all market participants simultaneously achieve relevantly constrained optimal positions. Consistent with this restriction of the scope of the discipline, attempts to account for dynamic processes have tended to take the form of what Professor Littlechild has aptly dubbed "clockwork" models, with the entire course of market events inexorably governed by the patterns of data fed into the model at the moment of its initiation.

The argument in this chapter, and in the book generally, calls in effect for widening the scope of economic analysis. I argue that, if the major teachings of received microeconomic theory are to be sustained, we must quite explicitly transcend the boundaries of merely optimizing decision-making. To understand the systematic forces at work in markets, we must introduce into our analysis the element of undeliberate but motivated *discovery*. At the level of individual market participants in general, I have elsewhere argued that this calls for extending the scope of analysis to embrace what Ludwig von Mises called *human action*. At the level of the analysis of market roles, this calls for incorporating analysis of the effect of the *entrepreneurial role,* not as a disturbing feature muddying the clear-cut outcomes mapped by economic theory, but as the essential driving force rendering that theory intelligible. The chapters that follow represent attempts to understand the systematic character of the capitalist process in terms of entrepreneurial discovery.

NOTES

1. See my "Classical Economics and the Entrepreneurial Role," in Israel M. Kirzner, *Perception, Opportunity, and Profit* (Chicago: University of Chicago Press, 1979).

2. For a survey and bibliography on theories of entrepreneurship during this period see F. H. Knight, *Risk, Uncertainty and Profit* (Boston: Houghton Mifflin, 1921), chap. 2.

3. W. J. Baumol, "Entrepreneurship in Economic Theory," *American Economic Review* 58 (May 1968): 64.

4. Robert F. Hébert and Albert N. Link, *The Entrepreneur: Mainstream Views and Radical Critiques* (New York: Praeger, 1982).

5. See Hébert and Link, *Entrepreneur.*

6. My earlier discussion on entrepreneurial alertness is contained in Israel M. Kirzner, *Competition and Entrepreneurship* (Chicago: University of Chicago Press, 1973) and

Kirzner, *Perception, Opportunity, and Profit*. See also Israel M. Kirzner, ed., *Method, Process and Austrian Economics: Essays in Honor of Ludwig von Mises* (Lexington, Mass.: D. C. Heath, 1982), chap. 12.

7. T. W. Schultz, "The Value of the Ability to Deal with Disequilibria," *Journal of Economic Literature* 13, 3 (September 1975): 827–46.

8. G. L. S. Shackle, *Epistemics and Economics: A Critique of Economic Doctrines* (Cambridge: Cambridge University Press, 1972), p. 364.

9. These sections owe much to Roger W. Garrison, "Austrian Economics as the Middle Ground," in *Method, Process, and Austrian Economics,* ed. Israel M. Kirzner (Lexington, Mass.: Lexington Books, 1982). Garrison's work was highly commended in G. L. S. Shackle, "Decisions, Process and the Market," *Journal of Economic Studies* 10, 3 (1983): 61.

10. See F. A. Hayek, "Economics and Knowledge," *Economica* 4 (February 1937): 33–54, reprinted in Hayek, *Individualism and Economic Order* (London: Routledge and Kegan Paul, 1949), for an early discussion of processes of equilibration treated as being processes of learning.

It is by now fairly well recognized that the mainstream of modern equilibrium microeconomics has, particularly since its decisive absorption of Walrasian influence, assumed a form in which scope for the entrepreneurial role is conspicuous by its absence.[1] One broad modern tradition in which the entrepreneur was never squeezed out was that which drew its source from Carl Menger and his followers. Writers with such sharply varied approaches to economics as Schumpeter and Mises shared, at least, a high disdain for the dominant perfectly-competitive-equilibrium view of price theory, and a lively sense of the crucial significance of entrepreneurship for an understanding of the capitalist-market process. Yet the history of economic thought does not, in its treatment of the place of entrepreneurship in economic theory, assign much importance to the founders of the Austrian School.

In the considerable economic literature, from the 1880's on, in which entrepreneurship and entrepreneurial profit were discussed, there were few contributions from the founding Austrians.[2] It is of some interest, therefore, to examine the writings of Carl Menger himself to determine rather carefully the extent to which his system, explicitly or implicitly, found room for the entrepreneurial role (or to which his system might, at the hands of his followers, be expected to lead to the clear identification and explication of this role).

This interest is perhaps heightened by the existence of some intriguing discussions concerning the extent to which Menger's work did, in fact, influence later writers on the problems of entrepreneurship. Knight, in his highly unsympathetic "Introduction" to the first English translation of Menger's *Grundsätze*, remarked that on the questions

From *Atlantic Economic Journal* 6, no. 4 (September 1978). Reprinted with kind permission from Springer Science+Business Media.

1. For an example see Baumol, p. 72.

2. Important exceptions were two monographs on profits by Mataja, *Der Unternehmergewinn,* and Gross, *Lehre vom Unternehmergewinn.* Hayek, Vol. 1 of *The Collected Works of Carl Menger,* p. xxiii, describes both Mataja and Gross as "immediate pupils" of Menger.

of entrepreneurship and profit, "Later economists got little help from Menger or his contemporaries, or even his successors in the Austrian School" (Knight, 1950, p. 30).[3] On the other hand, Streissler recently expressed the view that, while Menger's immediate followers ignored his emphasis on problems of information, Schumpeter built his own theory of entrepreneurial innovation largely on Menger's foundations (Streissler, 1972, p. 432f).

Now Streissler's view that Schumpeter built on Mengerian foundations is difficult to document. In his 1911 book, where his distinctive ideas on entrepreneurship were most definitively stated early in his career, Schumpeter hardly referred to any Austrian literature. Beyond a disparaging reference to Mataja (Schumpeter, 1934, p. 76), Schumpeter cited only Böhm-Bawerk's "friction" theory of entrepreneurial profit (p. 32); Menger's writings are not mentioned at all in regard to the entrepreneurial function. Even more revealing is Schumpeter's indirect, but very clear, dismissal—in his *History of Economic Analysis,* written so many years later—of Menger's work on entrepreneurship. Again, referring to Böhm-Bawerk's theory of entrepreneurial profit, Schumpeter remarked that "excepting Böhm-Bawerk, the Austrians had very little to say about the matter" (Schumpeter, 1954, p. 893). Nonetheless, Streissler's conjecture that Menger's ideas on information *may have* provided a broad source for Schumpeter's later ideas— even if it were to prove the case that in fact they did not so serve— remains a fascinating possibility.

We turn, then, to examine Menger's view of the market process in order both to explore Streissler's conjecture and also to confront this paradox: On the one hand, we have a flourishing modern Austrian tradition (claiming its paternity from Menger even more emphatically than from Böhm-Bawerk),[4] emphasizing entrepreneurial processes, while on the

3. Knight presumably meant by this, not that Menger altogether ignored these questions, or that he exerted no influence on later writers, but that he and his followers pursued an approach that Knight in his own work on the matter (1921), found unhelpful. This interpretation would fit in with what seems to be Knight's grossly inadequate references, in (1921), to the work on entrepreneurship of Schumpeter, presumably one of the "successors" to Menger, whom Knight had in mind in the citation in the text.

4. Hayek's remark is well known: "The reputation of the [Austrian] School in the outside world and the development of its system at important points were due to the

other hand we have in Menger's own work what appears at first glance to be a decided lack of attention to the nature of the entrepreneur, of his role, and of entrepreneurial profit.

In what follows, we shall successively discuss: first, Menger's own treatment of the entrepreneurial role; second, Menger's recognition of the importance of knowledge, of error, and of uncertainty, in the economic process; third, Menger's position with respect to the role of equilibrium analysis of economic phenomena; and fourth, Menger's understanding of the nature of competition, and of product quality variation, in market processes. We will then, in the light of these discussions, return to appraise Menger's system from the perspective of the purposes of this study, as described above. It should be mentioned at the outset that this study owes a great deal to several important papers by Professor Streissler (1969, 1972, 1973). Although we shall have occasion to take serious issue with several of Streissler's conclusions, it is to Streissler, rather than to the earlier and better known surveys of Menger's contributions,[5] that we owe an awareness of Menger's unique understanding of the crucial importance of knowledge, error, and uncertainty. Ultimately, any examination of the place for entrepreneurship in Menger's system must, as ours will, take this awareness as its point of departure.

MENGER ON ENTREPRENEURSHIP

Menger's explicit treatment of entrepreneurship is brief, consisting of two or three passages in his *Principles of Economics,* the longest of which is a footnote.[6] For Menger, entrepreneurial activity is a special kind of labor service. Such activity is, as a rule, valuable to economizing men. However, since these kinds of services cannot be bought and sold,[7] they do not have a market price

---

efforts of his brilliant followers, Eugen von Böhm-Bawerk and Friedrich von Wieser. But it is not unduly to detract from the merits of these writers to say that its fundamental ideas belong fully and wholly to Carl Menger" (Hayek, 1934, p. v.). See also Lachmann, pp. 145ff.

5. Hayek, 1934, Stigler, and Knight, 1950.

6. These passages appear in the English translation on pages 160, 172. The passage appearing in the English *text* on page 160 was a footnote in the original German edition.

7. Nonetheless, Menger at one point talks of the "entrepreneur himself" requiring "helpers" to assist him in his entrepreneurial activities, if the firm is large (p. 160).

(Menger, 1950, p. 172). A necessary prerequisite for the provision of such services, moreover, is possession of the appropriate amount of capital. Menger listed the specific functions constituting entrepreneurial activity as involving (a) *information* about the economic situation; (b) economic *calculation*—all the various computations that must be made if a production process is to be efficient . . . ; (c) the *act of will* by which goods of higher order . . . are assigned to a particular production process; and finally, (d) *supervision* of the execution of the production plan so that it may be carried through as economically as possible."[8] Menger is explicit in rejecting Mangoldt's view that risk bearing is the essential function of entrepreneurship (p. 161).

Entrepreneurship is a good of "higher order," that is, one of the complementary higher order goods needed for production. The "prospective value of the product determines the total [of the complementary goods of higher order] only if the value of entrepreneurial activity is included in the total" (*ibid.*).

It seems not unfair to understand Menger's entrepreneurial activities as being quite similar, say, to those of Marshall's entrepreneur-manager (Marshall, Book VI, Chapters VII, VIII). Despite the special (and quite unusual) attention paid by Menger to the "information," and to the "act of will" involved in the entrepreneurial function, we find no attempt (such as we find later in Schumpeter or in Knight) to distinguish the entrepreneurial role from that of the hired manager. And Menger had no qualms about treating entrepreneurial profit as a species of factor return, as the value of a useful service. In a long footnote discoursing on the "morality" of property incomes (in which Menger simply pointed out that given the social conditions of the moment, the efficient market simply assigns each factor its true economic value—whether or not we approve of it morally, Menger finds no need to give pure entrepreneurial profit any separate treatment. Nor is there any hint of a relentless competitive market process continually and repeatedly operating to grind down entrepreneurial profit to zero; nor of the associated possibility that "in equilibrium" there might be a situation in which no scope at all would exist for the entrepreneur. Certainly,

8. Menger, 1950, p. 160. In the citation here given I have omitted the word "obtaining" which appears in the English translation under (a) before the word "information." Streissler (1972, p. 432, n. 24) has valuably pointed out that "the German text does not make it clear whether [entrepreneurs] have to inform others or themselves."

insofar as any *deliberate* discussion of entrepreneurship finds a place in Menger, it is understandable that Schumpeter and Knight saw little from which either of them could draw inspiration.

MENGER ON KNOWLEDGE, ERROR, AND UNCERTAINTY

Despite the limited explicit attention Menger paid to the entrepreneurial function, it is nonetheless possible that Menger's exposition of the operation of the market system may embody implicit understanding of the pivotal role played by the pure entrepreneur in the capitalist process. Such implicit understanding must, if it is indeed found to exist, relate especially to the importance of changing *knowledge* as the propelling force behind the process; to the concomitant continual discovery in the market of earlier *errors* by decision makers; and to perception of the closely related phenomenon of *uncertainty* that necessarily conditions and suffuses all market decisions. We shall, that is, be searching for possible signs of recognition by Menger of the systematic tendencies generated in the markets by the dynamics of interacting decisions that are made under a wide range of degrees of mutual ignorance.

Menger's system provides, indeed, a fascinating opportunity for such a search. As emphasized by Streissler, Menger's *Grundsätze* provides numerous instances of his "constant stress on problems of information" with its variability "over time and, at any given moment, over individuals" (Streissler, 1972, p. 431f). Moreover, Menger's emphasis on the time dimension led him to pay a good deal of attention to the *uncertainty* which this dimension entails (Streissler, 1972, p. 433; 1969, p. 249 and p. 250, n. 44; 1973, *passim*). This Mengerian emphasis on the role of knowledge is a remarkable feature of his work, one to which (as mentioned above) commentators before Streissler unaccountably failed to draw attention. And even Streissler, it may be argued, does not quite do complete justice to the extent to which Menger's whole system revolves around questions of knowledge.

MENGER ON KNOWLEDGE

Menger's *Grundsätze* is not merely a treatise containing scores of references to knowledge. Nor is the crucial role of knowledge in Menger's system quite captured, it may be argued, even in his "remarkable sentence, 'the quantities of consumption goods at human disposal are limited only

by the extent of human knowledge.'"⁹ Menger's awareness of the importance of knowledge is central to an impressive variety of different aspects of
his theory, including (perhaps, for the purposes of our own study, most significantly) the very foundation of his system, that of "economizing" activity.

Menger stated, of course, that it is the *perceived* usefulness of goods
that makes them goods in the first place, and upon which the notion of
economic value depends (pp. 52f, 115). Changes in perception, correct or
otherwise, change value (p. 148). To the extent to which planful provision
for the future occurs, it must depend on foresight and expectations
(pp. 68, 80, 89). As mentioned, economic progress depends for Menger,
in the last analysis, on the progress of human technical understanding
(pp. 71–4). The very first component of entrepreneurial activity, we have
seen in a previous section, involves "information about the economic situation" (p. 160). Opportunities for mutually beneficial exchange, Menger
made very clear, can be expected to be acted upon only if both parties are
able to *perceive* the existence and worthwhileness of these opportunities
(pp. 179f, 188f, 195). Of particular interest, in this last respect, is Menger's
footnote reference to *advertising* as a means whereby producers can make
their products known to potential customers (p. 242, n. 9). Menger has a
highly impressive analysis of the spontaneous market process by means
of which a money can emerge. This process is one of spontaneous discovery, and is worth quoting at some length (pp. 260–1):

> The exchange of less easily saleable commodities for commodities of
> greater marketability is in the economic interest of *every* economizing
> individual. But the actual performance of exchange operations of this
> kind presupposes a knowledge of their interest on the part of econo-
> mizing individuals . . . This knowledge will never be attained by all
> members of a people at the same time. On the contrary, only a small
> number of economizing individuals will at first recognize the advan-
> tage accruing to them from the acceptance of other, more saleable,
> commodities in exchange for their own whenever a direct exchange
> of their commodities for the goods they wish to consume is impos-
> sible or highly uncertain . . . Since there is no better way in which
> men can be enlightened about their economic interests than by ob-
> servation of the economic success of those who employ the correct

9. Streissler, 1972, p. 431. The citation from Menger is from (1950, p. 741).

means of achieving their ends, it is evident that nothing favored the
rise of money so much as the long-practiced, and economically profitable, acceptance of eminently saleable commodities in exchange
for all others by the most discerning and most capable economizing
individuals.

Of special interest for our purpose is the place that knowledge occu-
pies in relation to the activity of *economizing*. Economizing is the basic
activity upon which Menger's elaborate microeconomic theoretical structure is built. (We shall, in a later section, have further occasion to comment on the character of the Mengerian "economizing individual.")
Knowledge appears to enter Menger's elaboration of the requirements
and characteristics of economizing activity in at least two different ways
(although it must be confessed that Menger does not himself articulate
these differences).

First, in order for economizing activity to take place, it is necessary
that the individual *perceive* that his needs exceed his means (p. 95).

> Wherever . . . men recognize that the requirements for a good are
> greater than its available quantity they achieve the further insight that
> no part of the available quantity, . . . may lose its useful properties
> or be removed from human control without causing some concrete
> human needs, previously provided for, to remain unsatisfied . . . A
> further effect . . . is that men become aware . . . that any inappropri-
> ate employment of particular quantities of this good must necessarily
> result in part of the needs that would be provided for by appropriate
> employment of the available quantity remaining unsatisfied.

At this level, *knowledge* of scarcity is called upon to impress upon the
individual the very need to economize, to *realize* that he lives, not in a
land of Cockaigne but under circumstances in which avoidance of waste
is of some importance.

Second, in order to effectively engage in provident economizing activity, it is required that that individual know not merely that he lives in a
world of scarcity, but also the specifics of his anticipated requirements
and of the expected quantities of goods that will be at his disposal. It is
at this level of discussion that we encounter some of Menger's remarks
concerning uncertain expectations. It is in relation to this kind of specific knowledge that Menger discussed the deliberate efforts of men *to*

obtain knowledge. "To the degree to which men engage in planning activity directed to the satisfaction of their needs, they endeavor to attain clarity as to the quantities of goods available to them at any time."[10] And it is here that Menger (no doubt drawing on his own earlier experience as an economic journalist surveying the state of the markets for the *Wiener Zeitung*) discussed the various concrete methods by which reports on commodity stocks in grain, sugar, and cotton markets are assembled and used by traders (pp. 92–3). And, in perhaps his closest linking of knowledge to entrepreneurship, Menger explains how a widening market permits "the development of a special professional class . . . [that has an interest] in compiling data about the quantities of goods, . . . currently at the disposal of the various people and nations whose trade they mediate . . . They have, moreover, an interest in many other general kinds of information . . ." (p. 91).

Menger's emphasis on knowledge is certainly of great significance and acquires even greater significance in the context of his parallel emphasis upon *ignorance and error* (to which we shall give attention below). Nonetheless, it must be pointed out that it is not enough, in order to declare Menger a pioneer in entrepreneurial theory, to cite his ubiquitous references to knowledge. It seems more likely that this aspect of Menger's system stems from his central concern to establish the *subjectivist* perspective on economic phenomena as the starting point in economic theory. According to the subjectivist point of view, economic change arises not so much from the *circumstances* relevant at the moment of decision, but from man's *awareness* of these circumstances. So that Menger's carefully constructed methodological individualism required him at each turn to emphasize the decision-maker's knowledge and awareness of economic constraints, rather than the force exercised by those constraints in and of themselves. This does not, at least without further extension, imply that a systematic process of adjustment exists in the market, set in motion and fuelled by continual entrepreneurial discovery. We shall find ourselves compelled to recognize the validity of this restrained interpretation of Menger, by a consideration of his treatment of ignorance and error, to which we now turn.

10. Menger, 1950, p. 90. The entire section, pp. 80–94, is relevant to this level of discussion.

MENGER ON IGNORANCE AND ERROR

As almost a corollary of his emphasis on knowledge, in economizing activity, Menger called attention to error and uncertainty.[11] If man's valuation of goods depends on his knowledge of his need and of their availability, then it follows that "men can be in error about the value of goods just as they can be in error with respect to all other objects of human knowledge" (p. 120).

Moreover, at one point, Menger recognizes that the gains from new trade, between individuals or between nations, are closely related to ignorance. If, Menger explains, "the full gains from the new trade are sometimes not immediately forthcoming, the reason is that . . . knowledge of the trading opportunities and power to carry through exchange operations recognized to be economic, are ordinarily acquired by the participants only after a certain period of time" (p. 188). While the context of this sentence clearly shows that Menger did *not* see that the high initial gains from new trade are associated with the very imperfection of knowledge to which he refers, the passage does see the market process as one which gradually overcomes ignorance.

One recent writer has in fact treated Menger's recognition of the possibility of error as a major characteristic of his system, distinguishing him sharply from his fellow pioneers, Jevons and Walras, in the so-called "marginal revolution." Thus, William Jaffé writes, "Veblen's strictures upon what he considered the Austrian preconception of human nature fit Jevons' or Walras' theory much better than they do Menger's. In Menger, man is not depicted as a hedonistic 'lightning calculator of pleasures and pains . . .' Man, as Menger saw him, far from being a 'lightning calculator' is a bumbling, erring, ill-informed creature, plagued with uncertainty, forever hovering between alluring hopes and haunting fears, and congenitally incapable of making finely calibrated decisions in pursuit of satisfaction."[12]

Jaffé's interpretation of Menger's economizing individuals is suggestive. To the extent we can agree with Jaffé's interpretation, we can

11. In an important sense Menger's treatment of uncertainty was simply as an aspect of the consequences of error. See, for example, his section (pp. 67–71) entitled "Time and Error," which in fact deals with uncertainty.

12. Jaffé, p. 521. Jaffé's reference to the "lightning calculator . . ." is, of course, cited from Veblen.

attribute to Menger's economizing individuals scope for precisely the same kind of "entrepreneurship" that, for Mises, is contained in the notion of individual human action.[13] This is not the place to embark on a full scale analysis of the role of economizing man in Menger's writings. Nonetheless, we may remark that Jaffé's position seems to be closer to the truth than that apparently taken by Knight in his Introduction to Menger's *Principles*. In that essay, Knight understands (or rather misunderstands) Menger's use of the notion of the economizing individual as "naive economism." Menger's "economizing man" is the "economic-man who has been the butt of so much sarcasm" (Knight, 1950, p. 16). Moreover, Knight appears to argue that error plays no role in Menger's theory! "Menger notwithstanding," Knight writes quite astonishingly, "economic behavior is more than mechanical cause and effect. Its indubitable affection by error proves that . . ." (p. 21). Certainly Jaffé's quite different understanding of Menger is closer to the truth.[14]

It is tempting, then, to seize on Jaffé's interpretation of Menger as the basis for maintaining that Menger's perception of the market process was indeed an entrepreneurial one—one that understands the market process to be a systematic modification of error on the part of market participants and of steadily improving mutual knowledge. Unfortunately, it does not seem possible to sustain such a reading of Menger.

This becomes apparent in Menger's famous fifth chapter, "The Theory of Price"—the chapter which Hayek describes as the "crowning achievement"

13. "The term entrepreneur as used by catallactic theory means: acting man exclusively seen from the aspect of the uncertainty inherent in every action" (Mises, p. 254).

14. In fact, in the translator's note to Menger's Preface—in the very edition to which Knight was providing an Introduction—it is carefully explained that Menger's economizing man is not a reference "to 'the profit motive' or to 'the pursuit of self-interest,' but to the act of economizing" (Menger, 1950, p. 48, n. 4). (For the classic reply to those ridiculing the role of economic man in economics, see Robbins, pp. 94ff. Robbins (p. 16n) cites Menger as the earliest source for his own conception of economics as dealing with "human behavior as a relationship between ends and scarce means which have alternative uses"—i.e., with economizing.) As is evident from the earlier discussion of the role of economizing activity, there is ample scope, as Jaffé believes, for interpreting imperfect knowledge in Menger as a context within which economizing activity may be carried on. Menger's reference, at one point, to "economizing individuals aware of their advantage" (p. 213) must, therefore, be understood to refer to economizing individuals whom, for the sake of a particular problem in hand, we *choose to imagine* to happen to be so aware.

of the entire work and as revealing "the clear aim which directs [Menger's] exposition" from the very beginning.[15] In Menger's entire theory of price error is carefully excluded—completely confirming Knight's reading of Menger! At all the stages of the argument, Menger abstracts from error—in the discussion of bilateral monopoly, of one-sided competition, and of bilateral competition. The possibility of error, in the decisions that determine price, is not forgotten. Instead it is deliberately brushed aside. Moreover, the possibility is not simply assumed away as a matter of analytical convenience, it is assumed away as being an abnormality! In concluding the theory of monopoly price policy, Menger declares that "of course, error and imperfect knowledge may give rise to aberrations, but these are the pathological phenomena of social economy and prove as little against the laws of economics as do the symptoms of a sick body against the laws of physiology" (p. 216). Menger's discussion of competition, too, explicitly proceeds on an assumption "[b]arring error and ignorance on the part of the economizing individuals involved" (p. 224).

Clearly, Menger's willingness to incorporate error into his system was neither as totally absent as Knight believed nor as complete as claimed by Jaffé. Either we have here a curious inconsistency in Menger, or else there is some subtlety here that has as yet to be plumbed. Certainly a theory of price in which error is assumed away as a pathological abnormality cannot qualify as a process theory of the modern Hayekian variety, involving *discovery* in some essential way. We turn our attention now to Menger's position in regard to the role of equilibrium analysis of economic phenomena.

MENGER ON EQUILIBRIUM AND DISEQUILIBRIUM

The discussions in the preceding section (and in particular our remarks on the apparent inconsistency, in Menger's treatment of error in his price theory as compared with his emphasis on error elsewhere) have considerable bearing on the question of the extent to which Menger's economics can be described as "disequilibrium economics." If it were indeed possible to show that Menger's theory was primarily "disequilibrium theory," then indeed Menger's credentials as a forerunner of the entrepreneurial theory of the market process would be strengthened considerably.

---

15. Hayek, 1934, p. xvii. For a view diametrically opposed to that of Hayek on this point, see Jaffé, p. 519.

The view that Menger's economics is disequilibrium economics has been put forward recently by Streissler (1972, p. 438f; 1973, p. 167) and strongly endorsed by Jaffé (p. 520). (An *apparently* contradictory statement by Schumpeter: "We must see in the Jevons-Menger utility theory an embryonic theory of general equilibrium . . ." [Schumpeter, 1954, p. 918], is itself too terse and the content not sufficiently clear to enable us to be sure that Schumpeter is disagreeing with Streissler. In any event, against Schumpeter's statement we may balance the recent statement by Hayek that there is in Menger's work an "absence . . . of the conception of a general equilibrium. If he had continued his work it would probably have become even more apparent . . . that what he was aiming at was rather to provide tools for what we now call process analysis than for a theory of static equilibrium" [Hayek, 1973, p. 10].)

Neither Hayek, Streissler nor Jaffé offer explicit citations from or references to Menger's work to support their view. Evidently they base their views on a general reading of Menger that found him, in Streissler's phrase, both "shirk[ing] away from too precise a statement of equilibrium theorems" (Streissler, 1969, p. 254), and denying in certain passages "That one and the same good had at a given moment of time *everywhere the same price.*"[16] Streissler and Jaffé both understand the disequilibrium economics which they attribute to Menger, not primarily as offering scope for an entrepreneurial process (or as evidence that Menger in fact saw the market process as an entrepreneurial one), but rather simply as a refusal "to glorify entrepreneurial ability into a high speed adjustment mechanism" (Streissler, 1969, p. 254). As Jaffé puts it: "With his attention unswervingly fixed on reality, Menger could not, and did not, abstract from the difficulties traders face in any attempt to obtain all the information required for anything like a pinpoint equilibrium determination of market prices to emerge . . ." (Jaffé, p. 520).

Nonetheless, even if the emphasis is more on the *delay* in the communication of information, reflected in disequilibrium (rather than the process of learning which equilibration might represent), the Mengerian refusal to be trapped in the equilibrium mold could at least *open the way* to a theory of the market process based on learning. Streissler does in fact refer to a *tâtonnement* process in Menger—one that takes a century (in contrast to Walrasian *tâtonnement* that takes a minute) (Streissler, 1972,

16. Streissler, 1972, p. 436 (italics in original). See also Streissler, 1973, pp. 169ff.

p. 439f). And this Mengerian tâtonnement is, as explained by Streissler, indeed a kind of social learning process, involving the standardization of goods, the creation of institutions for gathering information, and the emergence of a class of middlemen.

But here again we encounter the very same puzzle in Menger that we found in the section above. Surely, Menger's theory of prices, monopolistic or competitive, is emphatically *not* a disequilibrium theory! An examination of Menger's fifth chapter on the theory of price provides no hint of any time-consuming market process (entrepreneurial or otherwise) through which prices are systematically formed. On the contrary, as we saw in the preceding section, Menger explicitly assumed the absence of all error—an assumption guaranteeing instantaneous equilibrium, and one which in fact starts out by giving entrepreneurs little to do.

Now Streissler does seem to have been aware, at least to some extent, of this difficulty. "If Menger did not believe in equilibrium," Streissler asks, "how is it possible that we find in his founding treatise all the laws of the determination of price and especially of the determination of the prices of productive inputs?" (Streissler, 1972, p. 430). This is not, however, a clear statement of the difficulty we have encountered. Our difficulty is not so much that Menger offered a theory of price determination; our problem is that, in Menger's theory, prices are shown to be determined instantaneously and inexorably by the ruling economic circumstances. It follows that our puzzlement is not immediately lessened by Streissler's attempted answer to his question: "Menger would have replied that he had to show the fundamental causes that determined economic processes"—to which Streissler adds the (even more puzzling) remark that "Menger did not try to outline the equilibrium points, the solutions of a set of differential equations . . ." *Our* difficulty is that Menger's price theory surely *is* an outline of the equilibrium situation!

THE ROLE OF ERROR AND DISEQUILIBRIUM IN MENGER:
A SUGGESTION

We have encountered what appears to be a fundamental inconsistency between Menger's price theory, on the one hand, and the rest of his *Grundsätze* on the other. Except for his chapter on price, Menger's book displays a sensitive awareness of the inescapable influence of error and ignorance, and of the resulting continuous state of flux in which the economic system must always find itself. Yet in his chapter on price Menger seems unaccountably to lapse into a world in which equilibrium prices are instantaneously determined, under conditions from which any suspicion of less than perfect omniscience is dismissed as pathological. A possible solution to this difficulty may be suggested. The solution depends on the distinction which Menger implies at several points between "economic prices" and "uneconomic prices."

Menger's chapter on the theory of price does indeed assume the absence of error, and is, therefore, *not* a disequilibrium theory. But Menger does not claim that market prices will at any time in fact correspond to the prices whose determination this chapter explains. This chapter deals only with *economic* price, *the price which would emerge if economizing individuals in fact acted in their own best mutual interests without the hindrance of incomplete information.* Menger is fully aware that the world will, at any given moment, display prices that are, to greater or lesser degree, *uneconomic.* And Menger's later chapter seven, dealing with the "marketability" of commodities, is the locus for his insights concerning the imperfectly economic character of market prices in the real world.

So that the prices discussed in Menger's chapter five are not primarily *equilibrium* prices (in the sense that at any given moment Menger is especially concerned to postulate a powerful tendency for actual market prices to converge towards them). Rather they are "correct" prices in a normative sense, that is, the prices which sensible market participants would (each in his own interest) immediately agree to were they aware of all the relevant circumstances. "Uneconomic prices" are, in this sense, "wrong" prices.

The century-long tâtonnement to which Streissler has referred should be understood as a social process in which men devise institutions, and in the course of which specialists emerge, that help uneconomic prices to be avoided. Due to the complicated character of trading relationships, Menger explains in a footnote to his chapter on prices, "the formation of economic prices becomes virtually impossible" without the institutions of markets, fairs, and exchanges (Menger, 1950, p. 218, n. 7). "The speculation that develops on these markets has the effect of impeding uneconomic price formations . . ." (p. 219). This idea is expanded upon in his chapter seven in the course of the discussion on marketability. "The institution of an organized market for an article makes it possible for the producers . . . to sell . . . at any time at economic prices" (p. 249). In the successful achievement of economic prices *knowledge* is explicitly accorded an important role.

"If every consumer knows where to find the owners of a commodity, this fact alone increases to a high degree the probability that the commodity will, at any time, be sold at an economic price." The absence in retailing of local concentration of sellers "constitutes the major cause of less economic prices being established in this branch of commerce . . ."[17]

Most fundamentally, "economic prices" are those that faithfully reflect the underlying valuations, by market participants, of the relevant goods or resources. Uneconomic prices incorrectly, or distortedly, reflect these valuations. In a remarkable footnote to his chapter on the theory of value, in the course of which Menger declares the moral character of rent and interest to be beyond the scope of economics, he explains that wherever "the services of land and of capital bear a price, it is always as a consequence of their value, and their value to men is . . . a necessary consequence of their economic character. The prices . . . are therefore the necessary products of the economic situation under which they arise, and will be more certainly obtained the more developed the legal system of a people and the more upright its public morals" (Menger, 1950, pp. 173f).

It follows from all this, it may be suggested, that Menger had *every reason not* to introduce error into his chapter on the theory of price. For the determination of economic price, error is indeed to be viewed as a pathological aberration. The absence, therefore, of any hint in that chapter of the need and scope for an equilibrating process, should not be a source of bewilderment.

---

17. *Ibid.* It is worthwhile to cite at length Menger's discussion of the character of "economic prices," in his 1883 treatise on methodology. "There is scarcely need to remark that . . . as a rule *real* prices deviate more or less from *economic* ones (those corresponding to the economic situation). In the practice of economy people in fact endeavor only rarely to protect their economic interests *completely*. Many sorts of considerations, above all, indifference to economic interests of lesser significance, good will toward others, etc., cause them in their economic activity not to protect their economic interests at all in some cases, in some cases incompletely. They are, furthermore, vague and in error concerning the economic means to attain their economic goals; indeed, they are often vague and in error concerning these goals themselves. Also the economic situation, on the basis of which they develop their economic activity, is often insufficiently or incompletely known to them. Finally their economic freedom is not infrequently impaired by various kinds of relationships. A definite economic situation brings to light precisely *economic* prices of goods only in the rarest cases. *Real* prices are, rather more or less different from economic" (Menger, 1963, p. 69).

It should, despite our attempt to solve the apparent contradiction in Menger, not be thought that Menger's theory of *market* price determination is fully absolved from difficulties. Although Menger's theory has, as we have seen, been described as disequilibrium theory by several writers, it cannot be said that he gave us an adequate theory of price equilibration. The century-long tâtonnement that Streissler identified certainly does not give us such a theory. Rather, that glacial tâtonnement consists of slow but ultimately dominant forces which for Menger generate a climate in which the costs of avoiding error are reduced towards zero. This process is not, therefore, a learning process in the course of which prices are, through entrepreneurial grasping of arbitrage opportunities, gradually shaken down towards equilibrium. It is instead, a process that brings change to the environment within which prices are on each day—instantaneously—determined.

In this view of the market there appears no systematic process linking today's prices directly to those that prevailed yesterday. Yesterday's prices were struck in reflection of yesterday's valuations, as distorted (possibly) by yesterday's ignorance (or lack of "upright public morals"). Today's prices are struck in reflection of today's valuations as distorted (possibly) by today's ignorance. There is no hint that today's prices might reflect any process of learning (about other people's valuations) that might have been set off by the experience of yesterday's prices. If any link at all is to be seen, in Menger's system, between present prices and those of the past, this must be merely in that the superior present institutions facilitating the communication of information (for example, organized markets) evolved out of the inadequate results experienced in earlier environments.

Our conclusion, then, is that—at least as far as concerns the role of entrepreneurial alertness to existing error in bringing about adjustments in prices not yet in equilibrium—Menger's theory was *not* a disequilibrium theory at all. It did *not* make use of the phenomena of ignorance and error. This conclusion, it will be observed, does not necessarily deny the validity of what might seem the contrary view of Streissler and of Jaffé—that Menger's theory was distinguished precisely by its recognition of scope for the entrepreneur, of error, and of disequilibrium. That no such denial is necessarily involved can be shown most effectively by recalling Hayek's sharp criticism of Schumpeter, on a matter closely resembling those features of Menger's theory to which we have ourselves been drawing critical attention.

In one of the papers in which Hayek developed his ideas on the role of knowledge in market processes, he pointed to Schumpeter's view "that the possibility of a rational calculation in the absence of markets for the factors of production follows for the theorist 'from the elementary proposition that consumers in evaluating ("demanding") consumer's goods *ipso facto* also evaluate the means of production which enter the production of these goods.'"[18] Hayek reacts sharply (Hayek, 1949, p. 90f):

> What Professor Schumpeter's "*ipso facto*" presumably means is that the valuation of the factors of production is implied in, or follows necessarily from, the valuation of consumers' goods. But this . . . is not correct. Implication is a logical relationship which can be meaningfully asserted only of propositions simultaneously present to one and the same mind . . . To assume all the knowledge to be given to a single mind in the same manner in which we assume it to be given to us as the explaining economists is to assume the problem away . . .

Most significantly, Hayek can find an explanation for the circumstance that "an economist of Professor Schumpeter's standing should thus have fallen into a trap . . ." only in that "there is something fundamentally wrong with an approach which habitually disregards an essential part of the phenomena with which we have to deal: the unavoidable imperfection of man's knowledge and the consequent need for a process by which knowledge is constantly communicated and acquired" (Hayek, 1949, p. 91). That such a criticism can be levelled against Schumpeter in no way destroys our view of him as a pioneer in the explication of the entrepreneurial role. Quite similarly, our criticism of Menger's theory of market price determination—that it reveals no insight into Hayek's "process by which knowledge is constantly communicated and acquired"—does not rule out a possibly pioneering role for Menger in the economics of entrepreneurship, or of imperfect knowledge, or of disequilibrium.

MENGER ON COMPETITION AND PRODUCT VARIATION

Another aspect of economic analysis in which we may detect adumbrations of entrepreneurial processes in Menger's system, is the one that concerns the nature of competition and product variation. Both competitive

18. Hayek, 1949, p. 90. Hayek's citation from Schumpeter is from Schumpeter, 1942, p. 175.

activity in general and product variation as a form of competitive activity in particular, can be understood as manifestations of entrepreneurial search and experiment.[19] (In fact, perhaps the most powerful force which pushed entrepreneurship out of post-Marshallian price theory was the attempt to confine that theory within the perfectly competitive mold— within which product variation was excluded by definition, and in which competition became a state of affairs, not an activity at all.)

Here, too, Streissler and Jaffé have emphasized the difference between Menger and his non-Austrian contemporaries. "The important point to be remembered about Menger's vision of the market structure of an economy is that in contrast to most economists he did not consider monopoly as an odd exception to a world of competition. He much rather thought of *monopoly as the general state of the market and competition as a limiting* case to 'monopolies' . . . [M]ore precisely, Menger considers *isolated exchange* as the basic type of economic intercourse, . . . a particular case of *bilateral monopoly*" (Streissler, 1973, pp. 168f). Moreover, "Menger, as far as he thought of competition generally thought of it as *imperfect* competition in the modern sense: again and again he stresses *product differentiation* and *qualitative* dimensions in competition."[20]

For Streissler, in fact, product variation emerges as the *very central theme* of Menger's entire system. "Much more than a dissertation on utility," Menger's *Grundsätze* "is an *enquiry into the diversity of goods*. Its central thesis is the following: *The increase in the variety of goods* . . . enhances the wealth of nations just as much as the division of labour."[21]

Now it must be observed that this latter view of Streissler's is not only quite bizarre but appears to be wholly unfounded. There is a passage in Menger's opening chapter[22] in which he vigorously disputes Adam Smith's thesis that the economic progress of mankind is primarily the result of the increasing division of labor. Menger, on the other hand, argues that historically progress has resulted from the willingness of men to extend their attention to the provision of goods of progressively higher order, instead of continuing their activity merely to the acquisition of naturally available goods of lowest order. If "men abandon this

19. Kirzner, chapters 3, 4.
20. Streissler, 1973, p. 169; 1972, p. 435. See also Streissler, 1973, pp. 230f.
21. Streissler, 1969, p. 249. See also Streissler, 1972, pp. 427, 430f.
22. This is the passage cited by Streissler as the source for his assertion.

most primitive form of economy, investigate the ways in which things may be combined in a causal process for the production of consumption goods, take possession of things capable of being so combined, and treat them as goods of higher order . . . the available quantities of [consumption] goods will no longer be independent of the wishes and needs of men" (Menger, 1950, pp. 73f). In this process, Menger points out, not only will the volume of consumption goods expand but the more *varied* will also become the kinds of goods produced. (Menger appears to be moved to make this observation in order to explain how increasingly important becomes Smith's division of labor *as a result* of economic progress.) There is *no* suggestion here, as Streissler repeatedly asserts, that it is product variation that *is responsible for* economic progress. (Moreover, this entire passage in which Menger takes issue with Smith, was in the second edition of the *Grundsätze* (Menger, 1923) removed from the opening chapter and inserted towards the end of the fourth chapter, where it appears on pages 94–6—in a manner which hardly supports the view that this passage is of central importance to Menger's system as a whole.)

But Streissler's emphasis on product variation as a recognizable feature of Menger's economics is, of course, untouched by our criticism of Streissler's own excessive emphasis on this feature. And since it is entrepreneurial innovation that is surely responsible for experimentation with new products, new qualities and varieties of products, this feature of Menger's analysis certainly invites our examination from the viewpoint of interest in this paper.

Unfortunately Menger's perspective on the market—while it unquestionably transcends the perfectly competitive model with respect to numbers of market participants and to product homogeneity—offers little direct support for any discovery of recognition by Menger of the entrepreneurial role. While the perfectly competitive model later came to be viewed as the very core of neoclassical price theory, the truth is that the early post-1870 theorists worked in fact with more realistic perceptions of the market.[23] Menger certainly had his feet planted firmly in a world of heterogeneous products and of exchanges taking place between finite numbers of market participants (and, as Streissler points out), often between isolated buyers and sellers. But all this is, after all, entirely consistent with a perfect knowledge view of the universe in which no scope is permitted to exist for entrepreneurial alertness.

23. On this see Peterson, pp. 60–78.

THE ENTREPRENEURIAL ROLE IN MENGER'S SYSTEM

Our survey of the various aspects of Menger's economic system which relate to the entrepreneurial role, has yielded somewhat paradoxical conclusions. There can be no doubt that Menger—as shown and emphasized by Streissler—displayed remarkable insights about the role of *knowledge*, the phenomenon of *error* in economic activity, the resulting shadow of *uncertainty* in which economizing activity is carried on. Nor, again, can it be doubted that Menger perceived the economic world as an arena of dynamic, rivalrous competition—a world totally unlike the equilibrium world of the perfectly competitive model. Certainly Menger's world was one within which we would have expected the entrepreneurial role to have been not only clearly perceived but in fact boldly underlined. That we have found this is *not* to be the case is paradoxical enough.

This paradox became all the more puzzling when Menger's theory of price is examined. This theory, we saw, appeared to be constructed only through the careful *exclusion* of all error and ignorance. The prices explained by Menger's theory become, therefore, prices fully consistent with equilibrium, and totally inconsistent with competition understood as an entrepreneurial process generated by error and its spontaneous discovery. How are we to account for this surprising gap in Menger? How could a writer so steeped in non-equilibrium perspectives on the economic process, fail to recognize the pivotal character of the entrepreneurial role in this process?

Streissler, while not directly confronting this question, has already provided, it might be maintained, an answer to it. In a discussion of the sociological mileu from which the early Austrian economists sprang, Streissler attributes to them a "political" bias that must have operated against any thorough recognition of the role of the entrepreneur. The early Austrians faced the problem of explaining the great Austrian economic revival in the third quarter of the last century (especially after the military defeat of 1866). The question was: "to which social group does Austria owe its prosperity? In similar contexts the English classicists would have replied without hesitation: to the businessmen, the entrepreneurs. But this kind of answer could not be given by the three founders of the Austrian School, all of them sons of noble civil servants. This answer could only be given by Schumpeter, the son of a wealthy businessman. The answer would furthermore have enclosed political dynamite of the highest explosiveness. For who would have been responsible for the sole successes? An entrepreneurial class which in Austria was particularly strongly socially disparaged and which was, to boot, nearly exclusively of alien extraction: Germans, Protestants, Jews! Who would, on the other hand, have failed in their specific, the political, task? Their own class, the bureaucracy and the crown, the 'House of Austria'."[24] In this vein Streissler explains the emphasis of the Austrians (particularly of Wieser) upon marginal utility, as ideologically inspired. "In the shift of responsibility for economic prosperity from the embarrassing businessmen to the innocuous consumers, to everybody, the ideological charge of the idea of marginal utility can be found . . ." (Streissler, 1969, p. 259). But this approach can hardly be deployed to answer our question.

Not only is Streissler's suggestion little more than pure conjecture—and a conjecture not only bizarre but also highly uncomplimentary to the intellectual integrity of the early Austrians—it would not even be fully consistent with Streissler's own view of Menger's system. For Streissler, marginal utility was not at all the central theme of *Menger's* economics; it was only the later followers, particularly Wieser, who chose to emphasize this aspect of their system (Streissler, 1969, pp. 244–7). In Menger himself, Streissler maintains, the "idea of marginal utility is only of more or less secondary importance" (*ibid.*, p. 248). (In this regard it is therefore not quite clear why Streissler finds it important or even relevant to document that Menger—like Wieser and Böhm-Bawerk—belonged to the class of noble civil servants.)

A more intriguing explanation for the "entrepreneurial gap" in Menger has been suggested (in oral discussion with the writer) by Professor Lachmann. Schumpeter's recognition of the role of the entrepreneur, Professor Lachmann argues, arose out of his profound preoccupation with the Walrasian general equilibrium model. Precisely because of the more than obvious discrepancies between this model and the real world. Schumpeter discovered the source of these discrepancies in the dynamic role of the entrepreneur. Menger, on the other hand, not being encumbered by excessive attention to general equilibrium conditions, was not led to emphasize the specifically dynamic role of the entrepreneur—in fact he had no need to do so. Lachmann's suggestion is highly attractive, but it

24. Streissler, 1969, pp. 275f; and see relevant footnotes.

does not appear to take into account the extent to which (as emphasized in this paper) Menger's theory of price *is* an equilibrium theory and the extent to which he does in fact find it necessary to account for a process of *institutional* change that bears on the degree to which the real world has not yet attained the full equilibrium of Menger's "economic prices."

Perhaps a more simple but plausible understanding (of the unevenly profound recognition of scope for entrepreneurship in Menger) may be gained from the traditional view of Menger's system that Streissler finds so unacceptable. Surely the traditional view of Menger is wholly correct, if not in its emphasis of "marginal utility" as being the central theme of Menger's system, then at least in its emphasis upon subjective value. It is almost impossible to see how any reader of the *Grundsätze* can fail to agree that its single theme is the way in which all valuation in an economic system takes its source from the final valuations of those to whose desires the system is to minister. This theme was so profoundly important and exciting for Menger, and one so revolutionary, he believed, that it consumed all his energy and attention. Precisely because of this, Menger's view of economizing man is so complete, so sensitive to notions of knowledge, error, and alertness. Nonetheless, in pursuing this theme with single-minded concentration, Menger was simply not led to see the market *process* as an entrepreneurial one; he was not led to see how his own profound insights into the scope for error in economizing decisions provided the key to a view of the market as a process of social discovery—the very process through which the valuations of Menger's consumers come in fact to be translated into complex chains of production decisions ministering to their desires. It remained for later followers of the Mengerian tradition, in particular Mises and Hayek, to perceive the exact character of this process. In this task they were unquestionably able to draw upon a tradition—Mengerian in origin—in which error, uncertainty, diversity, and rivalrous competition were always, to some degree, in sight. But the process itself was not seen by Menger.

It should come as no surprise that Menger himself was unable to see how his own ideas pointed to these powerful insights concerning the entrepreneurial process. It is always so with great pioneers. And in the case of Menger we have direct evidence that he himself, in fact, saw how this was occurring! In his 1923 review article (of the second German edition of Menger's *Grundsätze*), Franz X. Weiss recalled an illuminating (and touching) conversation with Menger in 1910 (when the latter was, therefore, not quite seventy). When Weiss suggested to Menger certain ideas, built on Menger's own foundations, for the advancement of the theory of the value of money, Menger replied that he too saw how these ideas are the implications of his own teachings, yet he was unable to accept them! (Weiss, p. 154). Weiss uses this remark of Menger to throw light on Menger's general failure to cite or use almost any of the work of his own followers. The intellectual effort required to escape and to overthrow the deeply entrenched classical view of the economic system, Weiss believes, may have itself hindered Menger from being able to see and accept all the implications drawn from his own work by his followers. This appears to be the case, we would argue, in regard to entrepreneurship. As Weiss emphasized (ibid.), one's realization of this circumstance in no way diminishes in the slightest, of course, the greatness of Menger's own pioneering contribution to the history of economic thought—and, for that matter, to the development of the theory of the entrepreneurial market process.

REFERENCES

W. J. Baumol, "Entrepreneurship in Economic Theory," *American Economic Review,* 58, May 1968.

G. Gross, *Lehre vom Unternehmergewinn,* Leipzig, 1884.

F. A. Hayek, "Carl Menger," in Vol. 1 of *The Collected Works of Carl Menger,* London School of Economics and Political Science, 1934.

———, "The Use of Knowledge in Society," *Individualism and Economic Order,* London: Routledge and Kegan Paul, 1949.

———, "The Place of Menger's *Grundsätze* in the History of Economic Thought," in J. R. Hicks and W. Weber, *Carl Menger and the Austrian School of Economics,* Oxford: Clarendon Press, 1973.

W. Jaffé, "Menger, Jevons, and Walras De-Homogenized," *Economic Inquiry,* 14, December 1976.

I. M. Kirzner, *Competition and Entrepreneurship,* Chicago: University of Chicago Press, 1973.

F. H. Knight, *Risk, Uncertainty, and Profit,* Boston and New York: Houghton Mifflin Company, 1921.

———, "Introduction" to C. Menger, *Principles of Economics,* Free Press, 1950.

L. M. Lachmann, "On Austrian Capital Theory," in E. G. Dolan (ed.), *The Foundations of Modern Austrian Economics,* Kansas City: Sheed and Ward, 1976.

A. Marshall, *Principles of Economics,* 8th edition, London: Macmillan, 1920.

V. Mataja, *Der Unternehmergewinn,* Vienna, 1884.

C. Menger, *Principles of Economics,* translated and edited by J. Dingwall and Bert F. Hoselitz, Glencoe, Illinois: Free Press, 1950. Translation of the first edition of C. Menger's *Grundsätze der Volkswirtschaftslehre,* 1871.

————, *Grundsätze der Volkswirtschaftslehre,* 2nd edition, edited by K. Menger, Jr., Vienna and Leipzig, 1923.

————, *Problems of Economics and Sociology,* L. Schneider, editor, Urbana: University of Illinois Press, 1963.

L. Mises, *Human Action,* New Haven: Yale University Press, 1949.

S. Peterson, "Antitrust and the Classical Model," *American Economic Review,* 47, March 1957.

L. Robbins, *An Essay on the Nature and Significance of Economic Science,* 2nd edition, London: Macmillan, 1935.

J. A. Schumpeter, *The Theory of Economic Development,* translated by R. Opie, Harvard University Press, 1934.

————, *Capitalism, Socialism, and Democracy,* New York: Harper and Bros., 1942.

————, *History of Economic Analysis,* New York: Oxford University Press, 1954.

G. J. Stigler, "The Economics of Carl Menger," *Journal of Political Economy,* 45, April 1937. Also in G. J. Stigler, *Production and Distribution Theories,* New York: Macmillan, 1944, Chapter VI.

E. Streissler, "Structural Economic Thought, On the Significance of the Austrian School Today," *Zeitschrift für Nationalökonomie,* 29, 1969.

————, "To What Extent Was the Austrian School Marginalist?" *History of Political Economy,* 4, Fall 1972.

————, "Menger's Theories of Money and Uncertainty—A Modern Interpretation," in J. R. Hicks and W. Weber (eds.), *Carl Menger and the Austrian School of Economics,* Oxford: Clarendon Press, 1973.

F. X. Weiss, "Zur zweiten Auflage von Carl Menger's 'Grundsätzen,'" *Zeitschrift für Volkswirtschaft und Sozialpolitik,* N.F. 4, 1924.

METHODOLOGICAL INDIVIDUALISM, MARKET
EQUILIBRIUM, AND MARKET PROCESS

1. Contemporary price theory consists, to a large extent, of investigating the conditions that must be fulfilled in order for markets to be in equilibrium, under a variety of structural patterns. Whether the treatment be confined to a particular industry, or extended to consider interindustry relationships, the procedure is to extract, from the data relevant to the problem—tastes, incomes, technological possibilities, resource availabilities—that pattern of resource and product prices, of resource employments and of product quantities, that will permit all the plans of utility-maximizing consumers and of profit-maximizing producers to be successfully carried out.

The theoretical consequences of an autonomous change in the data are, similarly, explored, wholly on equilibrium lines, through the method of comparative statics. The conditions for equilibrium are determined first, for the data as they existed prior to the change, and then again, for the changed data. The data change is then viewed as bringing about an instantaneous jump from the old equilibrium situation to the new one.

More advanced work by mathematical economists has attempted to grapple with the problem of explaining how equilibrium is reached (and with related problems) under various headings, "dynamics," "problems of the path," the "stability of equilibrium." In all these attempts (none of them notably successful) these problems are seen as involving advanced work building on the firm foundation of equilibrium theory. It is the latter which is primary. Moreover it is the latter which still constitutes, as explained, the main body of much contemporary price theory.

This tendency has not gone uncriticized. A number of writers have vigorously objected to a theory of price confined to the conditions of

From *Il Politico* (Pavia, Italy) 32, no. 4 (1967): 787–99. Reprinted by permission.

Presented at a meeting of the Mont Pelerin Society held September 13, 1967, in Vichy, France.

Grateful acknowledgement is due to the Relm Foundation for a grant supporting research into certain aspects of entrepreneurship, from which this paper has developed.

equilibrium. Both Mises[1] and Hayek[2] have pointed out that preoccupation with equilibrium situations has tended, with unfortunate results, to avert attention from the true character of the market *process*. This preoccupation has led economists to ignore the character of the *market agitation* through which decisions are continually being reshuffled in the direction of equilibrium. It has led them to overlook the vital role played by the entrepreneur in the market process.

In the view of these critics, the appropriate starting point for a theory of price is not the configuration of prices and outputs at equilibrium, but the pattern of market adjustments set in motion by conditions of disequilibrium. It is the latter which should be primary, with equilibrium situations seen as special cases of some subsidiary interest to theorists (in that these situations represent the case where the market process, having run to completion, is at a standstill).

2. Hayek, in particular, in a series of justly noted papers,[3] has explored the underlying sequence of causes and effects responsible for the market process, and has contrasted this sequence with the state of affairs that prevails under equilibrium. The latter state of affairs is shown to mean "that the foresight of the different members of the society is . . . correct in the sense that every person's plan is based on the expectation of just those actions of other people which those other people intend to perform and that all these plans are based on the expectation of the same set of external facts, so that under certain conditions nobody will have any reason to change his plans. Correct foresight is then not, as it has sometimes been understood, a precondition which must exist in order that equilibrium may be arrived at. It is rather the defining characteristic of a state of equilibrium."[4] The market process, on the other hand, is one which "necessarily involves continuous changes in the data for the different individuals." The causal factor in this process has "the form of the acquisition of new knowledge by the different individuals or of changes in their data brought about by the contacts between them."[5]

1. L. Mises, *Human Action*, Yale, 1949, pp. 250–251.

2. F. A. Hayek, *Individualism and Economic Order*, Routledge and Kegan Paul, 1949, pp. 44f., 94f.

3. *Op. cit.*, Chapters II, IV, V. See also Chapter IX.

4. *Op. cit.*, p. 42.

5. *Op. cit.*, pp. 94–95. See also p. 50 for a reference to Mises in this connection.

In this view, then, the unique character of the market process is its ability to disseminate scattered pieces of information to those pivotal decision-makers to whom they are most relevant. The state of equilibrium, on the other hand, corresponds to the cessation of this process, all relevant knowledge having already become universal.

3. It may be observed that the shortcomings of an exclusively equilibrium approach to price theory, have reference not only to positive theory itself, but affect even more seriously the normative implications of the theory. The evaluation by economists of the achievements of the free market, turn out again and again to depend on whether the market is being appraised *in* the state of equilibrium, or whether its contributions are being considered in terms of the *systematic process* towards equilibrium of which it consists.

For the exclusively equilibrium approach the efficiency of the market is judged by the pattern of prices, outputs, allocation of resources prevailing under equilibrium conditions (for that market). All institutions, or utilizations of resources, that may be present in the real world, which do not correspond to the efficient pattern of resource allocation required of equilibrium, are immediately stamped as inefficient. It is of no matter that these institutions, or these utilizations of resources, may perhaps be precisely the vehicles through which the market process achieves its tendency towards equilibrium. To equilibrium theorists efficiency is judged against the background of equilibrium states of affairs. "Imperfect" competition, profits, advertising, the "wastes of competition"—all these are frequently attacked by economists on efficiency grounds. It is here being pointed out that all too often these (and other) attacks arise directly out of the exclusive preoccupation with equilibrium, and evaporate completely when introduced into the framework of the analysis of the market process.

Moreover, it is not only the case that equilibrium preoccupation is responsible for unjustified criticism of the market; this preoccupation has also been shown to be responsible for the mistaken notion that what is achieved by the market can, in principle, be achieved equally well by a system of central planning. Again, it is Hayek who has shown us[6] how the "solutions" to the problem of efficient economic calculation under socialism that was raised by Mises, turn out to misunderstand the real

6. Hayek, *op. cit.*, pp. 77ff, 88–91, 188.

contribution which the market makes. Too often it is implied that the economic problem facing society is that of allocating resources *on the assumption that all relevant information concerning preferences, technological possibilities, and resource availabilities is already possessed.* If this were the case, the problem would indeed be "merely" a matter of computation, and its solution *could* be consistent, in principle, both with a market in equilibrium, and with an economy under central planning. The real problem to be solved, however, and the one that is solved by the market process, and which has *not* been shown to be solvable under central planning, is "how to secure the best use of resources known to any of the members of society, for ends whose relative importance only these individuals know."[7]

4. The purpose of the present paper is to explore the underpinnings of the two approaches to price theory that have been thus exposed. It will be useful to have some handy labels, and I will use geographical ones (as is perhaps not inappropriate for an international gathering), albeit with full concession that the ones I use do some injustice to some writers, and are open to serious challenge on various grounds. Nonetheless I find that these labels do perform a useful service and will introduce them without further apology. I will call that approach that overemphasizes the state of equilibrium, the "Anglo-American" approach; the approach stressing the market process will be called "Austrian" (in both cases the quotation marks will be retained for purposes of self-defense).

It is of great importance to notice, before proceeding with our investigation, that *both* approaches share much in common from a methodological standpoint. Both approaches are *theoretical* (moreover both approaches *could* even be expressed entirely in an a priori garb). In particular both approaches are consistent with *methodological individualism* (and our own investigation, in fact, depends crucially on this shared methodology). In both approaches analysis begins with the individual decision-maker and proceeds to consider the interactions of numerous such decisions.

Why then, we must ask, is it that two approaches that have so much in common (as against competing economic doctrines) are able to yield such sharply diverging "pictures" of the economic universe, and lead to such sharply diverging views of the value of the contribution of the

7. *Op. cit.*, p. 78.

market? Besides the intrinsic interest attached to the answer to this question, our search for the source of this divergence may perhaps hold, in addition, some hope for a resolution of the conflict between the two approaches. The present paper, written frankly from an "Austrian" viewpoint attempts to answer the question here raised, and will attempt to exploit this answer as additional support for the "Austrian" approach.

5. It will be helpful to commence from the fact (cited in the preceding paragraph) that both approaches build on the individual decision. Both are content to work out the implications of the existence of numerous interacting decision-makers. Both approaches see the individual as *purposeful,* and as governing his acts by his logic. In neither approach, therefore, can a conscious individual act be seen as *undetermined.* Each such act follows rigorously and determinately from what the individual *wanted* to do, in the light of what he saw himself *able* to do. The planful individual decision, therefore, forms the basic unit of analysis on both of the approaches here under examination. But, it will here be submitted, it is at this point that agreement between the two approaches is exhausted. When one presses on further to inquire into the picture of the individual decision-maker under each of the two approaches, one discovers, it is our argument here, that the two approaches disagree, subtly perhaps, but nonetheless definitely, on the character of the most basic building block in the edifice of price theory, the nature of the individual decision. It will be our purpose to show that this is in fact the case, and to demonstrate how this disagreement is entirely sufficient to account for the other differences which we have seen to divide the two approaches in such important positive and normative respects.

In the "Anglo-American" approach the individual decision-maker is seen as an *economizer,* as adjusting purposefully (but essentially "passively") to the constraints inherent in his situation. In the "Austrian" approach the individual decision-maker is viewed as essentially active, in intent pursuit of courses of action which will make him "better off," not as an adjuster but as an actor. This concise expression of what appears to be the basis for the difference between the two approaches, calls for some elaboration. For this purpose it will be convenient to cite two important, well-known contributions to the modern literature on methodological individualism. These contributions are (quite correctly) often considered to have a very great deal in common. It will be shown here that it is precisely this common ground shared by these contributions that can point up most sharply a hitherto little noticed difference in emphasis between them, a difference which is of the utmost significance for the matter under present discussion. The two contributions are Lord Robbins' *Nature and Significance of Economic Science*[8] and Mises' *Human Action*.[9]

Both Robbins' and Mises' works emphasize the role of theory, based on the individual decision. There is much shared in common, not only in their views on method in economics, but also in their conceptions of the nature of the science. And Robbins, in particular, acknowledges a significant intellectual debt to earlier discussions with Mises.[10] Yet it must be insisted that a clear difference exists between the pictures presented in the two works of the individual human decision-maker. Robbins, it will be argued here, presents the decision-maker used in the "Anglo-American" approach; Mises' emphasis on human action fits naturally into an "Austrian" approach.

In Robbins, as is of course well known, the essence of the economic aspect of affairs is seen as involving the allocation of scarce resources among competing ends. Both ends and means, it is emphasized, are *given*. The juxtaposition of ends and means sets up the conditions for *economizing*, for the careful sharing out of means among the various competing end-gratifications. Insofar as men live in a world in which available means fall short of being able to satisfy all wants, it is universally necessary to plan, to budget, to allocate, to economize. The notion of purposefulness, never emphasized in Robbins, plays the role in his work only as being implicit in the formal concept of "ends." We start our analysis with our subject in possession of definite ends; purposeful, consistent decision-making in the light of these ends imposes definite constraints on the disposition of means. Economizing consists in so managing the available means, that their disposition reflects the given relative importance of the various ends.

In Mises, on the other hand, a careful perusal by the reader will reveal little emphasis on means-allocation as such. The emphasis is always on human *action,* on courses of action undertaken by the human being in order to remove uneasiness, to make himself, as he sees it, "better off." Of course such courses of action will necessarily involve planful

8. 2nd Edition, Macmillan, 1985.

9. Yale, 1949.

10. See his *Preface*. For what must, from the viewpoint of the present paper, be judged an incomplete comparative discussion of Robbins and Mises, see the writer's *Economic Point of View*, Van Nostrand, 1960, Chapters 6, 7.

calculation and allocation, but the discerning reader will discover that Mises' *homo agens* is something more than economizing man. He is not merely engaged in computing the pattern of means allocation that will most faithfully reflect the hierarchy of given ends. *Homo agens* is actively *seeking* out the best course of action; he is venturing, innovating, exploring, searching. He is constantly *testing* the nature of the constraints which circumscribe him. He is not tackling a problem imposed by a *given* pattern of means and ends; he is seen *before* any given pattern of means and ends has crystallized as *the* relevant one. He is seen *not only* as allocating means with respect to ends, where this can be unequivocally performed, he is seen always in active pursuit of new information as to which means are in fact available, and as to which ends he wishes to consider of greater importance. Even where ends and means have achieved definite status his pursuit of efficiency with respect to them is carried in with *full alertness to possible changes* in the circumstances of his decision.

That Robbins' economizing man represents someone who does not quite fill our flesh-and-blood picture of our fellowmen is of course an observation that has frequently been made, often, in our view, with little understanding of what Robbins was about. Soon after his work first appeared Robbins was subject to bitter attack by Souter on the grounds of "arid formalism." Parsons, similarly, raised questions concerning the validity of the concepts ends and means which are central to Robbins' conception of the economic problem.[11] Quite apart from Robbins' work, Professor Knight long ago emphasized that our very conception of human decision-making depends on the decision-maker *not* knowing with certainty all the relevant information.[12]

More recently Professor Shackle has again and again insisted on analysis of the decision that does not assume away the uncertainty in which it is invariably enveloped. Removing uncertainty, Shackle argues, denatures the decision into a mechanical calculation "determined" by data and tastes. Recognition of uncertainty, on the other hand, makes possible the viewing of the human decision as a creative, imaginative leap in the dark, that injects into history something that was not determined by previous history.[13]

11. See the discussion in the writer's *Economic Point View*, pp. 121–126.

12. See F. H. Knight, *Risk, Uncertainty and Profit,* Chapter 7.

13. See G. L. S. Shackle, *The Nature of Economic Thought, Selected Papers 1955–64* (New York, 1966).

While what we have asserted to be the "Austrian" dissatisfaction with economizing man bears some resemblance to these appeals for a less formal conceptualization of the economic problem, and for a concept of the decision that does not extrude all elements of uncertainty, the "Austrian" *homo agens* in fact differs from economizing man only in a somewhat more subtle sense. Some further discussion of this is in order.

6. The truth, after all, is that a theorist operating with Robbinsian economizing man, will have no difficulty in applying his model of decision-making to the world of Misesian human action. Precisely because the concept of economizing is formal and abstract it is able to be applied to different situations, both those with and those without uncertainty. *To the extent that* means and ends are clearly defined, human decision-making necessarily reflects the constraints imposed by the need to economize, if consistency is to be maintained. To the extent that uncertainty exists as to which means and which ends are relevant to a particular decision-situation, there is room within the Robbinsian framework for the deliberate, cost-conscious, but active search for relevant information. While all this will not go far at all in reconciling, say, Shackle, to such a scheme, it does seem to raise a question for our own assertion that the "Austrian" view of decision-making differs from the "Anglo-American" one (which we have exemplified by Robbins).

The defense for our assertion that such a difference does nevertheless exist, is as follows. The notion of economizing requires the *prior* existence of given ends and means. These do not, it is perfectly true, need to represent elements known with certainty to the decision-maker. It is perfectly in order to see economizing man allocating guessed-at quantities of means among alternative research projects (with guessed-at potentialities). But, with all their possible uncertainty, the ends and the means are *there already* at the time when the theorist begins his analysis of decision-making. *Before some image of ends and of means has been introduced, economizing cannot even begin.* Should a change in external conditions, or in tastes, or the appearance of new information, alter in any way the pattern of ends and means as seen by the decision-maker, then there will have been created a *new* economic situation calling for a *different* decision. The new ends-means configuration simply did not exist before for the decision-maker, and consequently, *there is no continuity* linking the new decision which will now be made, with the original situation as it faced the decision-maker. The exogenous change in data, or in information, simply wiped out one decision-making situation and replaced it with a different one. There can be nothing in the original decision-making situation that can be used to understand the decision finally made. The final decision has been made against a pattern of ends-means irrelevant to the original one. A discontinuity exists; an unexplained, exogenous alteration in conditions has generated a decision unexplainable in terms of the original economic problem. There is nothing in the formulation of the economic problem that tells us how, in the absence of such unexplained exogenous changes, one pattern of relevant ends-means can be replaced by another. So that where a series of such changes does occur, the corresponding alterations in decisions made, represents a series of disconnected discrete events, not understandable, within the exclusively economizing framework, as a logical sequence constituting a unified process. (Even, it should be noticed, where the solution of a "first" economic problem consists in searching for specific information, which is subsequently used in making later decisions, there is nothing *in the concept of economizing itself* which tells us how the discovered information alters the image of ends-means as seen by the individual. The later decision-possibilities, in this approach, gain their form only after the ends-means image has somehow been revamped, no doubt in the light of the new information.)

And it is at this point that the relevant aspect of the "Austrian" concept of the individual decision comes clearly into vision. By endowing the individual not only with the propensity to mould *given* means to suit *given* ends, but with the drive and alertness necessary for their discovery as well, the "Austrian" view points to the possibility of an entire logically-unified *sequence* of decisions, each one relevant to a pattern of ends-means as seen by the individual, that is the logical consequence of the experiences resulting from the earlier decisions. What must seem, in the "Anglo-American" view a disconnected series of discrete decisions, may turn out to be in the "Austrian" scheme, a systematic process.

Let us sum up our statement of the distinction between the "Anglo-American" and the "Austrian" views of the decision-maker. The former view is one in which the problem faced is essentially a computational one; it reaches us at a stage when the elements entering into the computation are both known and given. The latter view, while also embracing, where possible, the "computational" aspect of decision-making, sees it nonetheless more broadly as including also an element of alertness to possible changes in the data that has no place in the "Anglo-American" view. This additional element we shall call, without further explanation at this point, the *entrepreneurial element,* present in all decision-making.

7. An illustration from the most elementary problems in price theory will help clarify this distinction, and will explain why it is here being argued that this distinction is of relevance to the question of equilibrium preoccupation.

Let us imagine a single-commodity market in which many potential buyers and sellers are present. We draw a demand curve expressing the eagerness of buyers, in aggregate, to buy at various possible prices. Each point on the demand curve tells us the total quantity buyers will decide to buy if faced with the corresponding price. And we draw, analogously, the supply curve for the sellers. The intersection of the two curves marks the equilibrium situation for this market. At the price market by this intersection the quantity that would be sought to be bought will coincide with the quantity that sellers will be seeking to sell. The important question, however, is concerning situations at points other than the equilibrium one: what market process will be set in motion, and what accounts for it being what it is?[14]

Assuming, for the sake of simplicity in analysis, that we imagine a *single* price, p_1, to prevail throughout the market, but that this price is below the equilibrium price. Clearly buyers will make decisions to buy quantities which exceed, in aggregate, the quantities sellers as a whole will decide to sell. Each of the market participants will be making a decision, based on the (correct) assumption that the going market price is p_1. But the buyers make their decisions assuming that at the price p_1 they can each purchase *all* they want, and in this they turn out to be in error. They overestimate the willingness of sellers to sell at this price. The result is an unsatisfied demand, and we are accustomed to jumping immediately to the next step which is to say that prices will "therefore" rise. But why will prices rise?

Clearly prices will rise because the error will be discovered. Buyers will tomorrow, then, realize that they must offer a price greater than p_1 if they are successfully to coax sellers into selling all they will be prepared to buy. (Or equivalently, sellers will realize that they can successfully hold out for a price greater than p_1 and yet sell all they will be prepared to sell.)

14. For further discussion of this illustration, see the writer's "Rational Action and Economic Theory," *Journal of Political Economy* (August, 1962).

This is the basic character of the market process set in motion by the existence of a disequilibrium situation. *The crucial element here is the discovery of error and the resulting reconsideration by market participants of the true alternative now open to them.* The market process proceeds by communicating knowledge. *The all-important assumption is that men learn from their market experiences.* But on what basis do we make this assumption? Hayek calls this assumption and similar ones concerning how men acquire knowledge "apparently subsidiary hypotheses . . . which constitute the empirical content of our propositions about what happens in the real world."[15] He stresses that they differ from the "general assumptions from which the Pure Logic of Choice starts."

What we wish to submit here is that, within the "Anglo-American" context of the "computing" decision-maker, the assumption that yesterday's market disappointments will cause the buyers to realize that they must offer higher prices today, is indeed an arbitrary one, imported from the outside. *There is nothing, in the concept of economizing itself, which explains why buyers should offer higher prices today than yesterday.*

On the other hand, if one accepts what we have set forth as the "Austrian" view of human action, the higher price offered today is immediately seen as the logical consequence of yesterday's disappointments. The outline of the market process becomes very clear: there occurs a sequence of tentative guesses by buyers of the prices which they have to offer, and the process consists of the gradual discovery by buyers of where the equilibrium price lies. The precise "psychological" nature of the learning process is not the point here; all we wish to demonstrate is that the human action notion of decision-making leads naturally to the notion of market process, whereas the "Anglo-American" approach lends itself, even in this simple example, to the notion of process only after deliberate additional "external" assumptions are fed into the model.

In the special case of equilibrium, of course, both the "Austrian" and the "Anglo-American" views of decision-making coincide. Here the given market price does not engender any disappointments. Economizing buyers and sellers successfully carry out their plans; no changes in constraints occur. For the "Austrians," the situation at equilibrium represents the case where what we have labelled the "entrepreneurial" element in individual decision-making has no role to play. No matter how alert the

15. Hayek, *op. cit.,* p. 46.

individual may be he can and must remain content with the current pattern of decision.

Our insistence on what some may consider to be a possibly over-subtle distinction between the two notions of decision-making does not stem, however, from the above rather trivial example. Our concern with this distinction arises from a conviction that it has far more profound consequences in market theory, for which the above illustration will serve, however, as an excellent introduction. The link between the above simple illustration and the wider ramifications of the distinction which we wish now to explore, has to do with our labelling the additional element present in the "human action" notion (absent in Robbinsian economizing) as the "entrepeneurial" element. We turn to expand on this theme.

8. One of the simplest views of a price system is that which recognizes only three types of decision-makers. First there are *consumers,* who choose the consumption bundles which they *purchase* with their incomes in the products markets. Second there are *resources owners,* who, out of their nature-endowed supplies of resources, choose the bundles which they *sell* in the resource markets. Third, there are *entrepreneurs* who *buy* combinations of resources in the resource markets in order to *sell* the resulting products in the products markets. These entrepreneur-producers buy *all* the ingredients necessary for production.

There is a fundamental difference between the decision of consumers and resource owners on the one hand, and those of the entrepreneurs on the other hand. The former, seeking the best for themselves, do so by seeking to extract from the market the greatest possible value *for what they offer.* Consumers seek more and better goods for their money; resource owners seek the most money for their resources. Entrepreneurs, on the other hand, better themselves by discovering *discrepancies* between the prices they must pay in the resource markets, and the prices they can obtain in the products markets. They buy in order to sell.

Clearly the whole course of the market process, changes in prices of resources and of products, changes in quantities of particular outputs or of the employments of particular inputs, can result entirely from the initiative and knowledge exploited by the entrepreneurs. We may, if we wish, imagine that all consumers and all resource owners are passive price takers; we can never assume entrepreneurs as price takers. The essence of the entreprenurial role is precisely to discover and exploit price situations hitherto unexploited.

It is submitted that the entrepreneur so viewed does not fit at all into the "Anglo-American" notion of the allocating, computing, decision-maker. In a world of allocating, economizing, computing decision-makers, there is no room, without importing ad hoc elements from the outside, for a market system that is not in equilibrium. This is so because, in the absence of equilibrium, the brunt of the process, as we have seen, is borne by the alertness of the entrepreneur and his willingness and ability to profit from the opportunities so presented. Remove him from the scene, and you have removed from your theory the only element able to set into motion the tendency towards equilibrium.

On the other hand, the "Austrian" human action notion fits perfectly into the disequilibrium model. All we have done, in setting up the above simple picture of a price system, is to concentrate *all* the entrepreneurship into the hands of the entrepreneurs and (purely for simplicity of analysis) treat consumers and resource owners as if they were pure Robbinsian economizers. The *pure* entrepreneur *has* no "means" to start out with. His profit-making potential arises purely from his "alertness" to market changes and to price discrepancies.

It is for this reason that, in our earlier discussion of the "Austrian" view of the decision-maker, we labelled the element of alertness to possible new information (absent in the Robbinsian economizer) as the "entrepreneurial" element. It should be apparent now, why we consider the identification of this element so important, and why we (from the "Austrian" viewpoint) must insist always on a model of the price system in which this element has a clear place.

A theory of price viewed as the pure theory of choice is completely inadequate, from this point of view, if by "choice" no more is meant than "mere" computation and allocation. A theory of price must involve a broadened notion of choice to include the entrepreneurial element. (There is, as we have seen, no great harm done, if, for analytical purposes it is imagined that all the entrepreneurial element of choice is exercised only by a special group of entrepreneurs.)

For a market in equilibrium, there is no room for entrepreneurship, and the situation is entirely explainable in terms of Robbinsian economizing. But for the vitally important notion of market process, economizing is a grossly inadequate conception of decision-making.

Many of the mistaken attacks on the achievements of the free market turn out, as we saw at the outset of this paper, to stem from preoccupation with the equilibrium situation. Invariably, in these cases, what has been overlooked by the critics, is the entrepreneurial role in the market. The purpose of this paper has been to trace this tendency to overlook the entrepreneurial role, to a closely parallel tendency, even within the ranks of methodological individualists, to see decision-making as a matter of computing the answer to a maximization problem, with the constraints given and known.

9. It will perhaps be useful, in closing this paper, to relate its argument very briefly to certain recent contributions of other writers in this area. The writers we will refer to are (a) Professor Buchanan and (b) Professor Shackle.

(a) In an exceedingly interesting paper several years ago,[16] Buchanan called upon economists to renounce the Robbinsian emphasis on the allocation of scarce means among competing ends, and view their science, instead, as a *catallactics,* a science of exchanges, emphasizing the "unique sort of relationship . . . which involves the cooperative association of individuals, one with another, even when individual interests are different." The market, Buchanan points out, achieves much more than the mere "computation" of the efficient solution to a nation's "economic problem," it achieves social cooperation, a notion that is missed in the currently fashionable allocation economics.

Whether Robbins' emphasis on means-allocation problems is indeed to blame for the currently fashionable view of the market as performing a primarily computational function, need not detain us here.[17] Buchanan is altogether justified in criticizing the current view of the market. This view, it may be pointed out, fits in as one of the implications of the equilibrium preoccupation noticed earlier in this paper.[18] The market *does* achieve much more than mere computation.

While the focus of our own dissatisfaction here with Robbinsian allocation is a somewhat different one, the "Austrian" emphasis, we maintain, would remove what Buchanan finds objectionable. Buchanan objects to the "position of eminence in the economist's thought processes" held by

16. J. M. Buchanan, "What Should Economists Do?" *Southern Economic Journal* (January 1964).

17. On this see the writer's "What Economists Do," *Southern Economic Journal* (January, 1965).

18. See references in paper cited in preceding note, p. 259, ftn. 6.

the theory of choice. Choice, says Buchanan, is mechanical; a theory of choice is an applied mathematics or managerial science, not economics. It is submitted here that all this is true only for a mechanical, computer-type, notion of choice, *not* when choice is seen as human action in the above discussed sense. As soon as we broaden choice to embrace the entrepreneurial element, all that annoys Buchanan evaporates. The market, no longer confined to equilibrium, is seen not merely to compute efficient solutions, but to generate those cooperative actions by individuals that lead to the social results Buchanan wishes to emphasize.

(b) In a number of writings, referred to earlier in this paper, Professor Shackle has called for a view of the decision as *creative,* rather than determined. Shackle wishes to see history as having injected into it as each instant of decision-making, a novel element not predictable from and not determined by previous history.

The kernel of our own stress here on the "entrepreneurial" element in individual decision-making is rather different from what Shackle is seeking. The two approaches, Shackle's and our own, deal with different levels of discussion and *may* therefore both be simultaneously valid without coinciding at all. Shackle is concerned with the psychology of decision-making. He regrets that economics developed at the hand of Smith, Ricardo and Marshall, instead of at the hands of psychologists.[19] Much of Shackle's own contributions in this area are psychological in character.

Our own emphasis is quite different. We remain content to stay at the purely formal level at which economic theorists have always aimed their discussion. We still see economics as a theory of choice; we merely seek to have it recognized that the appropriate notion of choice for this purpose is the "Austrian" one which we have identified as embracing also the "entrepreneurial" element. Entrepreneurs, too, make choices; our theory cannot afford to leave them out.

19. Shackle, *op. cit.,* p. 130.

INDEX

Addleson, Mark, 34
Alchian, A., 81, 84–85
An Essay on the Co-ordination of the Laws of Distribution (Wicksteed), 101
Anglo-American approach. *See* price theory, Anglo-American *vs.* Austrian approaches
artifacts (tools), explanatory requirements, 6
Austrian economics. *See* subjectivism, overview

Baudeau, Nicolas, 125
Baumol, W. J., 88–89, 139
beaver-deer examples, 23, 26n3, 88–93
Becker, Gary, 7
Belidor, Bernard, 125
Bentham, Jeremy, 126
Blaug, M., 126, 128, 133
Böhm-Bawerk, Eugene von, 21–22, 23–24, 152
bread example, prices, 24
Buchanan, James, 6–7, 104–5, 188–89
bus transportation example, 5–6

Cannan, Edwin, 129–30, 131, 133–34, 136n6, 137n29
Cantillon, Richard, 125, 136n11, 137n29
capital-and-interest theory, in subjectivism, 112–14, 116–20. *See also* entrepreneurial element *entries*
Capital and Time (Hicks), 2
Capitalism, Socialism and Democracy (Schumpter), 16–17
central planning, 16–17, 51, 99n8, 177–78
choice. *See* human action
coal and iron production, 13–14
Cole, Arthur H., 135

The Common Sense of Political Economy (Wicksteed), 101
consumer needs/decisions: in central planning systems, 16–17, 51; in determinate market framework, 65–67; focus of, 186; Menger's arguments, 12–18, 24, 26n3, 49; in radical subjectivism, 53–54, 56–57. *See also* entrepreneurial element *entries;* human action
cost relationships, in Wicksteed's theorizing, 103–5. *See also* opportunity costs
Counter-Revolution of Science (Hayek), 1–2, 6

Davenport, H. J., 104
deer-beaver examples, 23, 26n3, 88–93
Defoe, Daniel, 124
discovery process. *See* entrepreneurial element *entries;* human action; human knowledge; subjectivism, overview
disequilibrium conditions: economizer model problem, 38–39; Hayek's argument, 8–9; in Menger's theorizing, 161–62, 166–67. *See also* entrepreneurial element *entries;* equilibrium conditions
dynamic subjectivism, static form compared, 31–33. *See also* Mises, Ludwig von (Hayek linkage)

Eagly, R. V., 132, 133
Ebeling, Richard, 35
econometrics: explanatory limitations, 3–4, 7, 63; as pre-reconciliation foundation, 66–67, 175–76

This book is set in Scala and Scala Sans, created
by the Dutch designer Martin Majoor in the 1990s.

Printed on paper that is acid-free and meets the
requirements of the American National Standard
for Permanence of Paper for Printed Library
Materials, z39.48-1992. ∞

Book design by Richard Hendel, Chapel Hill, North Carolina
Typography by Apex CoVantage, Madison, Wisconsin
Printed and bound by Worzalla Publishing Company,
Stevens Point, Wisconsin